The Refugee Connection

A Lifetime of Running a Lifeline

James L. Carlin

Preface by Congressman Peter W. Rodino, Jr.

MACMILLAN

First published 1989

Published by
THE MACMILLAN PRESS LTD
Houndmills, Basingstoke, Hampshire RG21 2XS
and London
Companies and representatives
throughout the world

Typeset by Footnote Graphics
Warminster, Wilts

Printed and bound in Great Britain by WBC Ltd, Bristol and Maesteg

British Library Cataloguing in Publication Data
Carlin, James L.
The refugee connection: a lifetime of running a
lifeline.
1. Welfare services for refugees. Biographies
I. Title
362.8'7
ISBN 0–333–49965–4

'He who saves a single human life is as though he rescued the entire world.'

The Talmud

Contents

List of Photographs

List of Tables

Preface

For the majority of my forty years in the United States Congress, I have been deeply involved in the many issues surrounding refugees and displaced persons. Without question – and I can say this from personal experience – I know of no more difficult and heart-wrenching problem than the millions of people worldwide who have been forced to flee from their homeland.

Without actually seeing the camps that house the refugees – many without families or hope – or the camps that provide shelter for those who have been displaced, it is difficult to appreciate the magnitude of the problem and the extent of human suffering that these people endure. It is a tragedy of immense proportions with which we all must be concerned.

This book by James L. Carlin provides a comprehensive review of the refugee flows and the dislocations of people caused by oppression, persecution and armed conflict since the Second World War. It also gives us a first-hand account of the humanitarian efforts of governments, voluntary agencies and dedicated individuals in responding to these emergencies.

At the same time, Jim's pen-sketches of individual cases – based on his long experience in the field – help reduce the issue to the starkest human terms that everyone can understand. These sketches most certainly will help the reader realize why it is imperative that the world develop an effective strategy to deal with this matter.

I can think of no person better qualified than Jim Carlin to write such a book. As an international civil servant and United States government official for more than four decades, he has been directly and continuously involved in the operational responses by governments to repeated refugee and migration crises. He has been an eye-witness to many of the events described in this book, starting as a 24-year-old United States Army officer on assignment to the United Nations Relief and Rehabilitation Administration. Subsequently, Jim served as Deputy Assistant Secretary of State for Refugee and Migration Affairs and, most recently, as Director General of the Intergovernmental Committee for Migration (ICM), an organization for which I have great admiration.

As I have worked with Jim over these many years, I have come to recognize that he has succeeded in his endeavors because he has a cool head, a warm heart and a finely-honed sense of what is possible and what is not. These qualities, combined with the fact that he is a loyal, discreet, and effective team player and leader, have made him an invaluable refugee expert whose advice and guidance is sought around the world.

I am confident the reader of *The Refugee Connection: A Lifetime of*

Running a Lifeline will find it to be interesting, informative and thought-provoking – as I did – for a variety of reasons. First, it provides a valuable historical overview of post-Second World War refugee and migration problems and demonstrates the utility of intergovernmental solutions to them. Second, it serves as a reminder that there is still massive human suffering caused by incredible cruelty throughout the world. Finally, it should also renew our faith in the essential decency of mankind. For despite the magnitude of the problem, there are thousands of people like Jim working tirelessly every day to provide a better life for the millions of people forced from their homes because of persecution, war or catastrophe.

September 1988

PETER W. RODINO, Jr.
Chairman of the Committee of the Judiciary
of the US House of Representatives

Acknowledgements

To friends and associates who, being aware of my extensive career in the field of refugees and migration, encouraged me to write an account of my experiences.

To Eugene E. Oja, now a vice president with Merrill, Lynch, Pierce, Fenner and Smith, who was my immediate commanding officer in the US military service during the Second World War, and who supplied me with copies of the situation maps used by our unit in the European theater of operations – maps which provided useful reminders of events described at the outset of this account.

To Roger Walon, a faithful and efficient colleague who served with me in the ICEM mission in Austria during the Hungarian emergency in 1956–57, and who helped me recall details of some of the more notable aspects of that tragic and exciting period.

To the ICM administration for making available the ICM photographs and the case histories included in this volume – and to Zilmo M. De Freitas of the ICM Library who managed to produce these items from the archives.

To Pat Norsky, a dear friend, who drew on her splendid Oxford training and many years of editorial work at the International Labor Office to blue-pencil my early drafts and provide professional advice on the layout and presentation of the material – and to her husband, Karel, a professional journalist and astute political observer, who offered sage advice on various parts of the presentation.

To Congressman Peter W. Rodino, Jr., Chairman of the Committee of the Judiciary of the US House of Representatives, a true champion of migration matters, who provided a kind and generous preface to my story.

To my dear wife, Annemarie, who with saintly patience worked and re-worked the manuscript through her personal computer until a final product was achieved.

Finally, to the subjects of this account – the victimized individuals whose turmoil and troubled situations gave me a special purpose in life – a constant challenge that provided the most rewarding career that anyone could ever expect to experience. Godspeed to each and everyone of those individuals wherever they may now find themselves.

JAMES L. CARLIN

Introduction

This is an account of homelessness and sojourning people. It reflects my personal involvement and experiences during more than four decades in the field of refugees and migration on both the national and international scenes. It extends from the latter months of the Second World War, when Europe was teeming with millions of displaced persons and prisoners of war, to the time of writing, when asylum countries throughout the world are burdened with massive flows of refugees, whether economic or political, victims of conflict and persons needing migration assistance.

For whatever reason – whether fate, happenstance or plain destiny – I have had an unbroken chain of involvement in organizations and programs concerned with uprooted and disenfranchised people.

While in some respects a memoir, this account is intended more particularly to illuminate a human problem – a problem that has absorbed my interests and energy, in and out of government, during most of my adult life. Though not a definitive study and certainly not a scholarly treatise, it is a factual story about refugee and migration problems – and my role in developing and implementing policies and programs to resolve them.

The saga of refugees and migrants is a harrowing but heroic one of people fleeing political oppression, persecution, war and, in some cases, economic deprivation to seek liberty and a better livelihood in the Free World.

Despite the staggering dimensions of the problem in human, economic and political terms, the fact that it has been growing in intensity over the past few decades, and the evident prospects of further massive dislocations in the years ahead – despite all of this, there are precious few individuals in or out of government who are conversant with the diverse aspects of the problem and who are practiced in remedial action.

Faust's servitor posed the question: 'How shall our counsel serve to lead mankind?' While feeling notably inadequate to respond to such a profound challenge, I believe, nonetheless, that I would be remiss if, taking account of my long involvement in service to refugees and migrants, I did not record my unique experience in the hope of arousing wider interest in, and ensuring closer attention being paid to, this ongoing human drama – a drama that each year touches the lives of millions of persons, affects the economic and political stability of many nations and costs the international community upwards of a billion dollars.

Should this account encourage any government to establish within its bureaucracy a training course on refugee and migration affairs for civil servants or foreign service officers; or should it prompt any college or

1

university to introduce the subject in its curriculum; or should it motivate any student to pursue a career in this relatively unexplored, but challenging and meaningful field of endeavor; or should it merely persuade one reader to concern himself with the plight of one uprooted individual – then the effort that went into this writing will not have been in vain.

In preparing this account I have relied on my memory as far as it has been able to serve me, and support from notes and records that have been gathered and maintained over the years.

1 The End of the Second World War in Europe

LAST DAYS AS A SOLDIER

The Second World War brought me to the European theater of operations, where I was assigned to Special Troops of the First United States Army commanded by General Courtney H. Hodges. I was a first lieutenant and platoon leader in a reconnaissance troop. The specific task of our unit was the gathering of military data for the G-2 (military intelligence) of the 69th Division. According to the training manuals this meant moving out front with all due regard for stealth and developing information about the characteristics and location of enemy forces, particularly enemy armor. In reality, more often than not, it meant moving forward to the point of drawing enemy fire. In any event the objective was to gather useful information and pass it back for processing by G-2, thus providing a basis for action by the First Army's air and ground forces. The following letter dated 15 April 1945 from our commanding officer reflects the nature of the assigned mission:

SUBJECT: Commendation
TO: Captain Eugene E. Oja
            CO Reconnaissance Troop

1. I wish to commend the Second Platoon of Reconnaissance Troop, commanded by First Lieutenant James L. Carlin, for their actions in Escherode, Germany.
2. On entering Escherode with infantry aboard their vehicles, they encountered heavy resistance from enemy small arms fire. Taking the enemy under fire, they silenced several enemy positions before being forced to withdraw by heavy artillery fire. After withdrawing, they supported the infantry in clearing the town in a very able manner.
3. The coolheadedness displayed by all members of the platoon is indicative of the highest standard of discipline, and their actions under fire show their ability to handle themselves in any situation.
4. My heartiest commendation goes to all members of this platoon. Their fine work reflects great credit on themselves and their organization as a whole.

        (*Signed*) Donald B. Miller,
          Lt. Colonel, Commanding

The path followed by our unit in the war zone reached from Normandy to the Siegfried Line, across the Rhine at Remagen, on to Kassel and eastward to Muhlhausen, Leipzig and the Elbe river.

The historic and memorable link-up of the American and Russian forces at Torgau on the Elbe river was reported in a dispatch from our parent division on 26 April 1945. It read as follows:

69th First to meet Soviets

THE FIGHTING 69TH MADE HISTORY YESTERDAY BY BEING THE FIRST UNITED STATES DIVISION TO MAKE CONTACT WITH THE SOVIET FORCES.

Elements of the 69th Division made contact with elements of Marshal Koniev's Army, the 58th Division, commanded by Major General Rusakov, at 1640 hours yesterday at the little town of Torgau. Contact was also made at Riesa.
A meeting was held at 10 a.m. this morning between Colonel Adams of the 273rd Regiment and a regimental commander of the 58th Division to make further plans.

Except for pockets of resistance in certain areas of the war zone and the occasional firing of a 'Panzerfaust' by a fanatical member of the Volksturm, the link-up of the American and Russian forces on 25 April signalled the end of hostilities in Europe. It was on 8 May 1945, however, that victory by the allied forces was officially declared. The official word read as follows:

SUPREME HEADQUARTERS
ALLIED EXPEDITIONARY FORCE (FORWARD)

8 May 1945

SUBJECT: Victory Order of the Day
1. The following Victory Order of the Day issued this date by the Supreme Commander to each member of the Allied Expeditionary Force is published for the information of all personnel of this headquarters:
VICTORY ORDER OF THE DAY
Men and women of the Allied Expeditionary Force:
The crusade on which we embarked in the early summer of 1944 has reached its glorious conclusion. It is my special privilege, in the name of all Nations represented in this Theater of War, to commend each of you for valiant performance of duty. Though these words are feeble they come from the bottom of a heart overflowing with pride in your loyal service and admiration for you as warriors.
Your accomplishments at sea, in the air, on the ground and in the field of supply, have astonished the world. Even before the final week of the conflict, you had put 5,000,000 of the enemy permanently out of the war. You have taken in [your] stride military tasks so difficult as to be classed by many doubters as impossible. You have confused, defeated and destroyed your savagely fighting foe. On the road to victory you have endured every discomfort and privation and have surmounted every obstacle ingenuity and desperation could throw in your path. You did not pause until our front was firmly joined up with the great Red Army coming from the East, and other Allied Forces, coming from the South.
Full victory in Europe has been attained.
Working and fighting together in a single and indestructible partnership you have achieved a perfection in unification of air, ground and naval power that will stand as a model in our time.

The route you have travelled through hundreds of miles is marked by the graves of former comrades. From them has been exacted the ultimate sacrifice: blood of many nations – American, British, Canadian, French, Polish and others – has helped to gain the victory. Each of the fallen died as a member of the team to which you belong, bound together by a common love of liberty and a refusal to submit to enslavement. No monument of stone, no memorial of whatever magnitude could so well express our respect and veneration for their sacrifice as would perpetuation of the spirit of comradeship in which they died. As we celebrate Victory in Europe let us remind ourselves that our common problems of the immediate and distant future can best be solved in the same conception of cooperation and devotion to the cause of human freedom as [has] made this Expeditionary Force such a mighty engine of righteous destruction.

Let us have no part in the profitless quarrels in which other men will inevitably engage as to what country, what service, won the European war. Every man, every woman, of every nation here represented, has served according to his or her ability, and the efforts of each have contributed to the outcome. This we shall remember – and in doing so we shall be revering each honored grade, and be sending comfort to the loved ones of comrades who could not live to see this day.

(Signed) Dwight D. Eisenhower

Lest any reader gain the impression that this is yet another war story, I hasten to note that such is not the case. Since, however, it was forward reconnaissance missions in the European war zone – missions during which I witnessed suffering, destruction and death on a scale beyond human comprehension – that caused my initial exposure to victims of persecution and conflict (displaced persons, prisoners of war, inmates of concentration camps, and others uprooted and dispossessed), it seemed appropriate to take such background as a point of departure for this account.

POST-HOSTILITIES ACTIVITIES UNDER SHAEF IN GERMANY, INCLUDING FIRST ENCOUNTERS WITH PEOPLE IN TROUBLE

Upon the cessation of hostilities on 8 May 1945 (V-E Day), our reconnaissance troop was dispatched to a camp in Germany near Grimma (a town located approximately 50 kilometers south-east of Leipzig), which housed upwards of 15 000 persons – mostly Russian and Polish prisoners of war, together with a sprinkling of male and female slave laborers from Poland and Russia who had made their way to the camp after hostilities had ended.

Our unit's basic task was to maintain order in the camp and to limit as far as possible looting and ravaging of the surrounding countryside by the camp inmates.

This in itself was no mean task, but soon, upon the arrival of a British colonel from SHAEF Headquarters (unfortunately his name is not recalled), we were made aware of our secondary role, namely organized repatriation. The colonel, a salty little Britisher with his well-tailored uniform and a moustache to match, was impressive with his keen sense of discipline and respect for orders from above. His orders, which in a real sense became our orders, were to co-ordinate and implement arrangements for the transfer of Soviet prisoners in the Grimma Camp to Soviet military authorities. As it turned out, this task entailed mustering and shepherding the Russian POWs on to trucks and delivering them to the hand-over point.

At the time this task seemed quite normal to those of us involved. While being duly patriotic in the war effort, I had uppermost in my mind the wish to see an end to the war in the Pacific, as in Europe, and to return to civilian life. I well recall being impressed by the news currently being reported in the *Stars and Stripes* that, with the war over in Europe, the Russians were transferring tens of divisions to the Manchurian border for action against the Japanese. How fitting, I thought, to get these Russian prisoners home for re-conditioning and possible help in that war effort.

In the prevailing circumstances the fact that many of our charges tended to resist embarking on their journey homeward was regarded as a general lack of discipline and in many cases attributed to their over-indulgence in the crude forms of alcohol that had been scrounged in the local community. While being cognizant of the fact that we were dealing with members of a friendly ally, it seemed relatively normal, nonetheless, for our troopers to have their pistols or carbines at the ready to ensure that the trucks were loaded and the transfers effected according to plan – and according to orders. In those cases where resistance was particularly strong, some of our more able-bodied troopers provided the necessary encouragement.

It was a relatively short trip (50 to 60 kilometers) from the camp near Grimma to the pontoon bridge over the Elbe river where the transfers were to be made. The far end of the bridge was visibly decorated with red banners bearing the hammer and sickle; Russian martial music provided what was thought to be a seemly welcome to the returnees.

Such was the state of affairs in those early post-war days. Being line troops, we were far removed from the high-level political decisions of the time and totally unaware that the orders from SHAEF concerning the transfer of Russian POWs stemmed from a secret agreement reached by Churchill, Roosevelt and Stalin at the Yalta Conference in February 1945. While in retrospect it appears naïve, we were equally unaware of the peril that might await these returnees upon their arrival in the Soviet Union – peril that has been so aptly described by Nikolai Tolstoy in *Victims of Yalta* and *Stalin's Secret War*. In later years I have often wondered about the fate of those Russians from the Grimma Camp who were our charges for a brief period.

Similarly I have had troubled thoughts about the Poles in that camp. Strangely enough, or so it seemed at the time, the orders from SHAEF about transfers applied only to the Russians. On 5 May 1945 a special message from SHAEF informed liberated Poles that they would have the opportunity to indicate whether or not they wished to return to Poland. All cases, the message indicated, would be dealt with individually. This seemed a commendable policy and a happy solution for the Poles who found themselves in what became the western occupation zones of Austria and Germany. It was less certain, however, what would befall those, such as our charges, who were deep in what was to become the Soviet occupation zone of Germany.

Our stint at the Grimma Camp was brief – a matter of only a few weeks – and while the bulk of the Russians were 'transferred' during our assignment there, several thousand Poles remained in the camp at the time of our departure and their fate is not known – at least not to this writer.

After Grimma, our troop received orders to proceed to Lutzen, a city with a population of approximately 6000 located some 18 kilometers southwest of Leipzig. There we quartered ourselves in a sugar factory on the outskirts of the city and in the absence of any particular mission members of the unit were assigned to little more than guard duty and organized athletics.

But our light schedule at Lutzen was to be short-lived. Within a few days of our arrival orders came for our troop to participate in the systematic procurement of any and all kinds of construction material such as lumber, cement and hardware to be found in the general vicinity. To carry out this assignment the area was carefully carved up on the grid squares of our situation maps, and segments were assigned to several mobile patrols, each comprised of a commissioned or non-commissioned officer, two troopers and a jeep. Trucks were on call as necessary. According to orders, the assigned areas were to be thoroughly searched and any appreciable amounts of new construction material were to be confiscated immediately and transferred to the nearest rail-head. The rightful owner was merely given a receipt, with no clear indication that compensation or reimbursement would ever be made. As I recall, the orders did not specify the ultimate recipient of the material, but it was commonly understood at the time that it would be shipped to the Soviet Union.

As with the POW transfers, action of this sort was undertaken in those early post-war days without too much concern for the motives. The Germans were the vanquished, the atmosphere was still hostile and it was recognized that the Russians, our ally, had indeed suffered extremely heavy losses in men and material at the expense of the Germans.

In later years and in a changed political climate I have often recalled how systematically that area was gleaned of useful material, and wondered whether the rightful owners of the property were ever compensated.

A few weeks later our unit was scheduled for re-deployment. Our departure from Lutzen, the exact time of which was supposed to be a military secret, turned out to be a memorable event, especially in the light of our local procurement activity and the then existing taboo on fraternization with Germans.

When we crossed the initial point at the specified time (0600 hours on a day in late June 1945), it is no exaggeration to report that the vast majority of the residents of Lutzen were at their open-shuttered windows waving white handkerchiefs and shouting 'Aufwiedersehen'. Many were in tears. How strange that seemed to us at the time. But they knew that the Americans would soon be replaced in the area by Soviet occupation forces – and they obviously had a good appreciation already of what it meant to have the Russians coming.

2 Fresh Fields and Pastures New

THE START OF A NEW LIFE WITH THE UNITED NATIONS
RELIEF AND REHABILITATION ADMINISTRATION (UNRRA)
IN AUSTRIA

The winter of 1945–46 was quite severe and the situation in Austria was difficult in terms of food and fuel shortages. Although Austria was considered 'liberated', the occupation forces of the Allied Powers were in place throughout the country – the British in Carinthia and Steiermark, the French in the Vorarlberg and Tyrol, the Russians in Burgenland and Lower Austria and the Americans in Land Salzburg and Upper Austria. Vienna, like Berlin, had been declared an international city, with all four occupying powers represented there. The United States forces in Austria (USFA) were under the command of General Mark Clark, and USFA's headquarters were in Vienna.

The reconnaissance unit to which I was then assigned was in Hallein, a town located about midway between Salzburg and Berchtesgaden. It is ironic to note that Hallein had two principal points of interest at the time. One was the Heimatmuseum, where the original lyrics of the Christmas carol 'Silent Night' were on display. 'Silent Night' had been composed by a native son of Hallein, Franz Gruber, who first presented it at the nearby St Nicola church in Oberndorf on 24 December 1818. The other main attraction was the local salt mine, in which caches of art treasures were found at the war's end. Many of these famous works had been owned by wealthy Jews and confiscated by the Nazi forces.

On one of those cold winter evenings a group of six civilians (three Americans, two Britishers and a Frenchman) arrived in a converted British staff car at our command post seeking accommodation for the night. They wore a mixture of military uniforms which were noticeably bare of any insignia. The only distinguishing mark was a red crescent shoulder patch bearing the initials UNRRA. This, they promptly explained, was the acronym for the United Nations Relief and Rehabilitation Administration. The group had been en route for several days from UNRRA's training base at Granville, France, and their destination was Salzburg, where they were slated to take over key positions in UNRRA's displaced persons operation.

The group was very appreciative of the warm food and quarters provided by our unit, and when they moved off the following morning the senior member, a distinguished-looking American with a name like Fatheringhill, encouraged me to contact him after he was installed at the UNRRA office in Salzburg.

9

Out of sight, out of mind, and scarcely any thought was given to UNRRA until a bulletin was circulated from USFA Headquarters a few weeks later announcing employment opportunities with UNRRA for military personnel having enough points to qualify for separation from the service. The point system was based principally on time in the service, with particular weight going to duty in a theater of operations during wartime.

UNRRA's qualifying criteria were rather sketchy, with preference being shown for persons with university-level education and experience in the fields of administration, management, social welfare or medicine. Mindful of the USFA bulletin and armed with the necessary point count, I decided to check UNRRA out on one of my not infrequent outings to the American Red Cross Club in Salzburg in search of coffee and doughnuts and the *Stars and Stripes*.

No difficulty was experienced in finding the UNRRA office, which was situated in the Residenz – an impressive building complex in the heart of Salzburg which had been constructed for the Archbishop Princes at the turn of the seventeenth century. I was warmly welcomed by the characters I had met a few weeks earlier in Hallein, and after several hastily arranged interviews I emerged with an official job offer: 'UNRRA Supply Supervisor – Upper Austria'. Because of British influence on UNRRA's administrative procedures, the grades and salaries of the organization's officials were equated to military ranks. In accordance with the responsibilities attached to the position to which I was being assigned, my grade corresponded to the rank of major. This incidental fact is mentioned only because, in the prevailing circumstances, assimilated ranks were of some importance in relation to official dealings with the military authorities in the zones of occupation and also in terms of accommodation in military facilities.

Upon assuming employment with UNRRA in February 1946 I removed the insignia and other paraphernalia from my uniforms and substituted UNRRA's red shoulder patch. While this change produced a sense of nakedness at the time, especially in an occupation zone where the military was the dominating element, the demands of my new job soon preoccupied me to the exclusion of other considerations.

Knowing practically nothing about UNRRA, I had used the few short weeks between receiving the job offer and arranging my separation from military service to read up on my new employer. I thus learned that UNRRA, the first international relief agency in world history, had been established at the White House in Washington DC on 9 November 1943. It was UNRRA's task to tackle the problems that were to emerge with the return of peace – the prevention of widespread starvation, the curbing of epidemics and the averting of economic collapse. UNRRA would operate in the seventeen countries most directly affected by the war. It was intended to give the world a breathing space in the struggle for recovery.

Soon after UNRRA's founding it was recognized that the organization would also have to give special attention to the millions of persons who had been uprooted during the war and scattered across Europe, the Middle East and Asia. Accordingly the UNRRA Council at its meeting in September 1944 had adopted a resolution authorizing operations in enemy and ex-enemy areas for the care and repatriation of displaced persons (DPs) who had been victimized by the war.

Some experiences as an UNRRA 'supply supervisor'

In Austria UNRRA had a dual purpose: to administer relief to the country in general and to provide care for the tens of thousands of DPs there. My assignment related solely to the latter. As 'Supply Supervisor – Upper Austria', I became part of the UNRRA area unit which had its base in the Rathaus (city hall) in Linz, the capital of Land Upper Austria. Although terms of reference for my job were non-existent and there was no one to interpret my duties and responsibilities with any appreciable measure of precision, early visits to several of the DP camps in the vicinity brought the needs of the assignment and indeed my responsibilities into clear focus.

When UNRRA's operations started there were about 1 650 000 refugees/displaced persons and other aliens in Austria, while the country's native population totalled only six million. Of the alien population, 1 000 000 were non-German speaking persons, who became UNRRA charges, and 650 000 were ethnic Germans from Czechoslovakia and Yugoslavia, for whom UNRRA did not assume any particular responsibility. The network of DP camps was spread throughout Upper Austria. There were Jews in Binder-michl and Ebelsberg on the outskirts of Linz, Poles and Ukrainians in Branau, Balts (Estonians, Latvians and Lithuanians) and Russians in Ried, Yugoslavs in Inns and Steyr, and a mixture of the same nationalities in several other smaller camps throughout the Land.

UNRRA teams, consisting usually of a team director, supply officer, medical officer, nurse and welfare officer, were in place in each of the DP camps. Working in close conjunction with the team directors and camp supply officers, my job evolved largely in the areas of procurement, promotional liaison, co-ordination, control and distribution of supplies. The principal sources of supply were the US Army, the Land government of Upper Austria, the military government, UNRRA itself and certain voluntary agencies such as the American Joint Distribution Committee (AJDC).

In order to assure a steady flow of essential items (foodstuffs, blankets, clothing and medication) to the camps and maintain any semblance of the prescribed 2000 calorie daily diet, promotional liaison with the supply sources was necessary on a day-to-day basis. Supplies were usually transported to the camps in UNRRA trucks – a mixture of used American, British and German military vehicles – and keeping them on the road in a satisfactory state of repair was a major task in itself.

The UNRRA supply officers were responsible for requisitioning, controlling and distributing supplies in the camps. In this connection they were obliged to prepare and submit detailed weekly reports reflecting camp population by age group, stocks in hand, etc. Moreover, they were expected to be responsive to the requests of the medical and welfare officers for special items required to meet the particular needs of children and persons with physical ailments.

While there was a generous outpouring of supplies to provide relief to the needy DPs, such action, as probably happens in most emergency situations, was not without its unusual and sometimes amusing aspects. For example, part of Norway's contribution to UNRRA had been in the form of five-gallon tins of cod-liver oil. That gift was unquestionably well-intentioned and indeed cod-liver oil represented a good nutritional supplement to the standard diet of the DPs, many of whom were or had been victims of malnutrition. Nonetheless, cod-liver oil in its natural form proved to be as distasteful to the DPs as it had been to those of us who had been subjected to it in our youth and there was an equal reluctance on the part of the DPs to consume the daily dosage. Thanks to the special efforts of UNRRA medical personnel by means of supervised feeding in some of the camps, limited amounts were put to good use but, as I recall, the bulk remained in the supply warehouses.

Then there was a shipment of 30 tons of used shoes from the people of the United States. On the face of it this contribution was most welcome, especially since there was a dire need among the DPs for all sorts of clothing. Upon opening the huge white bales, however, it was discovered, to the dismay of all of us concerned, that pairs had not been kept together, not even within individual bales. As may be imagined, the sorting and pairing of 30 tons of used shoes was a monumental task and while the bulk of the shipment eventually served a useful purpose, it can also be reported that the likes of high-heeled satin slippers did not exactly prove suitable for the DP women.

Special efforts for Jewish displaced persons

Since the majority of Jews among the DPs in our case-load had been inmates of concentration camps they were in need and deserving of special attention, and indeed special efforts were made on their behalf, particularly in terms of accommodation, rations and medical care. Within their groups they established camp committees to work in close conjunction with the UNRRA teams which were responsible for administering the camps. Then there was the so-called Jewish Central Committee, which was based in the Bindermichl camp. I recall with particular interest and pleasure the close contact I maintained with the chairman of that committee, Engineer Simon Wiesenthal, who has become widely known in more recent years for his tracking down of former Nazi war criminals. Engineer Wiesenthal was highly effective in interpreting to UNRRA and the US military authorities the special needs of the Jewish DPs. In retrospect I think it can truly be reported that those of us who were concerned with the problem at the time, whether in UNRRA, AJDC or the US military, were highly responsive to those needs.

To be or not to be: repatriation or resettlement

It seems well worth noting that at all six sessions of UNRRA's Council, held during the period 1943–47, it was ruled that the 'UNRRA administration, in the performance of its functions in respect of displaced persons, should bear in mind that the main task ... is to encourage and assist in every way possible their early return to their country of origin'. Indeed in the early months following the war there was a considerable amount of repatriation of DPs from Austria. The total exceeded 200 000.

However, as time moved on and the stresses and strains in international relations emerged and grew with the peace, there was growing reluctance among the DPs to return to their communist dominated homelands in Eastern Europe. Indeed, as it turned out, repatriation was not to be the primary aim of UNRRA's operations. Its major role, although not admitted in sessions of the UNRRA Council, proved to be the care of those DPs who did not choose to be repatriated.

Nonetheless, basing itself on the policy guidance of the Council, the UNRRA administration made one final effort to promote repatriation in the autumn of 1946. That effort was known as the Sixty-Day Ration Scheme (dubbed 'operation grubstake' by the US Army and 'operation carrot' by the British). It was designed particularly for the Polish DPs. Under this scheme those DPs who decided to return during the period October to December 1946 were to be given enough food for sixty days upon arrival in their homeland.

While this initiative met with modest success, the DPs' reluctance to accept repatriation persisted. At the same time their interest in being resettled in a third country heightened. Resettlement, however, was not a solution supported by the policy-makers in the UNRRA Council. This was made clear in late 1946 when UNRRA officials in the field were instructed that UNRRA would not sponsor any resettlement schemes, that UNRRA funds should not be used for resettlement purposes and that UNRRA staff should not participate in any selection activity for resettlement or suggest to any DP resettlement as an alternative to repatriation.

In practice, nevertheless, UNRRA officials in the field were more sensitive to the interests and needs of the DPs and, while resettlement opportunities were quite limited, they rendered considerable assistance to particularly deserving DP candidates by explaining to them the immigration laws and requirements of prospective receiving countries. Moreover, there was close co-operation in the field, certainly in Austria, between UNRRA officials and representatives of the Intergovernmental Committee for Refugees (IGCR) – the only intergovernmental entity dealing at that time with the resettlement of refugees.

INTERGOVERNMENTAL COMMITTEE FOR REFUGEES (IGCR)

IGCR had resulted from a meeting held in July 1938 at Evian, France, at the suggestion of the President of the United States, Franklin Delano Roosevelt. It was established to handle the resettlement of political refugees from Germany and Austria. In addressing that meeting, at which 32 governments were represented, the delegate of the United States, Myron C. Taylor, stated:

... Mr. Chairman: Some millions of people, as this meeting convenes, are, actually or potentially, without a country. The number is increasing daily.

A major forced migration is taking place, and the time has come when governments – I refer specifically to those governments which have had the problem of political refugees thrust upon them by the policies of some other governments – must act and act promptly and effectively in a long-range program of comprehensive scale.

Mindful of the harrowing urgency of this situation, President Roosevelt took the initiative of calling this meeting at Evian. The response of 32 governments which were invited to participate has been generous and encouraging, and the courtesy of the French Government in offering the hospitality of its territory to the meeting and in arranging the technical details of our reception calls for deepest appreciation and most profound thanks.

At the outset, we must consider that we are dealing with a form of migration which presents peculiar difficulties... Now we have a form of compulsory migration, artificially stimulated by governmental practices in some countries which force upon the world at large great bodies of reluctant migrants who must be absorbed in abnormal circumstances with a disregard of economic conditions at a time of stress.

... Accordingly, my government, in its invitation, referred specifically to the problem of German (and Austrian) refugees and proposes that, for the purposes of this initial intergovernmental meeting and without wishing to set a precedent for future meetings, persons coming within the scope of the Conference shall be: *(a)* persons who have not already left Germany (including Austria) but who desire to emigrate by reason of the treatment to which they are subjected on account of their political opinions, religious beliefs or racial origin, and *(b)* persons as defined in *(a)* who have already left Germany and are in process of migration.

IGCR's secretariat was in London under the direction of Sir Herbert Emerson, a Britisher. IGCR's representative in Austria was Mr R. A. Montgomery ('Monty'). Monty had been a major in the US army serving in the G-5 section of USFA – the military entity dealing with the DP problem in Austria. Monty, though small in stature, was big in terms of thinking and action. He got on well with the representatives of those governments willing to open their doors to at least limited numbers of DPs, and he took maximum advantage of any such opportunities for the benefit of the neediest among them. He maintained close contact, for example, with the representatives of the US War Refugee Board, which had been established at the request of President Roosevelt early in 1944 'to take all measures within its power to rescue the victims of enemy oppression who were in imminent danger of death, and otherwise to afford such victims all possible relief and assistance'. The operatives of this Board had been particularly active during wartime; they had assisted in arranging escapes, hiding and caring for refugees from the Nazis and for transporting them to safety. In the early post-war period they continued co-operative efforts with certain voluntary agencies and IGCR to assist the more needy persons among the escapees from Nazism. Some 900 such cases were moved to the United States. The Executive Secretary of the War Refugee Board was George Warren Sr., who continued for many years to be the US Government's foremost expert and spokesman on refugee and migration affairs.

IGCR operated on a shoestring with limited staff, limited financial resources and limited resettlement opportunities. Nonetheless, great significance lies in the fact that IGCR set in motion a process by which resettlement assistance could be rendered on an international scale to victims of oppression and persecution. Of equal importance, IGCR established a pattern of resettlement operations – a pattern that would usefully be followed in coping with massive dislocations of peoples in the future.

SOME PRACTICAL EFFECTS OF GROWING CO-OPERATION BETWEEN UNRRA, IGCR AND THE VOLUNTARY AGENCIES

By the spring of 1946 UNRRA's supply operations for the DPs in Upper Austria were functioning reasonably well considering the difficult circumstances of the time. The prescribed 2000 calorie daily diet was being provided to all the camps, thanks largely to US military sources. Important supplementary rations were being provided to the Jewish DPs by AJDC, while certain additional amenities, such as cigarettes and chocolate, as well as blankets, clothing and medication, were supplied to all of the DPs by UNRRA. UNRRA's doctors and nurses gave special attention to the health condition of the DPs and, much to their credit, it can happily be reported that no epidemics or widespread medical problems occurred.

The summer of 1946, however, held a surprise in store. The weekly reports from the supply officers in the Jewish camps reflected an increase in their population. The initial increases were not particularly significant, and it was assumed that some Jewish DPs from camps in the other Länder in Austria, or even Germany, had turned up for some reason or another in the camps in our area. However, in the days and weeks that followed, when the infiltration grew more marked, it became apparent that something out of the ordinary was happening. It was then discovered that the infiltrators were newly arrived Jews from Poland.

USFA's G-5 section was aware of this development and hastened to investigate the circumstances. I can recall a meeting with the G-5 officer in Linz, a certain Captain Wright, to discuss the problem. He shared with me a detailed report which his office had received from the US Counter-Intelligence Corps (CIC). CIC had dispatched an operative to Poland to learn as much as possible about the matter. The operative had done a thorough job and his report suggested not only that a continuing heavy influx of Polish Jews was to be expected but, more than that, it provided a detailed account of the arrangements for their escape from Poland and the routes for their illegal passage via Czechoslovakia to either Austria or Germany. The CIC operative had made contact with a representative of the BRICHA – a group of courageous Jews from Palestine who had taken on the difficult and hazardous task of locating the remaining Jews in Poland and organizing their escape. He actually accompanied a group of these Polish Jews along one of the escape routes. He experienced the safe-houses, the illegal night-time border crossings, the use of various guides and the contact with a sometimes friendly, sometimes hostile population.

His report prompted the G-5 military authorities in Austria and Germany to prepare for the influx and, since UNRRA was the military's operating arm for DP activities, the UNRRA teams in the areas concerned were called upon for special action.

While the US military authorities were not against the provision of assistance to these Polish Jews, they represented something of a problem, at least initially, to the UNRRA administration, which was authorized to assist nationals of member countries of the United Nations only if they had been displaced by the war and ex-enemy nationals only if they had been persecuted by the enemy. UNRRA, however, duly solved the problem by invoking the notion of 'internal displacement'. It was safe to presume that all Jews had been 'displaced' by the war; in fact the UNRRA administration finally decided that all Jews were automatically to be considered eligible for assistance under this ruling unless positive proof to the contrary was produced.

Tens of thousands of Jews were brought out of Poland under operation BRICHA. In fact it turned out that over 60 per cent of the Jews accorded UNRRA aid were persons who had come out of Poland and other Eastern European countries after the end of the Second World War.

In Upper Austria it was decided that Wegscheid, near Linz, a wooden-barrack camp that formerly housed slave laborers employed at the Herman Goering iron and steel works in Linz, would be made ready for these Polish Jews. I recall one particular week-end in the summer of 1946 when US soldiers, UNRRA personnel, representatives of voluntary agencies and Austrians from the Land government worked feverishly to this end. Wegscheid became the principal transit camp in Upper Austria for Polish Jews, although significant numbers were also housed and cared for in the Bindermichl and Ebelsberg camps.

While the BRICHA was responsible for arranging the escape to Austria and Germany of the Polish Jews, it was the Jewish Agency for Palestine (JAFP) that played the key role in facilitating their processing and onward movement to Palestine.

JAFP had been founded in 1921 essentially for the purpose of promoting Jewish immigration to Palestine. The agency's Constitution was signed on 14 July 1929 in Zurich, Switzerland. On that occasion it was suggested that not only would JAFP act for the benefit of Palestine but also ultimately knit together, into a new and rejuvenated body, the scattered members of the 'House of Israel'. In fact, prior to the founding of the State of Israel JAFP indeed functioned practically as a government in orbit. It assumed responsibility for stimulating the interest of DPs, such as the Polish Jews, in migration to Palestine, completing all the formalities and arranging transportation. Additionally it engaged in certain cultural activities and teaching for the benefit of the DPs.

Representatives of JAFP were very active in the Jewish camps, especially Wegscheid, and with quiet efficiency they organized periodic group movements to the port of Bari in Italy, from where the DPs were transported by ship through British surveillance to the shores of Palestine. JAFP, subsequently to become known as the Jewish Agency for Israel (JAI), was destined to play an important role in Israel's immigration affairs – a role that has continued most effectively to the time of writing.

THE TERMINATION OF UNRRA

UNRRA was a pioneering effort – a type of international organization doing a job of a scope and significance new to history. While the assessment of its overall achievements and value as an experiment in multilateral operations seems better left to the economists, political scientists and historians, the organization's DP operations must be regarded as a notable success – certainly in terms of care and maintenance. And I look back with pride in having been a part of that effort. I also have fond memories of my colleagues on the UNRRA staff in Austria – an interesting mixture of Americans, Belgians, British, Dutch, French, Latin Americans and Scandinavians – all imbued with a deep sense of purpose and a willingness to undergo rigorous work schedules and living conditions for the sake of the needy DPs.

While my duties and responsibilities were largely in the area of supply,

my tour of duty with UNRRA also afforded me exposure to the resettlement activities of IGCR, JAFP and the War Refugee Board – an exposure
which triggered my interest, and subsequent long-term involvement, in the
field of refugee resettlement and migration.

On the basis of a decision taken at the Fifth Session of the UNRRA
Council in Geneva in August 1946, a time-table for terminating UNRRA's
DP operations was drawn up. Accordingly, those operations were discon-
tinued on 30 June 1947, and shortly thereafter I received the communications reproduced below:

UNRRA

This Records

the Loyal and Valued Services of

James L. Carlin

to the United Nations Relief and Rehabilitation Administration in its Great
Work of Relieving the Suffering and Saving the Lives of the Victims of War
in the Liberated Countries

(*Signed*)　　Lowell W. Rooks
　　　　　　　Director General

Washington, D.C.
2 September, 1947

UNITED NATIONS
RELIEF AND REHABILITATION ADMINISTRATION

1344 Connecticut Avenue
Washington 25, D.C.

2 September 1947

Dear Mr. Carlin:

Because of the termination of UNRRA's activities, you are leaving the
services of the Administration. You have been a part of the large army of
employees whose efforts have allowed UNRRA to pioneer in the field of
international agencies, proving beyond any question of doubt the feasibility
of the United Nations to operate in concert. You have helped to avert
starvation for millions, to restore their health and to give them courage to
meet their problems. Your efforts have helped the war-torn nations to make
an appreciable start on needed rehabilitation of their national economies
which, unfortunately, will require years to complete.

For your loyalty and your devotion to the task of helping others help
themselves, I, personally, am most grateful. I am sure I speak for the
unnamed millions whom you benefitted by your labors.

I sincerely trust that the future may bring you happiness and an opportunity
to continue to serve in some capacity making fullest use of your experience.

Sincerely yours,

(*Signed*)　　Lowell W. Rooks
　　　　　　　Director General

3 Creation and Achievements of the International Refugee Organization (IRO)

The notion of creating an international organization to replace UNRRA's DP operations and IGCR's resettlement activities had been considered for more than one year in various international fora, and on 15 December 1946 the Constitution of the International Refugee Organization (IRO) was approved by the General Assembly of the United Nations.

The creation of IRO was described by the delegate of France to the United Nations, Raymond Bousquet, as 'the first real effort to gain a clear picture of a problem painful in its human aspect, delicate in its technical aspect and politically extremely difficult, and to find a solution for one of the most heart-breaking problems ... which ... has confronted the conscience of mankind'.

Speaking for the United States Government on that occasion Mrs Eleanor Roosevelt stated:

> Each member government of the United Nations has a direct selfish interest in the early disposal of this problem. As long as a million persons remain with refugee status, they delay the restoration of peace and order in the world... They represent in themselves political, economic and national conflicts which are symbolic of the work which lies before nations if peace is to be restored. While they remain a solid mass in assembly centres they deteriorate individually, and collectively they represent a sore on the body of mankind which it is not safe for us to ignore.

In general terms IRO was charged to care for, protect and re-establish in a normal life the refugees and DPs within its mandate. The term 'refugee' was to apply to recognized pre-war refugees, victims of Nazi, Fascist or Quisling régimes, victims of racial, religious or political persecution and persons outside their countries of origin or former habitual residence who were unwilling or unable to avail themselves of the protection of the governments of those countries. The term 'displaced person' was to apply to persons who had been obliged to leave their country as a result of actions of the Nazi or Fascist authorities.

With a legacy from UNRRA of some $2 million in cash and about $13 million worth of supplies and equipment, the Preparatory Commission of the International Refugee Organization (PCIRO) started operations on 1 July 1947. It was only in September 1948, however, that the requisite

number of governments had ratified the Constitution enabling the organization to operate officially as IRO.

IRO, like UNRRA, was to be a temporary organization. Its headquarters were established at the Palais Wilson in Geneva, Switzerland. The
organization got off to a reasonably smooth start owing mainly to its take-
over of many of the persons who had gained experience in UNRRA's DP
operations, both in the field and at headquarters. This take-over was
planned by PCIRO's first Executive Secretary, Arthur J. Altmeyer, who
had been seconded for a few months to the organization from his position
as Chairman of the United States Government's Social Security Board.
Altmeyer was succeeded by William Hallam Tuck, a distinguished American who became IRO's first Director-General and who, although he
served with the organization for only a limited period, did much to
establish IRO's policies and set the organization's standards and objectives. Tuck, in turn, was succeeded by J. Donald Kingsley, a dynamic
personality who came from the United States Government's Social Security Agency. Kingsley concentrated on making IRO function as an efficient
operational agency.

Along with many of my colleagues in UNRRA's DP operations, I was
transferred to this fledgling organization on 1 July 1947, and thus
embarked on a new and increasingly demanding phase of my career in the
field of refugee migration.

While IRO was charged with the vitally important task of providing care
and protection to the DPs and refugees, practically from its inception it
recognized the need to remove its charges from the debilitating camps –
and accordingly made vigorous efforts to promote their re-establishment,
especially through the process of resettlement. IRO's operations were
managed by a brilliant Frenchman, Pierre Jacobsen, who had the title of
Deputy Director-General. It was my good fortune to serve under Jacobsen's tutelage as Chief of the United States Resettlement Branch at IRO's
Geneva headquarters and to work in a challenging new field in which my
interest had been stimulated earlier during my tour of duty with UNRRA
in Austria.

IRO's resettlement activities were conducted principally within the
framework of government selection schemes, personal sponsorships and
the placement of individuals with employers on the basis of the former's
qualifications and the latter's needs. A response to IRO's appeals for
resettlement opportunities for the DPs and refugees came largely, in the
initial stages, from Western European countries, principally Belgium,
France and the Netherlands; British Commonwealth countries, principally
Australia, Canada, New Zealand and the United Kingdom itself; Latin
American countries, principally Argentina, Brazil and Venezuela; and, of
course, Israel in so far as Jewish refugees were concerned.

SPECIAL EFFORTS OF THE UNITED STATES ON BEHALF OF DISPLACED PERSONS, INCLUDING THE CREATION OF THE US DISPLACED PERSONS COMMISSION

Owing to the quota system embodied in the US Government's then existing immigration legislation (US Immigration Act of 1924), which was based on a formula of selection according to race and nationality and designed to preserve in a general way the ethnic balance of the US population, the United States was slow off the mark in opening its doors to any appreciable numbers of DPs.

While the Truman Administration and certain groups such as the American Council of Voluntary Agencies supported legislation to enable the intake by the United States of a fair share of the DPs, there was equally strong resistance to such a move within the Congress and from vocal entities such as the American Legion and the Veterans of Foreign Wars.

In his State of the Union Message of 6 January 1947 President Truman urged the US Congress to enact legislation to authorize the admission of greater numbers of DPs into the United States. On that occasion the President said:

> The United States can be proud of its part in caring for peoples reduced to want by the ravages of war, and in aiding nations to restore their national economies. We have shipped more supplies to the hungry peoples of the world since the end of the war than all other countries combined. However, so far as admitting displaced persons is concerned, I do not feel that the United States has done its part. Only about 5,000 of them have entered this country since May 1946. The fact is that the executive agencies are now doing all that is reasonably possible under the limitations of existing law and established quotas. Congressional assistance in the form of new legislation is needed. I urge the Congress to turn its attention to this world problem in an effort to find ways whereby we can fulfil our responsibilities to these thousands of homeless and suffering refugees of all faiths.

During the early months of 1947 several Bills designed to permit the admission into the United States of DPs and refugees were introduced in the Congress, but owing to the expression of strong views, both for and against them, within the Congress and by public interest groups, they almost all died in committee without public hearings. In July 1947 President Truman sent a further message to the Congress stressing the urgent need for legislation permitting the entry of DPs and refugees into the United States. In this second message on the subject President Truman reminded the Congress that there were still about a million DPs in Austria, Germany and Italy – 'persons with burning faith in the principles of freedom and democracy, persons who are unwilling to return to their homelands because of fear of persecution'. The President pointed out that several other free world countries had opened their doors to substantial numbers of these DPs. 'It is our plain duty to join with other nations in solving this tragic problem', he said. In concluding his message the President further reminded the Congress that the United States had been founded by immigrants many of whom had fled oppression and persecution. Many of the DPs now in question, he said, had strong affiliations with the United States, such as kinship, religion or national origin. He stressed the need for swift legislative action.

The then Secretary of State, George C. Marshall, was also a strong advocate of special efforts by the United States to assist in resolving the DP problem by joining with other nations in providing resettlement opportunities. In testifying before Congressional committees, Secretary Marshall observed that the majority of the DPs remaining in the camps in Europe were from countries which had become communist dominated. They did not wish to return to their homelands and their forced repatriation, he said, would be against American tradition and American belief in freedom and liberty. Secretary Marshall stressed the need for concrete measures by the United States: 'You cannot assert leadership and then not exercise it.'

In an effort to be responsive to President Truman's further appeal, a Congressional delegation, comprised of members of the House Committee on Foreign Affairs and the Committee on the Judiciary, travelled to Europe in the autumn of 1947 to gain first-hand knowledge of the DP problem and develop recommendations for legislative action. This Congressional delegation visited numerous DP camps in Austria, Germany and Italy, and consulted with representatives of Western European governments, IRO, voluntary agencies and US military and diplomatic officials. The group was thoroughly persuaded that repatriation no longer offered a viable solution to the problem, that a vigorous program of resettlement was essential and that the United States should not only take a fair share of the DPs for permanent resettlement, but also provide leadership for the international resettlement effort that was required.

Subsequently members of the Senate Committee of the Judiciary, together with members of the Senate Foreign Relations and Armed Services Committees, undertook a similar fact-finding mission to Europe and prepared a report which was to form the basis for consideration of the matter by the Senate.

In the months that followed there were frequent acrimonious debates on the issue in both the House of Representatives and the Senate. The main differences of opinion centered on the number of DPs to be admitted, the qualifying dates for eligibility, the proposed preference for DPs from annexed areas and the requirement of guarantees of employment and housing for the DPs, as well as the assurance that they would not become public charges. In the course of the protracted debates the US media were critical of the treatment by the Congress of the DP problem, suggesting a lack of due regard for the high humanitarian principles that are the American tradition. Moreover the voluntary agencies representing religious and nationality groups found that those Bills receiving the most serious consideration in the Congress were discriminatory and inadequate. The agencies representing Catholics and Jews considered discriminatory the preference proposed for DPs 'whose place of origin or country of nationality had been annexed by a foreign power'. This referred principally to persons from the Baltic states of Estonia, Latvia and Lithuania. It was thought that those areas were predominantly Protestant; moreover the suggested provision made it appear that the United States had recognized Russia's annexation of those Baltic countries and that part of Poland east of the Curzon line, which the United States Government has never done.

The proposal that an eligible DP would be one who had entered the American, British or French zones of Austria or Germany between 1 September 1939 and 22 December 1945 (arbitrary time-limits of no particular significance) was also considered discriminatory with respect to Catholic and Jewish refugees, since considerable numbers of both groups arrived in these zones subsequent to 22 December 1945.

In mid-June 1948, after many months of haggling and shortly before the 80th Session of the US Congress adjourned, the Displaced Persons Act of 1948 (Public Law 774), authorizing the admittance of 205 000 DPs over a two-year period, was approved and sent to the White House.

Apart from the restrictive measures mentioned above, the Bill as enacted established criteria in terms of preferences for agriculturists, household, construction and garment workers and blood relatives of US citizens or aliens residing permanently in the United States. Within these preferences priority was to be given to persons who had fought against the enemies of the United States during the Second World War plus their family members, and persons who were living in the refugee camps on 1 January 1948.

President Truman was not at all happy with the final product and, when signing it on 25 June 1948, he stated that elements of the Act 'form a pattern of discrimination and intolerance wholly inconsistent with the American sense of justice'. He added: 'I have signed this Act in spite of its many defects in order not to delay further the beginning of a resettlement program and in expectation that the necessary remedial action will follow when the Congress reconvenes.'

Notwithstanding its defects and shortcomings, the US Displaced Persons Act of 1948 represented a very significant development in the history of US immigration. As a result of the Act the US Government created an agency – the Displaced Persons Commission – to implement a planned resettlement program for the United States.

Passage of the Bill was also welcome news to IRO. Time had been marching on and while, as indicated above, several countries had been opening their doors to substantial numbers of DPs, the case-load in camps in Austria, Germany and Italy was still near the million mark, with a growing desire among many of the DPs for resettlement in the United States.

On 12 August 1948 President Truman appointed three Commissioners to administer the Displaced Persons Act. The headquarters of the Displaced Persons Commission was established in Washington DC and a Co-ordinator's Office was set up in Frankfurt, Germany.

PRACTICAL CO-OPERATION BETWEEN IRO AND THE US DISPLACED PERSONS COMMISSION

Contact was immediately established between IRO and officials of the Displaced Persons Commission, both in Washington and Frankfurt, and Commission personnel posted to the field were welcomed in IRO's various resettlement centers in Austria, Germany and Italy – centers which had long since been established to provide facilities and services to the selection missions of any government having a resettlement scheme for DPs.

The latter months of 1948 were used to establish regulations, formulate operational procedures and develop working relationships among the many elements involved in the new US program. While only a limited number of cases were fully processed and moved by the year's end, the machinery was geared to large-scale operation by the turn of the year and the level of movements reached several thousand per month during the first half of 1949 – a remarkable achievement, indeed, considering the complex nature of the program.

Step one in the long, involved procedure was the submission of an application by an interested candidate, usually channelled through a voluntary agency. At the same time provision of an affidavit was required, specifying that the applicant would be suitably employed in the United States without displacing some other person from employment, that housing would be provided without displacing some other person from housing and that the principal applicant and members of his family accompanying him would not become public charges.

Only once these basic conditions were met would processing begin. The Displaced Persons Commission itself was assigned responsibility for conducting a thorough investigation into, and preparing a detailed written report on, the character, history and eligibility of every person to be admitted to the United States under the Act. With regard to this investigation section 13 of the Act stipulated that no person should receive a visa who had been a member of, or participated in, any movement hostile to the United States or its form of government. To ensure that this

requirement was met, the Displaced Persons Commission took measures
to have every applicant checked by

the US Federal Bureau of Investigation,
the Counter-Intelligence Corps of the United States Army,
the Central Intelligence Agency,
the Provost Marshal General of the US Army,
the fingerprint record center in Heidelberg, Germany and
the Berlin Document Center.

Additionally, a special investigation was carried out in respect of DPs
whose country of origin had become communist dominated. In connection
with these security investigations special liaison was also maintained with
British Intelligence, France's Sûreté Générale and Italy's Questura.

Just as there were many entities involved in the security investigation of
the DPs, there were several entities working in conjunction with the
Displaced Persons Commission on the various other aspects of processing
for the United States program. The voluntary agencies, representing
various religious, nationality and non-sectarian groups, played an important role in locating sponsors at the United States end and assisting with
counselling; the United States Public Health Service had to satisfy itself
that candidates being accepted under the Act met the health requirements
of the basic US immigration legislation; similarly the Immigration and
Naturalization Service of the Justice Department had to be satisfied that
they met all other requirements of this legislation; consular officers of the
State Department, after ensuring that all requisites of the consular procedures had been met, issued US immigration visas to the accepted
candidates; and of course IRO played an important role at various stages,
including assisting in the preparation of documentation, assisting with
physical examinations, providing information to the Displaced Persons
Commission about the applicants' refugee status, calling forward applicants for processing and finally arranging the physical movement of the
accepted candidates to the United States.

In my capacity as Chief of the United States Resettlement Branch at
IRO headquarters, I maintained day-to-day contact with my counterparts
in the IRO resettlement centers in the field, as well as with the Office of the
Displaced Persons Commission's Co-ordinator in Frankfurt. Through
these close contacts, and with the benefit of carefully designed statistical
reporting from the field, we were able to maintain at Geneva headquarters
up-to-date pipeline reports and to co-ordinate the arrangements for
processing and movements.

While the time required for processing individual cases under the US
Displaced Persons Program ranged from three to twelve months, experience showed that on average sixteen weeks elapsed from the date of
introduction of an assured case into the processing pipeline until the issue

of a visa. This was an important factor in projecting shipping needs and arranging movement schedules.

In anticipation of a large-scale resettlement program IRO at an early stage had chartered, at a very favorable cost, a fleet of twelve United States Army transports (USATS) – ships that had been used to transport US military forces during the Second World War. These transports carried hundreds of thousands of DPs to new homelands during IRO's lifetime, including the majority of those accepted by the United States under the Displaced Persons Act.

Apart from its resettlement centers, IRO operated a staging center in Camp Grohn near Bremerhaven, Germany, through which the vast majority of the DPs accepted by the United States passed for embarkation and final movement. There was very close co-ordination between this center in Camp Grohn and my unit at IRO headquarters in order to ensure the timely movement of fully-processed DPs to the camp and compliance with shipping schedules.

SOME SPECIAL PROBLEMS

In June 1950 an amendment to Public Law 774 (the Displaced Persons Act of 1948) was enacted and signed by President Truman. This text introduced the following basic changes:

1   the eligibility date was changed from 22 December 1945 to 1 January 1949;
2   visa authorizations were increased from 205 000 to 341 000, including 4000 for Shanghai refugees, 18 000 for former Polish war veterans in Great Britain, 10 000 for Greek refugees, 500 for recent political refugees and 2000 for refugees from Venezia Giulia;
3   the 40 per cent preference for Balts and the 30 per cent agriculturist preference were eliminated;
4   selection of eligible DPs was to be made without discrimination in favor of or against a race, religion or national origin;
5   sponsors of DPs were required to be United States citizens;
6   the admission of 54 774 persons expelled from Germany was authorized;
7   provision was made for the admission of 5000 war orphans;
8   every person aged 18 years or over was required to take an oath upon arrival at the port of entry that he was not a member of a communist or other subversive organization; and
9   priority for DPs living in camps was eliminated.

The new deadline for completion of the program was 30 June 1951. This was subsequently extended to 31 December 1951.

Despite the complex nature of the US Displaced Persons Act of 1948, and the numerous offices, organizations and entities involved in its implementation, the program functioned remarkably well throughout the period 1949–51, with movements to the United States averaging about 10 000 per month.

However, because of the scheduled termination date for the program established under the Act – 31 December 1951 – and the planned closure of IRO at the same time, there was growing concern for certain categories of refugees in the remaining case-load whose resettlement was presenting difficulties.

The Kalmuks

One such category was the Kalmuks. These were members of the Mongolian race whose ancestors, thought to be remnants of Ghengis Khan's Golden Horde, had settled in the south-eastern part of Russia between the Don and Volga rivers at the beginning of the seventeenth century.

The Kalmuk community, a minority group considered to have been wanting in loyalty and dangerous to the Soviet State, was uprooted and dispersed by the Soviet authorities in 1944. While it is not known, at least to this writer, how and when the remnants of this community reached Austria and Germany, it is a fact that about 800 of them were in DP camps in Bavaria seeking resettlement in the IRO years.

Since the Kalmuks were members of the 'yellow' race, they were considered to be *prima facie* ineligible for admission to the United States under the provisions of the then existing US immigration legislation. Consequently my colleagues handling IRO resettlement programs to countries other than the United States made vigorous efforts to create resettlement opportunities elsewhere for them. Project proposals were developed and possibilities were carefully explored with the governments of Argentina, Bolivia, Brazil, Paraguay and Venezuela, but in the end these efforts were of no avail and the Kalmuks remained in their camps.

Mindful of the fact that IRO's time was running out, certain concerned individuals, notably Countess Alexandra Tolstoy and Tatiana Schaufuss of the Tolstoy Foundation, were not about to let Russian DPs, especially victims of Soviet oppression, languish indefinitely in the camps. At their urging I sought and received permission from IRO's Director-General, J. Donald Kingsley, to retain the services of a prominent immigration lawyer in Washington DC, Joseph Fanelli, to make a special effort to get the Kalmuks admitted into the United States.

Fanelli, who had served previously with the Immigration and Naturalization Service of the US Justice Department, was thoroughly conversant with US immigration legislation and the means of dealing with difficult cases under the appellate procedures of the Immigration and Naturalization

Service. He agreed to take on the task and promptly came to Europe. He stopped in Geneva to discuss the matter with myself and interested colleagues at IRO headquarters and he went to the Munich area in order to obtain first-hand information about the Kalmuks. During the ensuing few months Fanelli pursued a Kalmuk test case through the Immigration and Naturalization Service's (INS's) Central Office, INS's Board of Special Inquiry and INS's Board of Immigration Appeals.

Basing his arguments on the cultural background of the Kalmuks, which had been essentially European (Russian) during the better part of the previous three centuries, he argued that that fact rather than their oriental blood-line, should be the dominating factor in considering their admissibility. Fanelli won his case, and on 20 April 1951 the Acting Attorney-General of the United States rendered a favorable decision. Thereafter things happened apace and, by the time the Displaced Persons Act expired on 31 December 1951, 560 Kalmuk cases had been visaed for immigration to the United States.

The resettlement of the Kalmuks in the United States was facilitated by the Tolstoy Foundation, the Church World Service and the Brethren Service Commission. While there were early efforts to place them in Arizona and New Mexico, the arrangements in those states did not prove satisfactory and the majority of the group finally settled in the area of Farmingdale, New Jersey.

European refugees in China

Another group for whom IRO had assumed responsibility and for whom resettlement presented difficulties were the European refugees (principally Jews and White Russians) in China. The White Russians had migrated to China in the early 1920s following the Russian revolution, and the Jews had arrived in Shanghai following events in Europe in the late 1930s. While IRO had succeeded in evacuating from China and resettling about 9000 such persons during the period 1948–50, there was an identified case-load of some 5000 IRO eligibles remaining in the People's Republic of China in 1951, when the organization's termination was approaching.

Since the Displaced Persons Act of 1948, as amended, authorized the issuance of up to 4000 visas to DPs or refugees residing in China, and relatively few had been accepted under the Act by 1951, my branch at IRO headquarters made a special effort to facilitate the resettlement of more persons from the remaining case-load in China. In exploring this matter, however, it became apparent that the processing of interested and qualifying candidates from that case-load would be possible only if the individuals concerned could be brought to Hong Kong. Therein resided a problem.

We ascertained that the Hong Kong authorities, while being sympathetic to the problem and wishing to be accommodating, had no intention of becoming saddled with these refugees in the long term. In fact, upon being officially approached they agreed to permit the admittance to the Colony for resettlement processing of only those cases possessing end-destination visas.

Innovation was the linchpin for results in those early post-war years, and the problem called for an imaginative solution. We thus set out to devise a formula under which *prima facie* eligible candidates could be brought to Hong Kong for processing for the United States.

Our objective was to secure a block of un-nominated end-destination visas which could serve this transit arrangement and provide given cases from China with the opportunity to be admitted to Hong Kong and to remain there during the period of time required for the completion of their US immigration processing. An end-destination visa from the block would be used only in the event that an applicant was rejected for immigration to the United States. This course of action was approved by IRO's front office and an official communication carefully describing the problem and requesting twenty un-nominated visas from each of some twenty free world governments was dispatched over the Director-General's signature.

This rather unusual request prompted several queries and there was a considerable amount of back and forth between the governments which had been approached and IRO Headquarters. But finally several governments responded favorably and a pool of un-nominated, end-destination visas was made available to IRO. While it is not clear just how many of the European refugees in China were enabled, precisely through this scheme for processing in Hong Kong, to immigrate into the United States, it is a fact that about 3300 were eventually accepted in the United States under the Displaced Persons Act of 1948.

What is of further significance was the discovery, during the latter stages of IRO, when we were endeavoring to devise a novel arrangement for processing candidates for the United States, that the case-load of European refugees remaining in China was considerably larger than the 5000 on IRO's eligibility rolls. This discovery was of concern to IRO's member governments, and at one of the final meetings of the IRO Council it was decided that a trust fund be established upon IRO's liquidation to cover care and maintenance for needy refugees in China and to promote the resettlement of those refugees in China who had been under the legal and political protection of IRO. Accordingly, when IRO operations were terminated at the end of 1951, the organization transferred funds to the newly created Office of the United Nations High Commissioner for Refugees (UNHCR) and the Provisional Intergovernmental Committee for the Movement of Migrants from Europe – later to become the Inter-governmental Committee for European Migration (ICEM) – to permit the continuation of care and maintenance and resettlement assistance for refugees in China.

At the risk of getting ahead of my story, it is interesting to note in this regard that, between 1952 and the time of writing, about 26 000 refugees of European origin were resettled from the People's Republic of China to third countries via Hong Kong under the joint auspices of ICEM and the UNHCR – some 19 000 more than the residual case-load as identified by IRO. Even more remarkable, it is estimated at the time of writing that the case-load of such refugees still in China awaiting resettlement exceeds 2000.

THE TERMINATION OF IRO

During IRO's lifetime (1 July 1947 to 31 December 1951) the organization spent $428.5 million on the care, protection and re-establishment of refugees. A total of 1 038 750 persons were resettled under the organization's auspices in forty-eight receiving countries – the largest program of organized migration in history recorded up to 1951. Of this total, 328 851 persons went to the United States under the Displaced Persons Act – the largest number received by any one country.

The IRO resettlement machinery was the first experiment in co-operative international action employing selective procedures on a multi-lateral basis. Through this action it was possible to serve the best interests both of the countries concerned and the refugee migrants themselves. IRO demonstrated most vividly the potential of international collaboration when governments, voluntary agencies and dedicated staff are challenged to work harmoniously and effectively to achieve a valid humanitarian and social objective.

Beyond its achievements measured in terms of care and maintenance, protection and resettlement, IRO contributed from its experience to the drafting of the Statute of the Office of the United Nations High Commissioner for Refugees (UNHCR), the drafting of the Convention relating to the status of refugees and the drafting of the resolutions adopted in December 1951 at the Brussels conference on migration, which brought into existence the Provisional Intergovernmental Committee for the Movement of Migrants from Europe (PICMME), later to become the Intergovernmental Committee for European Migration (ICEM) and later still the Intergovernmental Committee for Migration (ICM).

Having broken new ground in multilateral diplomacy and opened new prospects for population movements on a large scale, IRO's operations were terminated on 31 December 1951.

4 'What Next?': the Intergovernmental Committee for European Migration (ICEM) – a Worthy Successor to IRO

The concern for further international action on behalf of refugees and displaced persons after the termination of IRO was reflected in various international fora by the recurring question: 'What next?'

NEW PROBLEMS, IN PARTICULAR SURPLUS POPULATION AND ESCAPEES FROM COMMUNISM

While the post-war emergency involving DPs and refugees had been largely resolved by IRO, there still remained pockets of these persons who required further attention. In Austria, Germany and Italy there were about 150 000 IRO eligibles awaiting emigration opportunities. There were lesser numbers in Greece, Portugal and Spain who had been unable to make arrangements for either emigration or permanent care. Further, as mentioned earlier, there was a remaining case-load of White Russians in the People's Republic of China, most of whom wished to emigrate.

In normal circumstances the Western European countries might have absorbed these refugees and DPs if the large, precipitate movement of German ethnics from Eastern Europe had not been taking place simultaneously. This movement was of crisis proportions, threatening order and stability in Austria and the Federal Republic of Germany.

Moreover the problem of so-called surplus population in several countries of Western Europe was already making itself felt. At a meeting in London in May 1950 the Foreign Ministers of France, the United Kingdom and the United States recognized that this was one of the most important elements in the difficulties and disequilibrium of the world. They expressed the view that it would be desirable to study the situation in order to determine whether there was a need for a fresh approach to the problem. To this end they agreed to designate experts to confer together and consult with the experts of other countries, such as the Federal Republic of Germany and Italy, having a major interest in the matter.

At about the same time the problem of expellees and refugees of

31

German ethnic origin was receiving special attention from a sub-committee of the Committee on the Judiciary of the United States House of Representatives under the leadership of Congressman Francis E. Walter of Pennsylvania. The sub-committee found that approximately 12 million persons of German ethnic origin – 'Volksdeutsche' and 'Reichsdeutsche' – had been expelled from Eastern European countries and former German provinces placed under Polish administration or occupied by Soviet forces. About 8.5 million of these homeless, uprooted persons were in the British, French and United States zones of occupation in Western Germany, where housing, job opportunities and land for farming were hopelessly inadequate to meet their needs. Allowing for a maximum effort to integrate these expellees into the German economy, the sub-committee estimated that at least one million of them should be offered opportunities for emigration.

THE 'IRON CURTAIN'

The situation was further aggravated by East–West polarization and the creation of what Winston Churchill in his Fulton, Missouri, speech of 6 March 1946 christened the 'iron curtain'. The Communist-established 'iron curtain' was approximately 3000 miles long, stretching across the girth of Europe from the Baltic to the Black Sea. It was diabolically designed to separate the Socialist countries of Eastern Europe which had fallen under Soviet influence from the free countries of the West. Restricted zones about five miles wide were established along the frontiers. They were heavily guarded and patrolled by mobile border police.

A narrower strip, usually about two miles wide and immediately adjacent to the border, was even more closely guarded. This was absolutely forbidden territory. Watch-towers were located at strategic points and wooded areas were levelled to provide a clear field for observation and gun-fire. The armed guards patrolling this area were frequently accompanied by trained dogs. Much of the border was blocked off with electrically-charged barbed wire, often equipped with signal devices that set off alarms in the nearby watch-towers. The system not only warned of attempted escapes, but also pin-pointed the location of the breakthrough. The immediate border area was also mined.

While the 'iron curtain' made escape a perilous enterprise involving the risk of death, the Eastern Europeans were already then voting with their feet and upward of 1000 per month were making their way to the asylum countries of Western Europe. They came by a variety of means from every part of the communist world, arriving in stolen army vehicles and commandeered planes and trains; they hid beneath shipments of freight; they bucked the fast-moving river currents; and they painstakingly felt their way across mine-fields. They came from Russia itself, the Ukraine, the Caucasus and the Soviet states of Central Asia. They fled from Albania, Bulgaria, Czechoslovakia, Hungary, Poland and Romania – and they turned up in Austria, the Federal Republic of Germany, Greece, Italy and Turkey.

RENEWED EFFORTS ON BEHALF OF REFUGEES, DISPLACED PERSONS AND MIGRANTS BY THE UNITED STATES

To arrange urgently needed emigration and at the same time cope with the new, continuing influx of refugees from the communist countries of Eastern Europe, the sub-committee of the Committee on the Judiciary of the US House of Representatives recommended the creation of an international organization to be composed of Western European emigration countries, overseas immigration countries and possibly some additional sympathizing countries. This new organization, the sub-committee thought, should be created outside the framework of the United Nations since most, if not all, of the Eastern European members of the United Nations were the source of political refugees and would thus be hostile to the activities of such an organization.

The sub-committee recommended that the United States Government should take the initiative by immediately convening an international conference to create such an organization. With this end in view it proposed the following text to amend the Displaced Persons Act of 1948 (Public Law 555 of 16 June 1950):

> The Displaced Persons Act (Public Law 774) is amended by adding a new section to read as follows:
> 16. Representatives of the Government of the United States are authorized to participate in a conference between affected nations for the purpose of studying and making recommendations providing for a satisfactory solution to the problems of persons of German ethnic origin who were expelled from the countries of their residence into Germany and Austria and are presently residing in those countries. The appropriation of such sums as may be necessary to carry out this section is hereby authorized.

In support of the sub-committee's recommendation the United States Congress passed the Mutual Security Appropriations Act (Public Law 249) on 31 October 1951. The conference report accompanying this Act included the following statement:

> Emigration of surplus manpower. Sec. 101 *(a)* (2). The House bill set a ceiling of $30,000,000 to be utilized for the emigration of surplus manpower. The Senate amendment set the amount at $10,000,000. The Conference agreement follows the Senate version. The Committee of Conference wished to make clear its intent that none of the funds made available pursuant to the proviso should be allocated to any international organization which has in its membership any Communist, Communist-dominated or Communist-controlled country, to any subsidiary

thereof or to any agency created by or stemming from such organization. It is vital to the security of the United States and to the success of the surplus manpower emigration program that no international body with Communist influence receive any United States assistance for the purpose of such program. It is the expectation of the Committee of Conference that steps will be taken as quickly as possible to get the program moving and that the funds made available will be used.

It is noteworthy that the above statement served to dampen, and indeed abort, the vigorous efforts of the International Labour Organization (ILO), under the leadership of its then Director-General David A. Morse, to establish operational machinery to launch a migration program for surplus manpower. While ILO's traditional role in the field of migration, especially as regards research and statistics, was recognized, there was concern that the composition of ILO's membership, including a number of communist countries, quite apart from its tripartite structure (consisting of government representatives, representatives of employers' associations and representatives of trade unions), would seriously prejudice policy decision making and obstruct operational aspects of program management – especially since the envisioned program would involve political refugees in addition to national migrants.

THE BRUSSELS INTERNATIONAL CONFERENCE ON MIGRATION AND THE CREATION OF ICEM

With enabling legislation and the start-up funds in view, the US Department of State acted promptly by suggesting that the Government of Belgium convene an international conference on migration. The Belgian Government responded favorably, and thirty-four governments were invited to attend the conference opening in Brussels on 26 November 1951. A total of twenty-seven governments attended, nineteen as full participants and eight as observers. The full participants were Australia, Austria, Belgium, Bolivia, Brazil, Canada, Chile, Colombia, France, Federal Republic of Germany, Greece, Italy, Luxembourg, Netherlands, Switzerland, Turkey, United Kingdom, United States and Venezuela. Argentina, Denmark, Guatemala, Israel, Norway, Paraguay, Peru and Sweden were present as observers.

After nine days of deliberations the participating governments adopted a resolution establishing the Provisional Intergovernmental Committee for the Movement of Migrants from Europe (PICMME), which was subsequently to become the Intergovernmental Committee for European Migration (ICEM) and, later still, with the global broadening of its scope, the Intergovernmental Committee for Migration (ICM).

Since there were strong diverse opinions at the Brussels conference concerning the selection of a director for the new organization, a compromise was reached at the final meeting whereby the powers of director were vested provisionally in Franz L. J. Leemans (Belgium) and George L. Warren, Sr. (USA) until such time as a director would be elected. It was further decided that Pierre Jacobsen (France), who had been in charge of operations in IRO and had demonstrated outstanding qualities of leadership and executive ability, would be appointed Deputy Director and assume responsibility for setting the new organization in motion.

The fledgling organization's headquarters were established at Number 63, rue des Paquis in Geneva, previously the address of the IRO.

At a meeting of the organization's Council in June 1952 Hugh Gibson, a former US ambassador of high repute, was elected as the first Director of ICEM. Pierre Jacobsen continued to serve as Deputy Director.

It seems altogether appropriate to observe that the delegates representing their respective governments at the Brussels conference demonstrated both vision and wisdom. They saw the need for an international mechanism, composed of like-minded governments, not only to facilitate the orderly migration of large numbers of displaced, unemployed or under-employed persons in Western Europe, but also to be ready and able to cope with new flows of escapees and refugees such as were starting from the communist dominated countries of Eastern Europe. Moreover they recognized, in the resolution establishing PICMME, which forms an annex to the organization's Constitution, 'that a close relationship exists between economic development and immigration'.

Thus a unique intergovernmental operational structure was created. Its stated purpose was and is to assist in and facilitate refugee resettlement and development-related migration through practical measures in the form of transport and related support services.

Four further key features should be mentioned.

First, the humanitarian motivation of the participating governments, resulting in the exclusion of divisive political attitudes in decision making and operational performance.

Second, the absence of rigid eligibility definitions, leaving it to member states, acting through the policy-making Council, to decide in which situations to provide assistance.

Third, the explicit acceptance of the twin notion that a) membership will be open only to governments with a demonstrated interest in the principle of the free movement of persons (in accordance with the provision of the Universal Declaration of Human Rights that 'everyone has the right to leave any country, including his own, and to return to his country) and b) each receiving country will retain control of standards of admission and the number of immigrants to be admitted.

Fourth, the right of any member government making a contribution to the operational budget to stipulate the terms and conditions under which that contribution can be used.

Against this background PICMME began operations officially on 1 January 1952, at which time IRO went into liquidation.

START OF MY WORK IN THE FIELD FOR ICEM, INCLUDING THE DEVELOPMENT OF CO-OPERATION WITH THE UNITED STATES ESCAPEE PROGRAM (USEP)

Along with several of my colleagues from IRO's resettlement staff, I was offered a post with the new organization and my initial assignment, as explained to me by the Acting Director Pierre Jacobsen, was to proceed to Frankfurt, Germany, make contact with the appropriate German authorities and establish a liaison and operational office in the Frankfurt area. In terms of program activity I was to work closely with the US Displaced Persons Commission in arranging transportation for 25 000 refugees of German ethnic origin admissible to the United States under the Displaced Persons Act of 1948, as amended. I was also instructed to establish and maintain contact with Australian and Canadian migration officials, as well as Latin American consular officers, and to be as responsive as possible to their interests and needs in the field of migration. Last, but certainly not least, I was alerted to plans of the US Government to establish a special program to assist refugee/escapees arriving in the asylum countries of Western Europe from the communist dominated countries of Eastern Europe. There were indications at the time that the operational headquarters of this new program would be in Frankfurt and that ICEM would have important functions to perform in relation to the program.

Taking account of the fact that many years later I was to be elected to the position of Director of ICEM – a development to be covered subsequently in this account – it is coincidental that just prior to my departure from Geneva for Frankfurt on that day in early January 1952, ICEM's Personnel Officer, a certain Red Murray, received from the printers a packet of ICEM employment contract forms and, since I was the first official of the new organization being assigned to a field post, it fell upon me to sign ICEM's contract No. 1.

ICEM was the first international organization in which the Government of the Federal Republic of Germany sought and was granted membership after the Second World War and, in view of its considerable potential usefulness, the German authorities, both at the Länder and Bund levels, were favorably disposed toward the organization. Consequently my task of establishing an office in Frankfurt was greatly facilitated. Within a few weeks office accommodation had been secured, staff employed, communications (telephone and telex) arranged and contacts with a range of working partners established.

In the early months of 1952, following the termination of IRO, it became increasingly apparent that the remaining displaced persons and the new refugees arriving in the asylum countries of Western Europe were receiving substandard treatment even though it was the most the host countries could provide, burdened as they were by over-population and, in the case of Austria and Germany, by their own unsettled national refugees.

These conditions were especially demoralizing for the new refugees who had risked their lives to escape to the free world – and moreover such conditions did not reflect the hospitality which the Western democracies desired to accord to those willing to sacrifice so much to regain their self-respect and to live in a free society.

Given this state of affairs, on 22 March 1952 President Harry S. Truman sent a message to the US Congress describing the inadequate and unsatisfactory conditions of reception and care awaiting new refugees from the Eastern European countries. He reported that they were arriving at a rate of 1000 a month to add to the 18 000 already in the asylum countries. Considering that the problem was of international concern he suggested that a US initiative was essential to stimulate and develop intergovernmental action. He asked Congress a) to provide aid for the victims of communism, b) to continue US participation in the intergovernmental effort to assist the emigration of refugees, and c) to authorize additional immigration of refugees into the United States.

Convinced of the necessity for further action, President Truman advised the Congress that, under the Mutual Security Act of 1951 (Public Law 165–82), he had authorized a program of assistance for refugees in fiscal year 1952 to which he had allocated some $4.3 million. His message to the Congress read in part as follows:

> I hereby notify you that I have determined that it will contribute to the defense of the North Atlantic area and to the security of the United States to initiate a program to improve the reception and treatment and to secure the resettlement of qualified persons who escape from the Iron Curtain area. This program will supplement, but in no sense supersede, the efforts being made by the countries bordering on the Iron Curtain area which carry the major responsibility for taking care of these people . . .

This move by President Truman provided the authority under which the Department of State established the President's Escapee Program (PEP) in April 1952. The name was subsequently changed to United States Escapee Program (USEP) and later still to United States Refugee Program (USRP). The principal objectives of the program were to improve reception facilities in the asylum countries, to provide care and maintenance assistance supplementing that being supplied by the host government and, most importantly, to assist the escapees either to emigrate overseas or to re-establish themselves in Western Europe.

It was envisaged that news of this program would seep back to people behind the iron curtain demonstrating the continuing interest of the people of the United States in their ultimate freedom and reassuring those persons choosing to escape from communism that they would be given assistance.

While the original PEP program was designed to assist refugees from communist countries in Eastern Europe, the language of the Mutual Security Act of 1953 was modified by the addition of the following words: 'or any communist-dominated or communist-occupied areas of Asia'. This amendment had the practical effect of authorizing assistance to Chinese refugees from Mainland China in Hong Kong and Macao.

The principal overseas office of the Escapee Program was established in Frankfurt, Germany. It was called the Office of Field Coordination (OFC) and was headed by Richard Brown, who had had extensive experience in various agencies of the US Government and in UNRRA. Brown had with him in OFC a team of US foreign service officers well practiced in the areas of programming, finance, management, political affairs and security.

As foreshadowed, my responsibilities in ICEM's Frankfurt office became largely centered on the United States Government's new Escapee Program. Having been on the scene from the outset, I attended practically all of the major meetings at which OFC officers discussed program implementation with representatives of a host of voluntary agencies, and I worked closely with OFC officers in developing procedures for the resettlement, processing and movement of those escapees found eligible for the program.

While country units for the Escapee Program were established within US diplomatic missions in all the major asylum countries – i.e. Austria, Federal Republic of Germany, Greece, Italy and Turkey – the OFC in Frankfurt had overall responsibility for the major aspects of the program, especially with respect to eligibility, finance and security. Thus procedures were established to ensure the exercise of control by OFC. For instance, when a *prima facie* eligible escapee case had been fully processed and visaed in one of the asylum areas, details of the case and a movement request were channelled from the Escapee Program country unit to OFC, Frankfurt, where control measures were taken before the case was finally approved and referred to my office in Frankfurt for movement processing by ICEM.

It is noteworthy that at the outset of the Escapee Program an official agreement was reached between the United States Government and ICEM whereby all approved escapee cases would be referred to ICEM for movement regardless of the point of origin or country of destination.

PEP was designed as a people-to-people program with the objective of ensuring the adequate reception, care and re-establishment of refugee/

escapees from communist dominated countries in Eastern Europe and China. While aiming to meet the immediate needs of the refugee/escapees, special attention was given to achieving the prompt and permanent re-establishment of eligible persons on the basis of personal dignity and self-reliance. PEP assistance projects provided for such things as welcome kits (containing toilet articles and other amenities), supplementary care and maintenance, counselling, resettlement documentation, language training and the funding of transportation to the country of resettlement.

The Program was implemented by means of contracts with a network of voluntary agencies representing the principal nationality and religious groups, including the following:

AFCR	(American Fund for Czechoslovak Refugees)
AJDC	(American Jewish Joint Distribution Committee)
APWR	(American Polish War Relief)
CWS	(Church World Service)
HIAS	(United Hebrew Sheltering and Immigrant Aid Society)
IRC	(International Rescue Committee)
ISS	(International Social Service)
LWF	(Lutheran World Federation)
NCFE	(National Committee for Free Europe)
NCWC	(National Catholic Welfare Conference)
ORT	(Organization for Rehabilitation through Training)
TF	(Tolstoy Foundation)
ULRFA	(United Lithuanian Relief Fund of America)
UUARC	(United Ukrainian American Relief Committee)
WCC	(World Council of Churches)
YM/YWCA	(Young Men's/Young Women's Christian Association)

Apart from the above-mentioned agencies, one called the American Friends of Russian Freedom (AFRF) was established to operate in Frankfurt and assist with the resettlement processing of Russian refugees and defectors after the completion by the competent authorities of their de-briefing.

With the increasing intensity of the Cold War in the early 1950s, there was a heightened interest in obtaining detailed information relating to economic, military, political and technological developments within the Soviet orbit. Refugees and defectors were regarded as one of the best sources for such information. Just as Frankfurt had been selected as the focal point for the various US programs for refugees (the Co-ordinator's Office of the Displaced Persons Commission was there from 1948 through 1952 and the PEP Office of Field Co-ordination was established there in 1952), so it was that US information-gathering entities were also duly represented there for obvious reasons.

The network of intelligence agents in the various asylum countries, as well as the defector committees in the various US embassies, were very effective in establishing contact with the newly arriving refugees and channelling those of evident interest to the Frankfurt area for de-briefing. These included high value people such as scientists and senior-level political and military personalities who went to the Frankfurt Defector Center, which had its headquarters in Frankfurt's IG Farben building. The less sophisticated but useful cases went to Camp King on the outskirts of Frankfurt, where the intelligence arms of the US military assembled a mosaic from the bits of information gleaned from the refugee/escapees. The persons involved received exceptional care and treatment during their stay in the safe-houses of the Defector Center and at Camp King.

The cases who had been at Camp King were usually shepherded back into the regular refugee channels after de-briefing and eventually processed for immigration by one of the voluntary agencies mentioned above. The cases who had been at the Defector Center received more careful handling, usually by an entity known as the Research and Resettlement Branch (R and R), which operated out of Frankfurt's IG Farben building. All such cases were treated as Escapee Program eligibles and practically all were moved under ICEM auspices. Since the R and R cases were of special interest to the United States, they qualified for expeditious visa processing, and my Frankfurt office was authorized to move them as full-fare passengers on scheduled flights ex-Frankfurt rather than by surface shipping, which was ICEM's usual means of moving refugees and migrants in those early years.

5 Operations in Austria

MY TRANSFER TO SALZBURG, AUSTRIA, IN CHARGE OF OPERATIONS

In the autumn of 1954 I was promoted and transferred to Salzburg to serve as Deputy Chief of the ICEM Mission in Austria in charge of operations. The armed forces of Great Britain, France, the Soviet Union and the United States were still in 'liberated' Austria at that time. However, progress toward agreement on the Austrian State Treaty was increasingly evident. The Treaty was in fact signed on 5 May 1955 and the military forces of the four powers departed from Austria a few months later.

Given Austria's geography – a country shaped somewhat like a tilted funnel with a broad mouth contiguous to three iron curtain countries – it was foreseen that, once free and neutral, it would become a major country of refuge for escapees from the communist dominated nations of Eastern Europe. Accordingly Salzburg, the apex of the funnel, appeared to provide a most suitable location for refugee resettlement activities.

In these circumstances, with the green light from ICEM headquarters in Geneva as well as encouragement from Washington, I developed detailed plans for a special refugee processing center in Salzburg, working to this end in close conjunction with the head of USEP's Austrian country unit, George Warren Jr. The existing facilities there, which had served the immediate post-war DPs, were in relatively poor condition and scarcely suitable for the anticipated influx of new escapees.

Since our plan involved the government of Land Salzburg as well as the federal government in Vienna, and called for co-operation with other Austrian Länder, the related negotiations were complex and time-consuming. However, by the spring of 1956 agreement was reached between the Federal Ministry of Interior and ICEM, and implementation of the project began.

In summary it encompassed the provision in Salzburg of housing for about 1500 persons in transit status, the setting up of a fully equipped processing center to accommodate selection missions from the refugee receiving countries and the ICEM operations staff, the preparation of dossiers on the so-called hard-core cases (physically and socially handicapped persons difficult to resettle), the establishment of a refugee documentation center and provision for the transportation of newly arriving refugees to the Salzburg center for resettlement processing.

Outside financing for the project came from the United States Government via ICEM, while the Republic of Austria provided land and covered

41

the cost of preparing the site for the center, including arranging for canalization, water and electricity.

As anticipated, Austria did become the major asylum country for escapees from Eastern Europe, and thus our thinking about and planning for the special processing center in Salzburg proved perfectly justified. However, events in the autumn of 1956 by far exceeded our expectations. During the summer developments in Hungary and at the Austrian/Hungarian border had created an atmosphere of suspense and excitement. Hungary's Prime Minister, Andres Hegedus, had stated that democratization would go ahead in the Hungarian People's Republic and that the 'iron curtain' would be lifted by the end of September. Indeed, according to some newspaper reports, dismantling was underway along the Austrian border. Thus, with somewhat relaxed conditions at the border, there was an increased flow of escapees from Hungary into Austria.

At that time Salzburg had a small Hungarian community comprised of a mixture of the Hungarian DPs remaining after the Second World War and some of the new escapees who had braved the iron curtain. As an aside it may be mentioned that the Catholics among them regularly attended an eleven o'clock mass said by a Hungarian priest in the Dreifaltigkeit Church – a magnificent baroque structure on Salzburg's Marktplatz. This mass followed the regular ritual through the final benediction, but then the Hungarian padre would step to the front of the altar; his little flock of parishioners would stand erect; and all would join in singing a Hungarian anthem. According to my informant, a Hungarian lady who was employed by the Australian Selection Mission, the English translation of the anthem was roughly as follows:

> God bless the Hungarian,
> give him gaiety and plenty,
> help him with Thy protecting arm
> when he fights the enemy;
> misfortune has befallen him;
> bring in a happy year for him,
> for these people have suffered in the past
> and already for the future too.

This brief interlude afforded these Hungarians the opportunity to exude pride in their national heritage and at the same time to show concern for their compatriots in the homeland. It was always an impressive and memorable occasion.

After the mass they would congregate either outside the church or at the nearby Cafe Bazaar on Salzburg's Schwartzstrasse and discuss the latest news reports. Understandably their interest centered on events in Hungary and related political developments – and here again the news was exciting. Hungary's communist party was in disarray; there was reported confusion and unrest in Prague; and a revolt had occurred in Poznan.

1. Construction site of the refugee reception/processing center in Salzburg, Austria, Spring 1956: (*left to right*) the author, a construction worker, and the Deputy Director of ICEM, Pierre Jacobsen

THE HUNGARIAN CRISIS, INVOLVING MY TRANSFER TO VIENNA

In the early autumn of 1956 it was being reported that Radio Free Europe, through its broadcasts and/or by means of pamphlet drops from balloons, was inciting the Hungarians to rebellion with veiled suggestions of outside assistance. It remains a matter of conjecture whether such reporting had any factual foundation, or whether it was merely a case of an anxious Hungarian people mustering false hopes based on the sound of a sympathetic voice.

The outbreak of the Hungarian revolution and its consequences for the international organizations concerned

Anyhow freedom fever was running high in Hungary, and on 23 October 1956 the Hungarian people revolted against their communist oppressors.

At the outset the manifestations, involving mainly students, were relatively peaceful with parades along the Danube, but soon Hungarian patriots who assumed the role of freedom fighters banded together and became increasingly aggressive. In terms of official action they demanded of Imre Nagy, the newly installed Premier, the immediate evacuation from Hungary of the Soviet forces. Moving swiftly they captured Budapest's radio station, as well as the headquarters of the Hungarian Secret Police (AVO) and, swarming into Budapest's Heroes Square, wrecked the huge bronze statue of Stalin. As another aside it is interesting to note that several of the freedom fighters who subsequently fled into Austria as refugees brought with them pieces of that statue. One such piece, representing a part of Stalin's foot, was eventually sold at auction in London during a fund-raising effort for Hungarian refugees.

The uprising, while centered on Budapest, quickly gained sympathy throughout the country. Guards on the Hungarian borders with Austria and Yugoslavia left their posts and, for the most part, the borders were open. However, during the actual period of the revolt only a limited number of Hungarians left the country. Most of them plainly preferred to remain in their homeland and participate in what they hoped would be the establishment of freedom.

Indeed for twelve glorious days Hungary was free. But on 4 November, just as negotiations were underway in Budapest for the withdrawal from Hungary of Soviet forces, events took a tragic turn. Instead of withdrawing, the Red Army, with massive reinforcements including tanks from its forces in the surrounding countries, went on the attack throughout Hungary and carried out a bloody suppression of the revolt. This action prompted an immediate exodus of Hungarian refugees, and during the All Souls/All Saints Day week-end (4 to 6 November) more than 10 000 Hungarians, mostly farmers, factory workers and students from towns and villages in the border area, poured into Austria. They passed the lifted barriers of the frontier posts in trucks, tractors and farm wagons piled high with luggage, or on foot carrying bundles and pulling or pushing hand-carts. It was a strange, pathetic procession.

Notwithstanding our plans and efforts to establish in the Salzburg area of Austria a special refugee processing facility, which incidentally was still in the stage of construction, the Austrian Government was scarcely prepared for such a massive influx of refugees – and the 10 000 who arrived that week-end represented only the beginning.

On Sunday 4 November Austria's Minister of Interior, Oscar Helmer, met with his senior staff to discuss measures to cope with the emergency. Accommodation for the new arrivals was a priority issue and it was decided, as a start, that the Judenau Castle, a camp at Eisenstadt and a large complex of two-storey stone barracks at Traiskirchen would be used as temporary housing for the refugees pending their processing for resettlement. Subsequently several other facilities were made available for this purpose, including a former hospital at Wiener Neustadt, a staging center adjoining Schwechat airport near Vienna, a staging center at Hoersching airport near Linz and the huge Roeder complex near Salzburg, which had been a US army facility.

The Traiskirchen camp, situated about 30 kilometers south of Vienna, which became one of the principal refugee centers, had been a military academy under the reign of Emperor Franz-Joseph. Indeed the stone entrance to the camp still bore the initials KuK, standing for 'Kaiserlich und Königlich' (of the Emperor and King). It is also interesting to note that the Traiskirchen facility had been used by the Soviet forces before they withdrew from Austria after the signing of the State Treaty.

Minister Helmer and his staff were quick to recognize that Austria would need considerable outside help to cope with the rapidly developing situation, and at that 4 November meeting they outlined a plan for international co-operative efforts. Their plan envisaged roles for three international entities, namely the United Nations High Commissioner for Refugees (UNHCR), the League of Red Cross Societies (LICROSS) and the Intergovernmental Committee for European Migration (ICEM). UNHCR would concern itself with the legal and political protection of the refugees and facilitate the local integration of those who could not emigrate. LICROSS, with help from the national Red Cross societies, would provide care and maintenance assistance and ICEM, working in close co-operation with its traditional partners, the voluntary agencies, would deal with the registration, documentation and movement of the refugees from Austria to other countries either for temporary asylum or permanent resettlement. As things turned out this assignment of responsibilities proved highly satisfactory and provided a model for subsequent refugee emergencies.

On 6 November, following receipt of an official request from the Austrian Government, the ICEM Director, Harold H. Tittman, dispatched a cable to 27 governments appealing for resettlement opportunities and special financial support to enable ICEM to handle effectively the processing and movement of Hungarian refugees from Austria.

Heightening of the crisis, involving transfer at 24 hours' notice to Vienna

ICEM moved swiftly in mobilizing its resources to meet the emergency. The Deputy Director, Pierre Jacobsen, made a flying visit to Austria over the 4 to 6 November week-end. After meeting with representatives of the Austrian Government and assessing the situation, he instructed me to proceed to Vienna immediately to take charge of the rapidly developing emergency operation. I, together with the medical officer, Dr Cleve Schou, a Norwegian national, and several local employees, moved to Vienna within 24 hours. Cliff Wyatt, a Britisher, with wide experience in refugee resettlement work, was my replacement at the Salzburg end.

It was a godsend that ICEM's Liaison Mission to the Austrian Government, headed by Gregory Esgate, was situated in Vienna's spacious Czernin Palais in the Friedrich Schmidtplatz just behind the Rathaus (City Hall). This most suitably located Palais became ICEM's central base of operations, and indeed the nerve center of the Hungarian emergency.

The emergency operation as handled by ICEM and the international response

Starting on the morning of 7 November ICEM, Austria, operated on a crash program basis. The mission staff was quickly increased from about 30 to well over 200. Experienced international officials were transferred temporarily to Austria from ICEM missions elsewhere in Europe and overseas, and several voluntary agencies generously loaned trained personnel to ICEM. For example a former British army brigadier, Leo Koenigsbert, was made available from the Paris-based World Association of War Veterans. His wife, Ingrid, a Danish nurse, also volunteered her services. Apart from the office in Salzburg field offices were established in Bregenz, Graz, Klagenfurt, Linz, Villach, at the Schwechat airport in Vienna and at the Hoersching airport in Linz.

A young Austrian lawyer, Kurt Teichman, who had previously worked for me in Salzburg, was our liaison officer with the Austrian Ministry of Interior. Teichman had come from that Ministry, was well-acquainted there and had close personal links with Minister Helmer. He was given an office, a desk and a telephone in the Ministry, and the close and effective connection thus created between our base of operations and the Austrian Government greatly facilitated meeting ICEM's needs for countless things, not the least of which were communications arrangements, rolling stock, inland transportation, camp space, police protection and special facilities at Schwechat airport.

From the outset of the emergency ICEM recognized the need to minimize the scattering and separation of Hungarian families, as well as the broader need to work toward the registration of the whole group and to maintain at least a minimum record of all the refugees being processed and departing from Austria under various schemes.

It was also realized that the refugees could not be expected to take irrevocable decisions regarding their final destinations so soon after leaving their homeland in such tragic circumstances. Therefore, in order to take account of these considerations while at the same time encouraging the rapid movement of the refugees out of Austria, ICEM agreed to arrange the on-movement at a subsequent date of those persons desirous of re-emigrating from countries of second asylum to other receiving countries.

The elegant salons of the Czernin Palais promptly became a focal point of ICEM's operations center. There was a battery of clerks and typists around the salons' long, polished tables to effect the basic registration and pre-processing of the refugees. Other rooms were made ready for selection missions, medical processing, general operations, communications and administration.

Despite the remarkable efforts of the Austrian authorities to provide adequate housing, the massive influx exceeded the capacity of the makeshift camps, and consequently large numbers of the Hungarians found themselves on Austria's open economy. In order to reach these Hungarians and get them into the resettlement pipeline, Austria's radio stations broadcast repeated messages urging them to report to the ICEM office at Friedrich Schmidtplatz for registration and processing.

Consequently, as from 8 November ICEM's operations center in the Czernin Palais was a beehive of activity. Throughout each day, from early morning until the evening hours, there were long queues of Hungarians lined up outside the Palais, and the sweeping staircase inside was crowded with them, scarcely leaving the ICEM staff and members of selection missions room to come and go.

Apart from the radio broadcasts, an information pamphlet in Hungarian was printed at an early stage of the emergency and distributed as soon as

2. Hungarian refugees awaiting registration for resettlement at the ICEM mission in Vienna, November 1956

contact was established to the newly arriving refugees. The text of this message (as translated into English) read as follows:

1. The Austrian government and international agencies are working night and day to help you in your desperate and needy situation.
2. The stream of your compatriots is increasing all the time; thousands come over the border every day. Please be patient, as the machinery dealing with your problem is severely strained.
3. Many of you will first pass through a transit camp where your most urgent needs will be cared for.
4. In the immediate future, perhaps in a matter of a few days, you can proceed to one of the countries which have offered you asylum, or you will be transferred to better quarters in Austria.
5. If you have relatives or friends willing and able to take care of you, private arrangements can eventually be made if you report to the Caritas or Red Cross offices.
6. Everything is being done to help you to take advantage of the generous invitation of countries outside Austria which have offered you a temporary or permanent home.
7. You are not in any way obliged to agree to go temporarily or permanently to another country, or to resettlement, unless you wish.
8. You will be shown every consideration in selecting either a temporary or permanent home.
9. Registration teams from the Intergovernmental Committee for European Migration (ICEM) are now operating throughout Austria.
10. These teams are equipped to register you for placement outside Austria, whether you are living privately or in a camp.
11. The following countries have offered you either temporary or permanent asylum: Argentina, Australia, Belgium, Brazil, Canada, Chile, Colombia, Costa Rica, Denmark, Dominican Republic, Ecuador, France, Federal Republic of Germany, Iceland, Ireland, Israel, Italy, Luxembourg, Netherlands, New Zealand, Norway, Paraguay, Portugal, Spain, Sweden, Switzerland, Turkey, Union of South Africa, United Kingdom, United States, Uruguay, and Venezuela.
12. When you are registered you will be given an opportunity to state your preference for either European or overseas placement.
13. The ICEM registration teams and missions of each country will visit the camps all over Austria.
14. Those of you who are not living in a camp can register at the ICEM offices at

   > Vienna: Friedrich Schmidtplatz 4, behind the city hall;
   > Salzburg: Hellbrunner Allee 18, Camp Hellbrunn;
   > Graz: Hofgasse 12, Landesumsiedlungsstelle;
   > Linz: Hauptplatz 6;
   > Villach: Camp St. Martin.

15. Do not be disturbed if you are not registered or seen by a registration team or selection mission immediately.
16. The world knows what you have gone through and what you have had to give up. There are outstretched hands from many countries to help you to find a new way of life and to ease your suffering.

While, as mentioned above, we had several experienced international officials working out of our hastily established operations center, there were also a number of secretaries who, at their own request, had been dispatched to Austria from ICEM headquarters in Geneva to lend a hand in the emergency situation. Several of these secretaries suddenly found themselves acting as leaders of impromptu teams, left to their own resources and having to use their imagination and rely on improvisation in order to cope with situations that they had never dreamt about in their well-organized headquarters existence. Suddenly they were faced with the stark reality that refugees were not just entries on a nominal roll but frightened, anxious human beings – bewildered people with countless questions to ask. Some were ignorant of the geographical location in Europe, or overseas, of the country in which their resettlement was being arranged, but all were desperate to get away – anywhere – from the closeness of the border, from the Hungarian secret police (AVO) and from the Russians.

By 8 November, when more than 12 000 Hungarians had fled into Austria, ICEM had five teams registering and documenting the refugees in the camps and border areas, as well as at the operations base in Vienna, and assisting the selection missions of receiving countries as soon as they arrived in Austria.

The response of governments to ICEM's appeal for resettlement opportunities and financial aid was rapid and generous. Among the first countries to offer to receive Hungarian refugees were Australia, Chile, France, Federal Republic of Germany, Italy, Netherlands, Sweden, Switzerland and the United Kingdon. Early pledges of financial support came from Argentina, Denmark, Greece, Italy, Union of South Africa and the United States. And of course the United States Escapee Program was on the spot providing a generous measure of material assistance from the outset of the emergency. The first country actually to receive Hungarian refugees was France, when on 7 November two planes sent to Austria by the French Red Cross loaded with first-aid supplies and blankets returned loaded with Hungarians.

Also on 7 November, within 24 hours of receiving the appeal, a Swiss team went to Traiskirchen to select Hungarian refugees for resettlement, coming on from there to ICEM's newly established operations center where, that same evening, nominal rolls were prepared and other documentation processed, thus enabling a train-load of some 400 to move off to Switzerland the following morning. So, with these early departures to France and Switzerland, a massive and dramatic resettlement operation was underway. During the next few days other groups were moved by bus and/or train to Belgium, the Netherlands, Sweden and the United Kingdom.

On 11 November our office received the following cable from the State Department in Washington:

> Department compliments ICEM on vigor with which it has moved in this crisis and further commends its efforts to co-ordinate with other agencies in the field. The President will confirm announcement Thursday that United States will endeavor to process up to 5,000 applicants under Refugee Relief Act from group which has fled Hungary since uprising. Request your transportation experts maintain twenty-four hour standby this week-end in event their services required for US movement.

At about the same time Canada announced a special scheme for Hungarians and ICEM detached 12 of its staff to work with the Canadian selection mission in Vienna's Tuchlauben Strasse.

In this kind of emergency situation ample communications were vital, and although there were insufficient telephone lines and telex machines in the early stages, ICEM's needs in this regard were soon met thanks to timely interventions on our behalf by Austria's Ministry of Interior. Moreover in order to expedite international calls ICEM was granted the privilege of making 'state calls' on a top priority basis.

With support from USEP, ladies from the US Embassy in Vienna established a makeshift kitchen in one of the small storerooms at the Czernin Palais. Hot soup and sandwiches were handed out to refugees, who stood in line for hours.

On 13 November the Council of Europe's Committee on Population and Refugees, meeting in Vienna, adopted a resolution in which it decided to 'support the efforts of ICEM and to approach the competent authorities of certain overseas countries in order that they may give asylum and employment to Hungarian refugees and their families'.

Although toward the middle of November movements out of Austria, mainly by bus and train, to other European countries were averaging about 800 per day, the daily influx was many times higher. By 16 November 36 000 refugees had poured into Austria, while 4703 had departed for countries of second asylum.

Fortunately offers of resettlement opportunities and financial aid continued to materialize. The United States, having decided to accept 5000 Hungarians from Austria under the Refugee Relief Act, received its first group of 60 aboard an ICEM flight on 19 November. The return leg brought a load of USEP welcome kits containing toilet articles, writing material and other useful amenities for distribution to the refugees.

ICEM's airlift to the United Kingdom also began on 19 November and soon after was operating at the rate of five planes per day.

The peak of the influx was reached on 23 November, when 8537 Hungarians fled over the border into Austria within 24 hours. By the end of November, less than one month after the influx had started, more than

100 000 Hungarians had sought refuge in Austria. About 30 000 of them had been processed and moved to other countries either for temporary asylum or permanent resettlement. At this stage average daily outgoing movements had jumped to 2600.

On 6 December another record was established when, within 24 hours, 6500 Hungarians were moved from Austria by air, bus and train. They went to Canada, France, Federal Republic of Germany, Ireland, Italy, Sweden, Switzerland, United Kingdom and the United States. For the first time since the emergency began, more refugees left Austria than entered it in the course of one day.

By the second week of December several countries had revised the figures they had given earlier respecting the number of refugees they were prepared to receive. For example the United Kingdom, which had originally announced an unlimited quota, was forced to call a temporary halt in order to allow time to absorb the more than 12 000 refugees who had already arrived there. Other countries, however, raised the number they had first specified. Canada, which had the second largest overseas program, requested ICEM to make all transportation arrangements for 6000 refugees before the year's end, the majority to travel by sea, the rest aboard eight flights.

By mid-December ICEM had a regularly scheduled airlift of 20 flights a day to overseas destinations, in addition to bus and rail movements within Europe and to the port of embarkation in Bremerhaven in the Federal Republic of Germany.

Vice-President Richard Nixon was among the dignitaries who visited Austria to observe the Hungarian refugee emergency at first hand. In his address to the staff when he called at the ICEM Mission in Vienna on 21 December 1956, he said, among other things:

Anybody could expect a certain amount of inefficiency in running a crash operation of this kind. But now that I have visited this organization and seen its efficiency, I can understand why this is the one operation which has raised no criticism.

In his message to Congress in January 1957 President Eisenhower stated:

Last October the people of Hungary, spontaneously and against tremendous odds, rose in revolt against communist domination. When it became apparent that they would be faced with ruthless deportation, or extinction, a mass exodus into Austria began. Fleeing for their lives, tens of thousands crossed the border into Austria seeking asylum. Austria, despite its own substantial economic problems, unselfishly and without hesitation, received these destitute refugees. More than twenty nations have expressed their willingness to accept large numbers of them.

On November 8, I directed that extraordinary measures be taken to expedite the processing of Hungarian visa applications under the provisions of the Refugee

3.   Vice-President Richard Nixon observing the departure from Austria of the first plane-load of Hungarian refugees to the United States, December 1956

Relief Act. On December 2, I directed that above and beyond the available visas under that Act – approximately 6,500 in all – emergency admission should be granted to 15,000 additional Hungarians through the exercise by the Attorney-General of his discretionary authority – and that when these numbers had been exhausted, the situation be re-examined.

On December 12, I requested the Vice-President to go to Austria so that he might inspect, first-hand, the tragic situation which faced the refugees. On January 1, 1957, following his return to the United States, the Vice-President made a personal inspection of our reception center at Camp Kilmer and then reported to me his findings and recommendations. He reported that the people who had fled from Hungary were largely those who had been in the forefront of the fight for freedom. He concluded that 'the countries which accept these refugees will find that, rather than having assumed a liability, they have acquired a valuable national asset'.

By the end of December 1956 more than 155 000 Hungarians had fled into Austria and nearly 88 000 had been processed and moved out of Austria under the auspices of ICEM.

The Hungarians who fled their country following the abortive rebellion in October 1956 came from all walks of life. There were farmers, students, shop-keepers, professional people including doctors, lawyers, architects and engineers and, of course, gypsies. During the latter months of 1956 and in early 1957 many of Vienna's hotels, bars and restaurants featured pleasing music from talented Hungarian gypsies. There were also a number of prostitutes who quite quickly managed to join the local 'ladies of the night' who paraded along Vienna's Kärntnerstrasse. Apart from being younger and rather more attractive than their Viennese counterparts, several of these Hungarian ladies distinguished themselves by carrying USEP welcome kits!

Just as there was a variety of components of the Hungarian case-load, there were diverse criteria for accepting the refugees applied by the receiving countries. The schemes of some countries were purely humanitarian and aimed solely at helping to relieve Austria of its hastily acquired burden. Others were selective and designed to serve given economic purposes of the country concerned. Still others were based on broader criteria and tended to satisfy both these requirements.

Sweden, for example, made a special effort to identify and select active tuberculars. On 29 November 1956 a group of such cases were moved in a specially arranged pullman car to Sweden's Halleby Sanatorium. Sweden also accepted many Hungarian students and teachers, in some cases entire classes. Among the more than 20 000 Hungarian refugees accepted by the United Kingdom there were about 2000 miners selected by the National Coal Board. The United Kingdom also granted scholarships to 150 Hungarian students to enable them to attend colleges and universities in Great Britain.

A Canadian migration mission had been firmly established in Austria before the Hungarian emergency to effect the processing of Austrian nationals and refugees seeking regular immigration into Canada. Thus the Canadians were well placed to be responsive in the emergency situation and indeed Canada, with a total of some 22 000 admissions, was second only to the United States in receiving Hungarian refugees. Canada's intake of Hungarians included about 500 members of the student body and faculty of the Forestry School of the University of Sopron. They had left Hungary in a body, and special arrangements were made to keep them together in Austria pending their processing by the Canadian selection mission. The acceptance of this particular group was personally authorized by Canada's then Minister of Immigration and Citizenship, Mr John W. Pickersgill, who visited Vienna at the time of the emergency. The group departed for Canada by ship on 29 December 1956 and eventually they were offered accommodation and facilities at the University of British Columbia, where they continued their forestry studies with their own professors.

South Africa's selection mission made a special effort to find craftsmen and skilled railway workers, so the majority of the 1300 Hungarians accepted for resettlement in South Africa were in these categories.

The bulk of the 900 refugees accepted by New Zealand were young, able-bodied persons who could be relatively easily integrated into the New Zealand economy. Among them was the 100 000th Hungarian refugee moved by ICEM from Austria – a former member of Hungary's international athletics team and one-time national 3000 meter hurdling champion.

Australia's migration mission, like Canada's, had long since been established in Austria to process Austrian nationals and qualifying refugees for regular immigration into Australia. Thus when the emergency struck the mission was in place and able to apply its selection criteria to the newly arriving Hungarians on a crash program basis. With an intake of some 7000 persons Australia was among the principal overseas receiving countries. Moreover that intake provided one of those 'now it can be told stories'. The story arose, in fact, out of an altogether different major crisis – that of Suez – which had, of course, a complex incidence on events in Hungary and the resultant refugee emergency.

The trouble in the Middle East had started in June 1956, following the withdrawal of British forces from the Suez Canal zone. A chain of reactions ensued in rather rapid succession. Upon President Nasser's nationalization of the Canal, France and Great Britain sought to place it under international control. Subsequently, despite a declared stance of solidarity with Egypt on the part of the nine-member Arab League, Great Britain, France and the United States announced agreement to establish an association to operate the Canal. When President Nasser indicated that he regarded this as an act to provoke war the matter was referred to the Security Council of the United Nations, where it was handled inconclusively with the Soviet Union vetoing a compromise resolution. Israel's invasion of Egypt soon thereafter prompted France and Great Britain to issue an ultimatum to the Egyptians and the Israelis to end the fighting, withdraw from a ten mile strip along the Canal and permit a Franco-British occupation of key points.

Back in the Security Council France and Great Britain vetoed a resolution calling for the refraining from the use of force and subsequently the British and French initiated military action in Egypt with the objective of safeguarding the Canal. Thereupon the Soviet Union threatened action to end the Suez fighting – a threat that caused President Eisenhower to order a global alert of United States armed forces. Moreover President Eisenhower sought and received authority from the US Congress to use US armed forces in the event of communist aggression in the Middle East ('the Eisenhower Doctrine'). In the light of such formidable measures France, Great Britain and Israel accepted a ceasefire, to be supervised by the newly created United Nations Emergency Force (UNEF). Upon the arrival of UNEF in the area the British and French forces withdrew from Egyptian territory, as did the Israelis except for the Gaza Strip and the area of Aqaba.

With a crisis of such proportions existing in the Middle East, the importance of the events in Hungary and of the resultant refugee emergency was magnified accordingly.

Reverting now to Australia's intake of Hungarian refugees, it so happened that among the initial cases accepted by the Australian selection mission there were several members of the orthodox Jewish community (Hassidim) from the Satamar region of northern Hungary. To respond to the prevailing pressures for the achievement of the maximum number of movements out of Austria as rapidly as possible and at the same time to respect Australia's desire to show early results under its crash program for accepting refugees, it was decided that one of the initial movements of Hungarians to Australia would be by air. (At that time normal migrant movements to Australia were effected by surface carriers.) This decision, however, created a problem. Because of the crisis in the Middle East we were under instructions not to emplane any Jewish cases on carriers over-flying Arab countries. ICEM's code number for the first flight to Australia of Hungarians, which was comprised mainly of the Hassidim Jews, was MIQAN 15/85, and it was indeed scheduled to over-fly certain Arab countries.

It was one of those hectic days in December 1956 when my very able Operations Assistant, Max Englaender, confronted me with the problem. It must be understood that at the peak of the Hungarian emergency, when there was a wide variety of movements involving several thousand persons per day, countless decisions on operational matters were made on the spur of the moment. We were under great pressure to keep out-movements at the highest possible level and there was not always time to weigh up all of the circumstances in a given situation. In the case of the Hassidim Jews going to Australia, the hasty answer was to show them as Roman Catholics (RCs) on the relevant ICEM movement nominal rolls. These documents, which provided personal details of individual migrants for the benefit of the competent authorities of the receiving country, interested voluntary agencies and, of course, ICEM's basic records accompanied all group movements.

Because this was the initial plane-load of Hungarians departing for Australia, there was particular interest in it for publicity purposes at the Australian end, and consequently a summary of the nominal roll details was telegraphed to Canberra a day or so in advance of the plane's arrival. The summary included among other things a breakdown of the group by religious denomination and in the event all were shown as Roman Catholics. Consequently, when MIQAN 15/85 landed at Melbourne Airport there was a host of dignitaries on hand to welcome the refugee migrants, including the Minister for Immigration Athol Townley, the Secretary for Immigration Tasman Hayes, and two of Australia's prominent Catholic leaders, Archbishop Mannix and Monsignor Crennan. There was, to put it mildly, considerable consternation when a bevy of orthodox Jews in their black hats and long black coats descended from the plane. Thank God, they arrived safely.

While certain countries, particularly European ones, were quicker off the mark in agreeing to accept Hungarian refugees for resettlement, the United States, once it got going, made up for lost time and took for permanent resettlement far more of them than any other receiving country. During the period of the emergency (28 October 1956 to 28 June 1957) the United States accepted a total of 33 205 Hungarian refugees from Austria.

As already indicated, the United States Government initially took advantage of the then existing Refugee Relief Act of 1953 and issued RRA visas to the first 5000 Hungarians accepted. When the quota under this source of visas was filled, it continued to accept Hungarians under the parole provision of the Immigration and Nationality Act – the first time that this authority had been utilized on such a massive scale. Formerly it had been reserved for individual cases such as ship-jumpers and political refugees finding themselves within the continental limits of the United States and requesting asylum.

Practically all of the Hungarians accepted by the United States, whether with immigration visas or on parole, were sponsored by relatives residing there or – the majority of them in fact – by interested voluntary agencies. In order to expedite movements out of Austria and at' the same time give more time to the voluntary agencies in the United States to make suitable placement arrangements, a part of Camp Kilmer in New Jersey was made available to serve as a reception and transit center for Hungarians arriving in the United States.

While there was considerable interest among the Hungarian refugees in immigration into the United States – indeed many regarded it as an obligation on the part of the United States Government to accept them on the basis of what they had understood from Radio Free Europe broadcasts – officials of the US consular and immigration services did not impose any particular selection criteria, simply satisfying themselves that the basic requisites of US immigration legislation were met.

Glimpses of just a few of the 33 205 Hungarians accepted by the United States

Any Hungarian arriving in Austria could apply for immigration into the United States – either directly or with the help, counselling and sponsorship of a voluntary agency. Thus those accepted for resettlement there represented a cross-section of the case-load. That each and every case represented a human drama is illustrated by the following examples:

Dr A and his wife were destined for Cleveland, Ohio, where they were to be reunited with her son, who had been a member of the Hungarian Olympic ski team in 1948. The doctor was an author and had been a newspaperman, but he said: 'I haven't published a word since the communists took over Hungary. My wife and I bought a knitting machine. In recent years we've supported ourselves making socks. I used to write for the Hungarian Radio League and I belonged to the Hungarian Pen Club. But when the communists took over I dropped them both. How could I write those lies? I'd rather make socks and be an honest man'. Escape for the couple took nine days and included being arrested by Russian soldiers in Körmend. 'But they offered to let us go if we'd return home. What did they expect us to say? We were over the border within hours. It was half-past three in the morning of 5 December 1956 and we knew it was Austria. We saw a sign that said "Gemischtwaren Handlung" and my wife began to cry.'

B had been a railway engineer in Hungary. On 21 November 1956 he commandeered an engine at the Szentgotthard railway station and, with his wife and his brother-in-law's family of four, steamed the one kilometer to the Austrian border – and freedom. They were going to Reseda, California, where the engineer's brother resided and where he hoped to work in his profession but on more modern-type trains.

The home of young *Dr C* faced the Kilian Barracks in Budapest and during the two-week siege of the barracks many wounded freedom fighters streamed through his door seeking medical attention. According to him many of those he treated were scarcely in their teens: 'One, a 12-year old with a piece of shrapnel in his cheek had a gun that was almost too big for him to carry.' The doctor, his paediatrician wife and their 3-year old son made their escape to Austria on 18 November 1956.

D, a 24-year old dental technician and a member of the Seventh-Day Adventists, had already had a brush with the Hungarian military authorities before the revolt because of his religious beliefs. He had been sentenced to five years' hard labor in a coal mine in northern Hungary. Although in ill health he seized the opportunity afforded by the uprising and made his way to the border. He was to be received by the General Conference of Seventh Day Adventists in Tacoma Park, Washington, and it was his hope to pursue his profession of dental technician in the United States.

E had been an eminent scientist in Hungary, doing research in the field of soil conservation. His work had been valuable to the régime and, despite the fact that he came from an upper class family, he was treated fairly well by the communist authorities. Still, he sensed that he was always under suspicion, and he was prevented from doing all he wished with his research. Part of his difficulty stemmed from the fact that he preferred to read whatever American and English scientific journals he could lay his hands on rather than those of Russian origin which were readily available to him. He and his wife fled to Austria early on in the uprising.

F, a midget who had worked for the state controlled circus in Hungary, was 32 years of age at the time of the uprising. He rode his miniature bicycle all the way from revolution-torn Budapest to freedom in Austria. He was fed up with the communist form of government and longed to go to a free country where he might continue with circus work and earn more than the barest of livings.

The *Gs*, a young Hungarian couple practiced in the art of dressmaking, were prevented from engaging in private enterprise under the communist régime. Instead they made a meager living out of periodic odd jobs. They joined the flood of refugees and arrived in Austria in early December 1956. They looked forward to a reunion with an uncle in the Bronx, New York, and an opportunity to work as dressmakers in the United States.

H had worked as a motor mechanic in Hungary. Thus he was able to 'borrow' a truck when the opportunity for escape presented itself. With his wife, two young children and three friends hidden under fruit boxes in the back of the truck, he lit out for the Austrian frontier. Near the border they abandoned the truck and covered the rest of the way on foot. They were going to Sioux Falls, South Dakota, where a cousin resided and where *H* hoped to find suitable employment.

The young gypsy, *I*, sold his beloved violin to pay for the arrangements for his own escape and that of a friend's family of ten from communist terror in Hungary. Before the revolution he had played his gypsy music at a tavern in a village near the Roumanian border. He was eager to get a job in the United States and save enough money to buy another violin.

J, a young Hungarian doctor, had been in difficulties with the communist authorities because of maintaining contact with his cousin, also a doctor, in Philadelphia, Pennsylvania. When the revolution began he worked for the Hungarian Red Cross. He made several trips to the Austrian border to fetch medical supplies. Then on 7 December 1956, by which time he had lost hope that the revolt would succeed, he, his fiancée and his parents joined the flow of refugees into Austria. He was hopeful of continuing his profession in Philadelphia.

K, a former member of Hungary's Olympic equestrian team, was one of Hungary's top horsemen, but he had been deprived of competing in his favorite sport because he was considered by the régime to be politically unreliable. He had been arrested on a false charge of conspiring against the state and deported to a small village on the Roumanian border where he had to work as a farmhand. He and his wife fled to Austria on 20 November 1956. A job awaited him at a stud farm in Skillman, New Jersey.

L was a pianist/composer who suffered under the stifling atmosphere of the communist régime. Owing to his known anti-communist attitude, he was denied meaningful employment as a musician. To make ends meet he played the piano at an espresso bar in Budapest. After the failure of the revolt he, his wife and their three children fled to Austria. All he carried with him were his musical compositions. They were destined for Summit, New Jersey, where *L* had a brother.

M worked as a carpenter and lathe operator in Budapest. The most impressive thing about the revolution, he said, was that it was the young people, who scarcely knew any way of life other than communism, who fought against the régime. *M* and his wife, with their 23- and 20-year old son and daughter, fled to Austria in late November 1956.

Despite several mishaps, including a brush with a Russian patrol, the *Ns*, Budapest ballet dancers, together with their 5-year old son, reached the Austrian border – and freedom. They were eagerly looking forward to a reunion in Columbia, South Carolina, with the wife's parents, from whom she had been separated for 12 years – and to the opportunity of pursuing a ballet career in the United States.

Dr O had been an ear, nose and throat specialist in Budapest. He had always refused to become a member of the Communist party and at the outset of the uprising he had worked with the freedom fighters. Having been warned by friends that the Hungarian Secret Police (AVO) were hunting for him, he and his wife kept themselves in hiding until 19 November 1956, when they could make their way to the Austrian border. They were going to Passaic, New Jersey, where the doctor's sister resided. *O* was hopeful of pursuing his medical career in the United States.

P had been a bus driver in Esztergom (Cardinal Mindszenty's home city). On the morning of 11 November 1956 he loaded his wife and seven friends on to his bus and headed for the Austrian border. The *Ps* looked forward to being reunited with his sister in Tallmadge, Ohio. He was confident of finding suitable employment and starting a new life in the United States.

Q was a craftsman in the old and meticulous art of porcelain-painting. For years he had been trying to arrange his family's immigration into the United States, but they were always denied exit permits. On 31 October 1956 he saw his chance to get away. He went by truck to the Austrian border and crossed at Jennersdorf. With help from the Red Cross, his wife and their two children were reunited with him a few days later. They were eagerly looking forward to joining her parents in Hillside, New Jersey, and to starting a new life.

R, a young architect, used a fake authorization to inspect construction work in a border town in order to flee from his homeland. He arrived in Austria on 20 December 1956 and promptly sought resettlement in the United States, where he was known to Father Kelemen Kiraly in Dewitt, Michigan.

S, a pharmacist, said he kept his pharmacy open at all hours of the day and night to provide badly needed medicaments during the uprising. But, once the outcome became apparent he, with his wife and 12-year old daughter, like tens of thousands of others, headed for the frontier. They arrived in Austria on 26 November 1956 and were promptly processed for resettlement in the United States, where they were going to be received by friends in Erie, Pennsylvania.

On 5 December 1956 a young railway engineer, *T*, drove a runaway freight train from Budapest to the border station near Andau and conveyed some 500 freedom fighters, students and other escapees to freedom. He was headed for Chicago, Illinois, where he had friends to help him start a new life.

Six months of solitary confinement had left an indelible impression on 30-year old *U*, a jockey, who had been on the communist black list from the time he had first tried to escape to the West in 1948. Thereafter he was not permitted to work with his horses, though this had been his vocation for 11 years, and was obliged to labor in the coal mines for very low wages. He joined the wave of escaping refugees and reached Austria on 21 November 1956. After prompt processing for resettlement he was destined for Arcadia, California, where he hoped to work with horses again.

After a frightening brush with Soviet soldiers that almost cost him his life *V*, a well known make-up man from Budapest, promptly decided to flee. Together with his wife and one-year old child he crossed the Austrian border near Andau on 17 November 1956. They were going to Hollywood, California, where his sister ran a shop for all kinds of theatrical make-up for the movies. He and his wife, whom he had trained, hoped to work in the make-up field on the Hollywood scene.

W, although only 16 years old, had worked as a butcher in a slaughter-house on the outskirts of Budapest. When the revolution broke out he, along with several of his fellow workers, joined the freedom fighters and were militarily active in the area around the slaughter-house. After several days of gallant resistance their little group was forced to break up. On 18 November he set out for the Austrian frontier on his bicycle and a day or so later he crossed into Austria near the village of Pamhagen. He was destined for South Bend, Indiana, where his aunt resided.

Newly qualified, 26-year old *X* had only just begun to work professionally as a medical practitioner in a small village near Budapest when the uprising started. During the ensuing week or so he divided his time between a few patients in the village and attending to wounded freedom fighters in Budapest. He continued to do this until 12 November 1956, when he learned that the AVO was looking for him. Afraid to return to his home, he set out for the Austrian border. An official looking pass that authorized him to transport medical supplies got him through. He looked forward to visiting a friend in Falls Church, Virginia, and to preparing himself to practice as a doctor in the United States.

Two Hungarian Olympic coaches, *Y* and *Z*, together with the athletes currently training under them, were activists in the uprising. But on 28 November 1956, when it was apparent that their efforts were in vain, they and their families took a train to Győr and then made the rest of the way to the Austrian border by farm cart and on foot. Between them they had coached several distinguished Hungarian Olympic record holders in field and aquatic events. They were destined for California, where they had relatives in Topanga Canyon and Monterrey. Both men hoped to renew their work as coaches in the American sports world.

On 7 November 1956 young *AZ*, a mechanical engineer, rode his motorcycle across the Hungarian border into Austria close to the little town of Ritzing. He had received his diploma from the Budapest Technical Institute just a few months earlier, after which he had worked in an automobile factory at Gsepel. But, he said, the pay was very low and the chances for advancement very limited. He had hopes of getting a good job as an engineer in the United States. His initial destination there was to be Chicago, Illinois, where his uncle resided.

Dr BY was working in a Budapest clinic for internal diseases when the uprising began. In the early days of the fighting the wounded poured into the clinic. According to the doctor they included not only Hungarian freedom fighters, but also Russian soldiers and members of the AVO. All were treated and cared for equally with the dwindling supply of medicines, he said. On 23 November 1956 he decided that he could be of no further use to the clinic. With his wife and small daughter he made his way to the border, and walked out of Hungary to freedom in Austria. The family looked forward to visiting a friend in Long Beach, California, and the doctor was hopeful of pursuing his medical career in the United States.

CX, a 32-year old freedom fighter who worked with the Revolutionary Committee Organizing the Resistance, struggled desperately to keep alive the Voice of Free Hungary. He and a handful of his fellow patriots in Dunapentele set up and kept in operation until the last minute a portable broadcasting station – Radio Rakoczy – the final free voice of Hungary to be heard in the Western World. They broadcast in four languages – English, French, German and Italian. *CX* fled to Budapest on 16 November 1956 after the Soviet forces had over-run Dunapentele and silenced the radio. He remained on the run from the AVO until he could locate his wife. They finally found each other and made their way to Austria, crossing the border at the village of Lutzmannsdorf on 21 December. They were destined for Sacramento, California, where a relative resided.

DW, an 18-year old freedom fighter, was sitting in a bus outside the ICEM office in Vienna waiting to depart to Switzerland when he spotted his wife, parents, sister and smaller brother on a street nearby. He had not known that they too had escaped from Hungary. They were waiting for their visas to go to the United States. With special help from ICEM and the co-operation of US officials, *DW*'s destination was switched and his processing for the United States was expedited so that he could join the rest of his family in immigrating there. DW was a mechanic, and his wife sang in the chorus of the Budapest Opera, but they earned scarcely enough to support the family. On 22 August 1956 they had all made a first attempt to escape, but failed, and the parents were jailed for eight weeks. On 9 November they tried again, but were stopped before they got out of Budapest. On 14 November *DW* decided to chance his luck alone and, after a brush with AVO agents in the town of Zalalovo, managed to proceed from village to village. He arrived in Gussing, Austria, on 17 November. Meanwhile the rest of the family tried yet another time and this time their luck, also, turned.

End of the emergency

On 22 April 1957, for the first time since the Hungarians had begun their flight to freedom across the Austrian border after the uprising, no new escapee arrivals were reported by the Austrian authorities. By way of explanation the Austrian newspapers were reporting tightened controls, including barbed wire fences, minefields and armed patrols on the Hungarian side of the border. The iron curtain was once again firmly in place.

Measuring the emergency from 28 October 1956 to 22 April 1957, a total of 171 189 Hungarians fled into Austria. Of these, 131 892 had been resettled from Austria as of 22 April. A breakdown is given in Table 5.1.

Table 5.1   Breakdown by receiving country of movements of Hungarian refugees from Austria

Country	Number of persons received
Argentina	621
Australia	5 842
Belgium	3 206
Brazil	415
Canada	18 436
Chile	162
Colombia	78
Costa Rica	3
Cuba	2
Denmark	1 106
Dominican Republic	581
France	9 161
Fed. Rep. of Germany	11 611
Iceland	52
Ireland	541
Israel	1 764
Italy	3 813
Luxembourg	205
Netherlands	2 973
New Zealand	922
Norway	1 034
Spain	14
Sweden	5 183
Switzerland	10 337
Turkey	505
Union of S. Africa	1 225
United Kingdom	20 532
United States	31 497
Uruguay	3
Venezuela	68

BACK TO SALZBURG

With the influx of Hungarians practically cut off, ICEM's operations in Austria resumed a more normal pace. Consequently it was possible to shift our operational base back to Salzburg. This transfer was effected gradually during the late spring months of 1957.

During the five to six months of the Hungarian emergency construction work on the refugee reception and resettlement center in Salzburg had continued apace, and indeed this installation was officially opened on 22 July 1957 in the presence of Austria's Minister of Interior, Oscar Helmer.

As indicated earlier, this center was intended to service new refugee/escapees arriving in Austria from Eastern European countries – and to facilitate their onward movement to a third country. Moreover the overall project provided for a survey of the entire foreign refugee case-load in Austria and the center was designed also to house documentation on each individual refugee case.

The survey of Austria's foreign refugee case-load

Upon return to Salzburg one of my major tasks, apart from supervising the ICEM mission's on-going operational activities, was to organize this survey. However, the situation had changed markedly from the time when the special refugee project was originally conceived. In addition to the 33 000 or so refugees of various Eastern European nationalities estimated to be in Austria at that time, there were about 38 000 Hungarians remaining from the recent influx.

After completion of the planning work implementation of the survey got underway in the summer of 1957. Teams composed of interviewers, interpreters and counsellors, and equipped with mobile X-ray units, fanned out across the various Austrian provinces to reach, register and X-ray the foreign refugees, whether they were residing in camps or existing on the open economy. The survey soon revealed that Austria's remaining case-load of foreign refugees included a high percentage of persons with either physical or social handicaps – persons designated as falling into the 'hard core' or 'difficult to resettle' categories. Consequently it became necessary to include medical practitioners and nurses in the teams to carry out a complete physical examination of all such cases.

The detailed information thus obtained on practically all of the foreign refugees in Austria, which covered not only negative aspects such as physical and social handicaps but also positive features respecting skills, occupations and employment qualifications, was particularly valuable in terms of promoting resettlement opportunities.

4, 5 and 6.   Ceremony for the opening of the refugee reception/processing center in Salzburg, 22 July 1957: (*above left*) Oscar Helmer, Austrian Minister of Interior; (*above right*) Dr Helmer and myself; (*below*) the author

In the wake of the Hungarian emergency, after so many countries had generously opened their doors to large numbers of refugees, there was a tightening in the attitude of the traditional refugee-receiving countries: schemes and quotas for refugee resettlement became comparatively limited, especially for 'hard core' cases. Consequently new approaches were called for and indeed new, imaginative techniques for promoting resettlement were developed.

The refugee/migrant catalogue

One such technique was our so-called refugee/migrant catalogue. Drawing on the wealth of data compiled through the survey we produced a series of loose-leaf catalogues listing in capsule form the pertinent personal details, both positive and negative, of the individual refugees in our case-load. Copies of these catalogues were circulated to a wide range of entities in potential refugee receiving countries, such as ICEM missions, voluntary agencies, UNHCR representatives, refugee councils and government offices concerned.

The introductory page of the catalogue provided a numerical breakdown of Austria's foreign refugee case-load. Beyond that there was a brief description of each case showing the individuals concerned as uprooted persons, who had been deprived of their job, home, property, place in society; many of whom had lost their parents, children, husband or wife; some of whom were physically or socially handicapped; and all of whom, for one reason or other, had been rejected for normal refugee/migrant resettlement schemes. The introduction to the catalogue stressed, however, that these persons had not lost faith in the possibility of having a new life, despite long and frustrating waiting periods in camps and the inevitable hardships of refugee existence, and expressed the hope that the information about them provided in the catalogue would serve to generate resettlement opportunities enabling them to gain their rightful place in a new society.

Recipients were advised that they would be informed as and when successful placements were effected so that they could make the necessary deletions. Similarly details of new cases would be dispatched to them from time to time for inclusion in the catalogue. With no names mentioned and photographs obliterated, the following are some typical examples of the thousands of cases that were catalogued for resettlement:

SKILLED JOINER, CABINETMAKER PARTIALLY CRIPPLED

... *has fully overcome physical handicaps*

Few humans could have survived the experiences that left *A*, aged 32, a partial cripple and brought him to Austria in 1956 as a refugee. Triple surgery was required to repair a badly injured spine, four broken ribs, and loss of most of his upper teeth. His recovery has been remarkable, sufficient to permit him to carry on his skilled occupation without difficulty.

A man of proven courage, occupational skill, and strength of mind, he is willing to accept a visa from any country that will offer him a resettlement opportunity.

FATHER ONCE HAD TB, NOW CURED, FAMILY AWAITS CHANCE TO MIGRATE AS A UNIT

... *skilled shoemaker, experienced in farm work, construction, and transport*

Strong family ties have held the *Bs* together through sickness, unemployment and the deadly boredom of refugee-camp life since November 1956, when they were granted asylum in Austria.

The father is 37 years old; in addition to 11 years' experience as a shoemaker, he has made his living as a farmer and as a bricklayer. Despite his TB history, he is in excellent health, energetic, and has proved himself capable of heavy work.

A first-class housekeeper, the mother has managed on next to nothing to keep up the morale and appearance of the family. The daughters aged 12 and 10, are recognizable immediately as attractive, intelligent, well brought-up children, devoted to their parents.

MASTER JOINER, CARPENTER, MISSING TWO FINGERS ON LEFT HAND

... efficient, skillful worker despite handicap

C, aged 48, lost two fingers in an industrial accident more than 20 years ago; most of his experience as a master woodworker was acquired after the accident, yet the loss of two fingers has disqualified him as medically unfit for all the resettlement programs he has applied for. He is in excellent health, industrious and intelligent.

POLIO LEFT HIM LAME, BUT HE WALKED 80 MILES TO ASYLUM

... then rejected for resettlement as a 'cripple'

D, aged 33, a skilled basket-weaver, has been a refugee for over three years now and has tried everything possible to qualify for migration. But regulations are regulations, and 'cripples' are excluded by them. He has a good basic education and is a man of exceptional character and determination.

FATHERLESS BOY, 9, SEEKS PLACE FOR MOTHER AND SELF

... mother and son called 'uneconomic' family

E, aged 9, and his widowed mother, aged 34, have been refugees since 1958. The son goes to the camp school and is reported to be a bright, well-behaved boy. The mother is a farm woman; she does housework when she can find a job. Mother and son are in perfect health.

MOTHER OF 2 YEAR-OLD GIRL IS QUALIFIED TEXTILE ENGINEER

... spinning machine technician and pattern designer

While working in a textile mill as a technician, *Mrs F*, aged 37, attended night classes at the University of Budapest to earn a degree in textile engineering. She is an expert on weaving machines and fabric production.

Mrs F has been a refugee in Austria since 1956 and is alone with a 2½ year-old daughter; the father was killed recently in an accident. In very good health, she speaks German and is improving her English with study.

FAMILY OF SIX, FATHER SKILLED, HAS SPECIAL PROBLEM

... mentally deficient daughter must be institutionalized

The *Gs* are caring for a mentally retarded daughter, aged 25, child of *Mr G*'s first marriage. Efforts to place this unfortunate girl in an Austrian institution have failed. The family cannot migrate until some provision is made for her care.

A highly skilled roofing and tile-setting expert, *G* successfully operated his own contracting firm for many years. The Austrians granted him and his family asylum in 1956; he has been working as a tile-setter since then. He is 53 years old, his wife, 47. The daughters, aged 17 and 15, are high-school students, and the boy, aged 8, is in grade-school. All are in excellent health.

MASTER TAILOR RAN OWN SHOP FOR 9 YEARS

... not limited in work by physical handicaps

A hunchback from childhood and without sight in one eye, *H*, aged 44, unmarried, has been a refugee in Austria since 1954. He works for a high-class tailoring firm making men's suits and overcoats, but his refugee status keeps him from establishing himself as an independent artisan. Aside from his physical handicaps, which he learned to accommodate years ago, *H* is in excellent health; he can supply first-class references from his present employers.

BORN BLIND, HIGHLY SKILLED ELECTRO-MECHANIC WITH 10 YEARS' FACTORY EXPERIENCE

... technical school graduate, specialist in appliance and telephone assembly, repair

I has been a refugee in Austria for two years. His work record is outstanding, proving beyond doubt that once he has a job he is fully capable of taking care of himself – he possesses all of the compensatory faculties of the highly intelligent, intensively trained totally blind.

Other measures for difficult cases

Apart from the catalogue there were other measures initiated to promote placement opportunities for our difficult cases. Complete dossiers were prepared on many of the physically handicapped cases and our medical officer, Dr Cleve Schou, who had performed heroically during the Hungarian emergency, travelled widely, making special efforts to interpret such cases to the competent authorities of prospective receiving countries. These efforts paid dividends and several European countries, in particular Belgium, Denmark, Netherlands, Norway, Sweden and Switzerland, established special schemes for accepting and placing appreciable numbers of these persons.

The Council of Europe's Committee on Population and Refugees, which had followed the Hungarian emergency with keen interest, was invited to Austria to gain first-hand knowledge of the serious refugee problem still existing in the country. As a further measure we staged a seminar in Salzburg and assembled a wide range of persons concerned, including representatives of the Austrian Federal and Länder governments, UNHCR, USEP, voluntary agencies, selection missions and our own ICEM staff. This seminar gave careful attention to the refugee case-load, particularly its hard core aspects, and ways and means to promote more placement opportunities. Recognizing that Austria would continue to be a principal country of refuge for asylum-seekers from Eastern Europe, much of the discussion also focused on procedures for facilitating the prompt resettlement processing of new escapees.

Visit of Mrs Eleanor Roosevelt

In mid-May 1957 Mrs Eleanor Roosevelt came to Austria to gain a first-hand impression of the refugee problem. Her host in the Salzburg area was

7. Briefing the Council of Europe's Committee on Population and Refugees on ICEM's refugee/migrant catalogue project, 1957

8. Participants in the ICEM seminar in Salzburg in 1957 to promote refugee resettlement: (*left to right*) Myself, Dr Hantschk, Chief of Section, Austrian Ministry of Interior, Paul E. Kelly and George L. Warren, Jr., USEP, and Arnold Rohrholt, UNHCR, Austria

George Warren, Jr., head of the USEP unit in Austria. Mrs Roosevelt was taken to various refugee installations, including Camp Glassenbach, which housed an assortment of Eastern Europeans, Camp Hellbrunn, the site of ICEM's new refugee reception/resettlement center, a refugee old people's home in Hellbrunn and Camp Roeder on the outskirts of Salzburg, which still housed several thousand Hungarians.

In Camp Roeder a surprise was in store for Mrs Roosevelt – a hunger strike on the part of the Hungarian refugees there who had not been accepted for resettlement in the United States, even though they allegedly were brought to the camp with that expectation. They were an embittered lot and a representative group of them presented a petition to Mrs Roosevelt which read, in essence, as follows:

We beg you, as one of the most respected political personalities of the free world, to accept our plea and help in solving our difficult case. Please support this request of the mentally and physically tortured Hungarian refugees. Please intervene with the competent authority or authorities in our serious situation. We are sure you will do your best to help us.

The inhabitants of the Hungarian refugee Camp Roeder in Austria, after careful and conscious consideration, came to the conclusion that we want to show in this memorandum our situation to the people of the United States of America, at the same time as we are starting our hunger strike, with a view to the solution of this unbearable problem as soon as possible.

The nearly 3,000 refugees of Camp Roeder made up their minds to go on hunger strike until all the Hungarian refugees who are in Austria and intend to migrate to the United States have the prospect of suitable arrangements being made by the Government of the United States.

In the heroic days of the Hungarian revolution, the entire Hungarian nation felt that all the free world – and above all the United States of America – was on our side, with its moral support.

Our war of liberty was quelled by the blood-thirsty Russians – as is well known – and the best of the Hungarian people, its most valuable members from the point of view of freedom, were compelled to leave their homes and seek shelter in the Western World.

The first weeks after our defeat proved that the free world, under the leadership of the United States, felt sympathy and was ready to help the refugees, not only with shelter but also giving them new homes in their countries.

The people of Hungary trusted steadfastly at the time of the revolution and soon afterward in the help of the people of the free world, especially the Government and people of the United States. The best sign of this help was – and should be in the future, too – for the United States to be ready to admit all the Hungarian refugees who intend to settle there – except those who prove politically unworthy. . .

The main criterion for acceptance should not be a medical but a thorough political examination.

At the same time we beg you to re-examine all the cases refused under your immigration legislation. We are not simply immigrants, but refugees.

> *(Signed)*   The Hungarian refugees of
> Camp Roeder

9 and 10.   Mrs Eleanor Roosevelt visiting refugee camps in Salzburg in May 1957

In accepting the petition Mrs Roosevelt assured the Hungarian refugees in Camp Roeder that she would do everything possible to persuade the United States Administration to continue a generous policy in terms of providing assistance and resettlement opportunities for needy refugees. With this assurance, she advised the refugees to stop their hunger strike and take the best possible care of themselves in order to be well prepared for resettlement when the opportunity arose.

Mrs Roosevelt was deeply moved by the problems of the refugees in Austria. Toward the end of her stay in Salzburg she met with representatives of the UNHCR, USEP, ICEM and the voluntary agencies and, while observing that her influence with the Eisenhower Administration had never really been tested – and mentioning in passing that she had never been invited to the White House since General Eisenhower had assumed the presidency – she agreed nonetheless to bring her influence to bear to the fullest extent possible, to help resolve the remaining refugee problem in Austria. 'It does not seem quite right', she said, 'that the United States, which was built by people of many different nationalities, should not rise to this emergency, which is not a very big one and which involves not too many thousand people'. She observed that this would be especially fitting since some Western European countries were accepting old people, putting them on relief for the rest of their lives and giving them places to live. Others had admitted the blind, tuberculosis sufferers and permanently incapacitated persons for the rest of their lives. 'The free world', she said, 'owes the Austrian Government a debt of gratitude. It took on a great temporary burden when its economy was not yet well re-established.'

Mrs Roosevelt was true to her word, and upon returning to the United States she made a special effort to interpret to the American people and the Administration the nature of the remaining refugee problem in Austria and the need for a further response from the United States in terms of resettlement opportunities.

The letter reproduced below was received from her and several of her 'My Day' columns, which were syndicated in many American newspapers, were devoted to the subject.

Mrs Franklin D. Roosevelt
211 East 62nd Street
New York 21, N.Y.

Dear Mr. Carlin: May 15, 1957

I want to thank you again for all your kindness during my visit to Salzburg. All of us had a wonderful time and we feel you contributed a great deal to the warmth of our welcome.

I was glad to have an opportunity to see the camps and to hear about some of your problems and I hope the columns I have written will be helpful.

With deep appreciation and my good wishes,

Very sincerely yours,

(Signed) Eleanor Roosevelt

While Mrs Roosevelt's personal efforts in this regard cannot be measured precisely, the US immigration authorities undertook further processing of the cases in Camp Roeder in the ensuing months and eventually the majority of them were accepted for resettlement in the United States.

Establishment of the United Nations Refugee Emergency Fund (UNREF)

Our local initiatives and the measures such as those just described were geared essentially to the case-load in Austria, but the refugee problem existed in various other European countries and also in China, so in an effort to tackle it on a broad front the United Nations Refugee Emergency Fund (UNREF) was established.

UNREF was meant to provide permanent solutions and was to be used primarily to deal with the difficult cases in camps in Austria, the Federal Republic of Germany, Italy and Greece, as well as with the evacuation and the re-establishment of refugees of European origin in China. It was to be directed mainly to the reduction of the number of refugees in camps. The basic principle for recourse to it was that contributions from outside sources were of a supplementary nature and were not intended to relieve countries of their responsibility for finding a solution for the problem of the refugees residing within their territory. At the same time it was recognized that certain countries of asylum, due to their geographical situation, were burdened with continuing influxes of refugees and thus were not able to support alone the expense and social problems resulting from the presence of large numbers of them on their territory. There was concern that if these countries did not receive adequate outside aid they might be compelled to adopt a more restrictive attitude toward asylum seekers. Consequently a *modus vivendi* was established whereby the granting of asylum would be accepted at least as a moral obligation and be matched by appropriate aid from the international community.

In the use of UNREF particularly close ties were developed and maintained between the UNHCR, ICEM and USEP. Monthly meetings were held between these three bodies to ensure the co-ordination of their work on the re-establishment of the refugees coming within their respective mandates. In this context an agreement was reached between UNHCR and USEP under which USEP paid two-thirds of the grants for USEP eligible cases requiring permanent institutional care.

Thanks to all these efforts the majority of the backlog of foreign refugees in Austria were eventually resettled in third countries or integrated within Austria, many of the aged and physically or socially handicapped cases being placed in institutions for permanent care.

Although at the same time there was a continuing influx of new refugees from Eastern European countries, it is gratifying to note that, with the benefit of the considerable experience it had by now acquired, the machinery to handle their prompt processing for resettlement, which involved the Austrian Länder and federal authorities, the voluntary agencies, USEP and ICEM, functioned with optimum efficiency.

PROMOTION AND RETURN TO VIENNA

In August 1960 I was promoted and appointed Chief of the ICEM Mission in Austria, which meant transferring from Salzburg to Vienna, back to the Czernin Palais at Number 4 Friedrich Schmidtplatz – our nerve center during the Hungarian emergency.

The Vienna assignment was somewhat more prestigious than my previous positions with ICEM since it involved frequent negotiations with the representatives of various Austrian federal ministries, as well as close liaison with ambassadors of ICEM member states and other members of the diplomatic community in Vienna. By choice I also retained personal responsibility for supervising all of ICEM's operations in Austria.

By this time the mission staff had gained considerable experience of all aspects of refugee resettlement and migration operations; consequently the mission was relatively easy to manage, with the various regular programs running smoothly. ICEM's principal challenge in Austria remained that of coping with the continuing, albeit somewhat reduced, influx of asylum seekers from Eastern European countries. However, through prompt registration and processing for resettlement, we were able to keep pace with the flow.

Fresh efforts for migration, including vocational training

At the same time ICEM was under some pressure from the traditional migrant receiving countries, principally Australia, to promote the emigration of Austrian nationals. With the Austrian economy already showing signs of favorable growth, and life in the country returning to normal and thus becoming increasingly pleasant, the Austrians were not wildly enthusiastic about emigrating. Nonetheless some interest could be detected, and with imaginative efforts there was a surprising number of potential candidates to be reached. One such effort involved the utilization of CARITAS's network of counselling offices throughout Austria.

Austria is mainly catholic, and CARITAS is the principal catholic agency in the country, concerning itself with both the spiritual and social welfare of Austrian catholics. Contact was established and close liaison maintained with CARITAS's headquarters in Vienna and the head of the office, Monsignor Unger, while not agreeing to promote emigration did see value in having the counsellors in CARITAS's field offices well informed on the possibilities of immigration into other countries in order that

11. The Hirtenberg Vocational Training School building in Austria

12 and 13. Refugees receiving vocational training at the Hirtenberg School in 1960

candidates might be duly counselled. Accordingly arrangements were made to supply those offices with all available information and documentation on existing immigration schemes, and this proved to be a very useful means of reaching those Austrians with a yearning to emigrate. Over the years upwards of 30 000 Austrian nationals were moved abroad under ICEM auspices, mostly to Australia and Canada.

At about the same time heightening interest was evidenced among ICEM's Latin American member states in making greater use of the organization in order to receive skilled European migrants to meet particular needs of the developing economies in the Latin American region. Although the major recruitment efforts for this purpose were undertaken in other Western European countries, principally Italy and Spain, we sought and received authority from ICEM headquarters in Geneva to explore the possibilities of recruitment for the skilled workers' schemes for Latin America among the Eastern European refugees in Austria.

While a hasty survey of the refugee existing case-load suggested some enthusiasm for Latin American immigration, it also revealed a need for training potential candidates, both in the use of modern equipment and machinery and in the Spanish language. The Austrian Government, through its Ministry of Interior, not only showed interest but also manifested its willingness to co-operate generously in such a program by making available a vocational training school at Hirtenberg, just south of Vienna near the Traiskirchen refugee camp. The Hirtenberg school was well staffed and equipped with modern machinery for training carpenters, cabinet-makers, welders, lathe operators and automotive mechanics. The Austrian authorities also assisted ICEM in finding suitable candidates among the refugees and having them transferred to the Hirtenberg school for training.

Interlude in Hong Kong

In the autumn of 1962, while serving as ICEM's Chief of Mission in Austria, I was approached by a representative of the US State Department and sounded out about my possible interest in leaving ICEM to take up related work with the US Government (State Department). Having given a positive response, I received an official offer of this employment in the winter of 1962–63. However, because of a commitment in the meantime to the Director of ICEM to undertake a trouble-shooting mission to Hong Kong, the duration of which was to be about six months, my swearing-in as an officer in the foreign service of the US Government did not take place until the autumn of 1963.

I went to Hong Kong in the early spring of 1963 to assume temporary management of the Joint ICEM/UNHCR Office and deal with some administrative and operational problems which were of concern to the respective headquarters of the two organizations in Geneva. Earlier in this account mention was made of the problem of refugees of European ethnic origin in China and of measures taken or planned to facilitate the evacuation and resettlement of those wishing to leave China. Having had a hand in developing the original plans for such an operation in 1951, I welcomed the opportunity to go to Hong Kong in early 1963.

After coping with the staff problems which had caused disruption in the Joint Office, I was able to concentrate on establishing contact with more of the European refugees in mainland China and arranging for their out-movement. Drawing on IRO records and information from voluntary agencies, principally the National Catholic Welfare Conference (NCWC), the United HIAS Service (UHS) and the World Council of Churches (WCC), further letters and personal data forms were dispatched to all of the identified European refugees in China.

Despite the fact that communications and mail service in China were irregular and unpredictable at that time, our efforts to reach more of the refugees were relatively successful, resulting in the receipt of an increased flow of completed personal forms, usually in Russian, at the Joint Office. These forms were promptly translated into English and submitted, according to where the refugees had relatives or a willing sponsor, to the authorities of the resettlement countries concerned. Upon receipt of a visa promise from a receiving country the Joint Office would apply to the Hong Kong immigration authorities for transit visas for Hong Kong to permit the refugees to enter the Colony for resettlement processing.

At the same time it would send a further communication to the refugees instructing them to send their travel documents to the British Chargé d'affaires in Peking, or the British Consulate in Shanghai (as directed by the Hong Kong Immigration Office) for the issue of Hong Kong transit visas. They were further advised to seek exit permits from the Chinese authorities in their particular area once they had their Hong Kong transit visas in hand, and then to present themselves to the China Travel Service (CTS) for movement by rail to the New Territories adjoining Hong Kong. The refugees were met at the Hong Kong border by staff members of the Joint Office and escorted to the Kowloon section of Hong Kong, where they were accommodated in hotels or apartment units on lease to the Joint Office for the purpose.

Soon after their arrival they were taken to a medical clinic for a physical examination, and to the consulates concerned for visa processing. During this transit period in Hong Kong food, accommodation and medical care were provided by the Joint Office. Once the resettlement visas were issued the Office arranged transportation for the refugees, either by air or sea, to the receiving country and prepared nominal rolls covering each departure for distribution to the parties concerned, that is the competent authorities of the receiving country and the representatives of the sponsoring voluntary agency.

As already indicated, the European refugees in China were mostly a mixture of White Russians who had left Russia after the revolution and Jews who had fled from Nazism in the 1930s. Many of the White Russians were members of the Old Believers sect, whose ancestors, a few centuries earlier, had refused to accept the reform of the rites of the Russian Orthodox Church. The Old Believers, or Old Ritualists as some regarded themselves, while gentle people, were strong-willed. They sought resettlement where they could be with members of their flock, live a simple but wholesome and dignified life on the land, and maintain their ancient culture and religion. They were distinctive in appearance. The men, practically without exception, had full beards and usually wore brightly embroidered blouses ('rubashka'). Most of the women wore long, peasant skirts and colored blouses; their hair was invariably done up in braids and they usually had their heads covered with scarfs.

Given the modalities of the program and the uncertainties experienced by the Joint Office in reaching the refugees in China and arranging for their evacuation to Hong Kong the Old Believers, like others, arrived on a case-by-case basis rather than in organized, scheduled groups. Since the Office was under pressure to get them processed for resettlement as expeditiously as possible, taking advantage of any existing placement opportunities, their movement from the Colony was likewise handled on a case-by-case basis. Consequently they went off from Hong Kong to various destinations, mainly Australia, Brazil and the United States. Owing, however, to their gregarious nature, as well as their social and religious beliefs – and with occasional assistance from agencies such as the Tolstoy Foundation – they tended to find one another. It is interesting to note in this regard that many of them in the meantime migrated onward to the Kenai Peninsula of Alaska, where they successfully established their own rural settlement. These particular Old Believers have almost gone full circle.

6 Assignment to the Foreign Service of the United States

FIRST STEPS IN GENEVA, INCLUDING THE STREAMLINING OF USEP

Having completed my special mission to Hong Kong, I departed from the Colony in August 1963 and proceeded to Washington DC to be sworn into the foreign service of the United States and be briefed on my new assignment at the United States Mission in Geneva.

The diplomatic title of my job was Counselor of Mission. The principal duties entailed overall responsibility for supervising the foreign operations of USEP – a function formerly handled by the Office of Field Co-ordination in Frankfurt – and day-to-day liaison with the headquarters in Geneva of ICEM, UNHCR and the International Red Cross (ICRC and LICROSS). My unit at the US Mission was composed of four to five foreign service officers, two secretaries (American) and between eight and ten local employees.

While the range of my responsibilities, as interpreted to me in Washington, seemed forbidding, the subject-matter was for the most part familiar to me – and thus I took up my work with measured confidence.

Just as it had been a curious chance that part of my work during my temporary assignment to Hong Kong had related to my involvement years before in developing plans for the evacuation and resettlement-processing of European refugees from China, so it was an interesting coincidence that my new assignment with the US Government included as a major component the management of the United States Escapee Program – a program with which I had been closely associated at the time of its initiation when I was in charge of the ICEM office in Frankfurt.

When I transferred to Geneva in autumn 1963 the tensions of the Cold War had diminished somewhat and, although the flow of refugees from Eastern Europe into the asylum countries of Western Europe – USEP's *raison d'être* – was still quite considerable, the decision was taken in Washington to change the program's name from United States Escapee Program (USEP) to United States Refugee Program (USRP). This change was favored in most if not all of the countries where the program was operative – certainly in Switzerland where the word 'escapee' reinforced notions of the Cold War and represented a potential irritant to the Swiss in terms of their neutrality – even though the United States Mission in Geneva, from which USEP operated, was accredited to the European headquarters of the United Nations rather than to the Government of

Switzerland. Incidentally, it had been perfectly logical to re-locate USEP's headquarters abroad from Frankfurt to Geneva, since by this time Geneva had become the center of humanitarian activities, with the headquarters of UNHCR, ICEM, the International Red Cross and a host of voluntary agencies established there.

In the course of my briefing in Washington I had received rather firm instructions to streamline the USEP administrative structure. As already mentioned, USEP country units were attached to the US embassies in practically all of the asylum countries. They were staffed with foreign service officers, American secretaries and local employees, who represented a considerable expense in terms of salaries and related costs.

Soon after taking up my assignment I visited all of the asylum countries in Western Europe and the Near East (Greece, Lebanon and Turkey) and made plans to close all the USEP country units, concentrating control of the program in Geneva. Arrangements were made for a liaison link with each of the embassies – usually through one of the political officers on regular assignment. This streamlining, completed within six months of my arrival, resulted in very substantial financial savings and indeed increased efficiency.

USEP, or USRP as it was known by this time, with its basic aim of facilitating the prompt resettlement of asylum seekers from the Eastern bloc countries after having provided adequate reception, care and maintenance facilities for them, was an important part of the total United States assistance effort for refugees. In administering the Program great reliance was placed upon the voluntary agencies and, following the closure of the country units, USEP contracts were drawn up and issued each year from the Geneva office to a host of such agencies, in particular the American Fund for Czechoslovak Refugees (AFCR), the American Joint Distribution Committee (AJDC), the International Catholic Migration Commission (ICMC), the International Rescue Committee (IRC), the Polish/American Immigration and Relief Committee (PAIRC), the Tolstoy Foundation (TF), the United HIAS Service (UHS) and the World Council of Churches (WCC).

The USRP assistance projects covered by these contracts related to the provision of food, clothing, dental and medical care, counselling, resettlement documentation and language training. Separate contracts, covering transportation assistance for the refugee/escapees, were concluded with ICEM. During the decade 1964–74 USRP annual allocations totalled between $2.5 and $3 million in an average year and the case-load of persons eligible for USRP aid ranged from 4000 to 40 000.

All refugee/escapees from Albania, Bulgaria, Czechoslovakia, Hungary, Poland, Romania and the Soviet Union were regarded *prima facie* as eligible for USRP aid and in accordance with established procedures the voluntary agencies, which had a network of offices in all of the asylum countries, were authorized to start granting assistance to newly arrived refugee/escapees as soon as their USRP registration cards had been completed. These registrations, which covered all pertinent personal details of the individual refugees, were filled out in duplicate, with one copy being forwarded immediately to my office in Geneva. Background investigations were initiated on each case upon receipt of the registration cards. In the event that derogatory information of a serious criminal or political nature came to light the case was dropped from the USRP eligibility rolls and the voluntary agency concerned was notified accordingly.

FURTHER LEGISLATIVE ACTION BY THE UNITED STATES

By the time of the Kennedy presidency the Government of the United States, and indeed the American people, had come to realize that the problems of refugees and migration were here to stay. President Kennedy's inaugural address included a ringing restatement of the US position respecting the concept of freedom for the individual human being. He said: 'Let both sides unite to heed in all corners of the earth the command of Isaiah – to undo the heavy burdens . . . and let the oppressed go free'. On another occasion President Kennedy also said:

> A steady stream of refugees pouring forth into the free countries of the world represents a continuing challenge to the sincerity of our offers of help and to our status of leadership in the Free World. What we do and how we meet the challenge will affect not only the personal lives of the refugees, but the cause of freedom in millions of hearts.

During the President's first year in office he sent to the Congress a Bill which, when enacted by the Congress, became the Migration and Refugee Assistance Act of 1962 (Public Law 87–510). This law simplified and codified the US Government's refugee and migration activities and centralized them in the Department of State. In submitting his Bill to the Congress President Kennedy, in an accompanying letter, summarized the foreign policy rationale for US Government refugee and migration programs. His letter read in part as follows:

> The successful re-establishment of refugees is importantly related to free world political objectives. These objectives are: *(a)* continuation of the provision of asylum and friendly assistance to the oppressed and persecuted; *(b)* the extension of hope and encouragement to the victims of communism and other forms of despotism, and the promotion of faith among the captive populations in the purposes and processes of freedom and democracy; *(c)* the exemplification by free citizens of free countries, through actions and sacrifices, of the fundamental humanitarianism which constitutes the basic difference between free and captive societies.

Public Law 87–510, which remains the law of the land at the time of writing, reads in part as follows:

Sec. 2(a) The President is hereby authorized to continue membership for the United States in the Intergovernmental Committee for European Migration in accordance with its Constitution approved in Venice, Italy on October 19, 1953. For the purpose of assisting in the movement of refugees and migrants and to enhance the economic progress of the developing countries by providing for a co-ordinated supply of selected manpower, there are hereby authorized to be appropriated such amounts as may be necessary from time to time for the payment by the United States of its contributions to the Committee and all necessary salaries and expenses incident to United States participation in the Committee.
(b) There are hereby authorized to be appropriated such amounts as may be necessary from time to time
    (1) for contributions to the activities of the United Nations High Commissioner for Refugees for assistance to refugees under his mandate or in behalf of whom he is exercising his good offices;
    (2) for assistance to or in behalf of refugees designated by the President (by class, group, or designation of their respective countries of origin or areas of residence) when the President determines that such assistance will contribute to the defense, or to the security, or to the foreign policy interests of the United States.

While Public Law 87–510 established permanent authority for the US Congress to appropriate funds for assistance to refugees and migrants, it was also recognized in the Kennedy Administration – and certainly among the leaders of voluntary agencies – that US immigration legislation was in drastic need of reform. For more than four decades the granting of immigration visas for the United States had been tied to a system of quotas based on nationality and weighted in favor of certain Europeans. Asians had been almost entirely excluded.

In a special message to the US Congress in July 1963 President Kennedy called for 'urgent and fundamental' reform of the immigration system. Abba P. Schwartz, who was the Administrator of the State Department's Bureau of Security and Consular Affairs in the Kennedy Administration, actively pursued the matter. In one speech on the refugee aspects of the law Mr Schwartz stated

Flexibility in the authority of the President to admit groups of refugees without delay is important to our foreign policy interests ... regardless of their race, creed or national origin. We feel that provision for admission of refugees should be embodied in our basic immigration law to reflect our traditional and continuing concern for refugees.

The resulting amendment of the Immigration and Nationality Act (Public Law 89–236), while continuing to limit the total number of immigrants, not only eliminated the national origin concept but also made specific provision for refugees.

President Kennedy did not live to see the enactment of this law but President Johnson, who had continued to press the matter, regarded it as so significant that he travelled to New York Harbor to sign it in a ceremony conducted on 3 October 1965 at the base of the Statue of Liberty and in sight of Ellis Island, where so many immigrants of earlier times had been received and processed. On that occasion President Johnson said: 'It is one of the most important acts of this Congress and this Administration, for it repairs a very deep and painful flaw in the fabric of American justice. It corrects a cruel and enduring wrong in the conduct of the American nation.'

Action on behalf of Cubans

President Johnson also took the opportunity at the Statue of Liberty to announce that, beyond the refugee provisions of the new law, he was opening the United States to all Cubans who wished to enter. Within two months of that announcement negotiations in Havana between the Swiss Ambassador (Switzerland representing US interests in Cuba) and Dr Fidel Castro resulted in the organization of an airlift which brought to the United States two plane-loads of Cubans a day, five days a week. In total, some 260 000 Cubans took advantage of the offer to flee the Castro régime and be resettled in the United States.

DAY-TO-DAY INVOLVEMENT WITH UNHCR AND ICEM IN RESPECT OF NEW REFUGEE AND MIGRANT PROBLEMS EMERGING ACROSS THE WORLD

General management of USRP continued to be my major responsibility and preoccupation. However, from my vantage point at the US Mission in Geneva I was also charged with day-to-day involvement with the head-quarters of UNHCR and ICEM in order to follow closely the activities of those organizations and to keep the State Department well informed on significant developments in the field of refugee and migration matters in which the US Government had an interest in political as well as human-itarian terms. Noteworthy developments were numerous.

UNHCR efforts for African refugees

In the wake of decolonization and wars of national liberation the early 1960s were marked by the emergence of many new refugee situations, particularly in Africa. There were some 300 000 refugees from Angola in the Congo (Leopoldville); 160 000 from Rwanda in Burundi, the Congo, Tanzania and Uganda; 60 000 from Portuguese Guinea in Senegal; 150 000 from the Sudan in the Central African Republic, the Congo and Uganda; 20 000 from Mozambique in Tanzania; 30 000 from Ethiopia in the Sudan; and 65 000 from the Congo in Burundi, the Central African Republic, the Sudan, Uganda and Tanzania.

The Office of the UNHCR was alert and promptly responsive to the newly emerging refugee problems in Africa. Apart from providing emergency assistance in the form of food, shelter and medical care, the Office wisely supplied the refugees with seeds and farm implements to enable them to become self-supporting in their new environment as rapidly as possible. This approach, geared to the maintenance of peace and stability in the countries in which the refugees found themselves, won warm support from member governments of the Executive Committee of UNHCR which were funding the programs, certainly including the United States Government.

ICEM's Latin American selective migration program

In 1964 ICEM, at the request of its Latin American member governments, established a Selective Migration Program in order to provide highly qualified manpower essential to the development of the Latin American economies, but unavailable in the local labor markets. This program, which won strong support, both financial and political, from the United States Government, was geared to the development policy and to the general economic and social conditions of each country.

Further assistance to Cubans

There were also further developments with respect to the Cubans. When the possibility of direct migration to the United States, mentioned earlier and taken advantage of by large numbers of them, was blocked, those still desirous of leaving their communist dominated homeland sought exit permits, purchased ostensibly round-trip (Havana–Madrid–Havana) tickets in hard currency (US dollars) and arrived legally in Spain, where they were treated as refugees, receiving care and maintenance assistance from the voluntary agencies and UNHCR and resettlement assistance from ICEM. The large majority – upward of 20 000 – then sought immigration into the United States where many of them had close relatives.

Asia and the Middle East

Large-scale refugee problems were also affecting Asia. After an influx during 1962 and 1963 of more than 300 000 Chinese from mainland China into Hong Kong, some 75 000 Chinese refugees entered Macao in 1964 and required assistance from the international community. And in Vietnam, with the infiltration of North Vietnamese, guerilla operations escalated to open warfare. By 1968 almost one million Vietnamese had fled from insecure areas and, being displaced, were in need of care and maintenance assistance.

A case-load of Tibetan refugees (40 000 in India and 12 000 in Nepal) also became the concern of the international community. However, as a result of some well designed assistance projects – financed for the most part by UNHCR and/or the United States Government and supervised by certain voluntary agencies – and thanks to the resourcefulness of the Tibetans themselves under the spiritual and temporal leadership of the Dalai Lama, this case-load was largely self-supporting by 1966.

And of course the refugee situation in the Middle East remained critical. As a result of the Six-Day War in 1967 about 500 000 Palestinians fled from the Israeli occupied territories.

New problems of Polish Jews

Back in Europe events in Poland were receiving close attention. Soon after the Six-Day War of 1967 in the Middle East Premier Gomulka publicly questioned the loyalty of Jews remaining in Poland. This put pressure on the Polish Jews, forcing the majority of them to renounce their right to Polish nationality, seek legal exit permits and arrange their departure from the country. While transit facilities were generously provided by the traditional asylum countries of Western Europe the Jews, who departed from Poland legally, were not regarded as refugees in the legal sense of the term under the UNHCR mandate but rather as economic migrants. Thus they remained outside the official refugee channels. Nonetheless they were treated as USRP eligibles and assisted by the Jewish voluntary agencies (AJDC and HIAS). ICEM arranged their resettlement from the countries of temporary asylum – some 2500 in 1968 and about 4000 in 1969.

United Nations Declaration on Territorial Asylum

By this time refugee problems throughout the world were receiving greater attention in international fora. For example on 14 December 1967 the General Assembly of the United Nations adopted a Declaration on Territorial Asylum. Accession to this Declaration reflected the growing concern of governments of countries where new refugee problems had arisen, especially in Africa.

The Czechoslovak crisis

Then 1968 brought a particular surprise. In the early hours of 21 August I was awakened by a telephone call from my immediate supervisors in

Washington DC, namely Clement Sobatka, Director of the State Department's Office of Refugee and Migration Affairs, and Ambassador Graham Martin, who was then serving as Special Adviser to the Secretary of State for Refugee and Migration Affairs. They were calling from the State Department's Operations Center to inform me of developments in Czechoslovakia. They said that a massive invasion of Czechoslovakia by the armed forces of the Soviet Union and other Warsaw Pact countries was in progress, and that all concerned should get braced for a new refugee emergency. I was instructed to establish contact immediately with USRP's voluntary agency working partners and ICEM to ensure that all possible measures were taken to respond to the needs of Czechs who might be victims of this development. Meetings were promptly arranged and, as in the case of the Hungarian emergency twelve years earlier, all concerned showed willingness to do whatever was necessary. The field missions of ICEM and the offices of the voluntary agencies in all of the asylum countries in Western Europe were alerted and instructed to be responsive to the needs of any Czechs who had been victimized by the onslaught on their homeland. USRP funds were made available on an emergency basis.

This event, which brought to an abrupt end the short-lived political freedom in Czechoslovakia – the so-called 'Prague Spring' which was Alexander Dubček's effort to create 'socialism with a human face' – aroused immediate widespread concern and sympathy for the people of Czechoslovakia. Dubček's ill-fated reform movement had obviously represented a major ideological threat to the Kremlin and, apart from the military invasion and occupation of Czechoslovakia, it led to Brezhnev's proclamation of the doctrine of 'limited sovereignty', whereby Moscow took upon itself the right to intervene in the affairs of other Eastern European countries in order to safeguard Soviet-type socialism.

For those of us directly involved in refugee and migration affairs the events of August 1968 in Czechoslovakia produced an unprecedented situation. They not only generated a heavy flow of Czechs out of their country into asylum countries, particularly Austria, the Federal Republic of Germany and Italy, but also caught by surprise, in various Western European countries, thousands of Czechs who had taken advantage of the 'Prague Spring' to secure passports and travel abroad as tourists.

It was estimated that on 21 August 1968 there were upwards of 80 000 Czechs travelling legally abroad in Western Europe. During the early stages of the invasion the borders with Austria and the Federal Republic of Germany were open and there was heavy traffic in both directions. Some of the tourists, who had left their children or other close family members behind, were understandably concerned about their welfare and returned home for this reason. Many of them, as soon as they were reunited with their relatives, seized the opportunity to return as family units to the West. During the summer and autumn months of 1968 an average of 1500 persons per day were crossing from Czechoslovakia into Austria and another 150 per day into the Federal Republic of Germany.

However, many of the Czechs in the asylum countries cherished the hope that they might soon be able to return home. Many of them did not qualify, nor did they necessarily desire to qualify, for the formal definition of 'refugee'. Rather, they chose to cling to their Czech passports and adopt a wait-and-see attitude.

This state of affairs created something of a dilemma not only for individual cases but also for the authorities of asylum countries and organizations willing to give counsel and aid. A fair number of Czechs took advantage of the amnesty granted by the Government of Czechoslovakia to those who had overstayed the duration of the validity of their exit permits and eventually returned home. However, with the passage of time, many others abandoned the hope of return, became *de facto* refugees and sought resettlement abroad. During the year following the invasion of their homeland some 16 000 Czechs were processed by the USRP-supported voluntary agencies and resettled by ICEM. Australia, Canada and the United States were the principal receiving countries.

The problem of East Pakistani refugees and UNHCR's role as focal point for co-ordination of assistance

The outbreak of civil strife in East Pakistan in the spring of 1971 produced a dramatic flight of millions of persons (the Indian Government estimated eight million whereas the Government of Pakistan cited a figure in the vicinity of two million) from there into India. Following a request for assistance from the Government of India to the Secretary-General of the United Nations, the UNHCR was designated as the focal point for the co-ordination of assistance from all the organizations and programs of the United Nations system as well as from other interested intergovernmental and non-governmental entities. In this capacity the UNHCR was entrusted with a) mobilizing and securing international support and contributions; b) arranging for the procurement of supplies and for their delivery to India; and c) maintaining close liaison with the Government of India, which was responsible for the actual relief operations.

From the beginning it was recognized that the solution of the problem lay in the voluntary repatriation of the East Pakistani refugees. That view was supported by both India and Pakistan. At the conclusion of hostilities the UNHCR in his above-mentioned capacity made a further appeal in January 1972 to the international community for assistance in meeting the cost of repatriating the refugees. By the end of March 1972 practically all of them had been repatriated.

Jewish emigrants from the Soviet Union

The last quarter of 1971 marked the beginning of the flow of Jewish emigrants from the Soviet Union – a flow that was to average about 3000 persons per month during 1972 and to have its peaks and valleys in succeeding years depending upon the political climate prevailing between the Super Powers.

Like the Jews from Poland mentioned earlier, those from the Soviet Union travelled with legal exit permits, having renounced their Russian nationality; thus they, too, upon their arrival in Austria, were considered to be outside the scope of the regular refugee channels. They were, however, regarded as eligible for USRP assistance, and a contract was negotiated with the American Joint Distribution Committee (AJDC) to cover the costs of their care and maintenance during their stay in Austria. During the early stages of this emigration (1971–78) a large majority of the cases arriving in Vienna were processed for onward movement to Israel.

With such a heavy flow of Soviet Jews throughout 1972, and indications that it would continue and even increase, it became apparent that special measures were needed to cope with the situation both in Austria during the transit phase and in Israel as regards the reception and absorption of the persons concerned. Consequently, with support from certain US congressional quarters, additional funds were appropriated to the State Department to ensure that the needs of these emigrants were met without over-burdening the already strained Israeli economy.

Having closely followed the situation from the outset in 1971 I was assigned for temporary duty in Washington in the early spring of 1973, to assist in developing the initial grant agreement covering assistance to the emigrants concerned during the various stages of their movement and integration in Israel. After careful consideration of the matter in the State Department an agreement involving a commitment of $31 million was negotiated and signed on 6 April 1973 with the New York-based United Israel Appeal (UIA) – the US counterpart of the Jewish Agency for Israel (JAI) mentioned earlier. This grant agreement, which has been renewed annually up to the time of writing, albeit at a somewhat reduced financial level, and which was amended to include oppressed Jewish emigrants from other areas, covers such things as care and maintenance, transportation, reception assistance, housing including the construction of absorption centers, language training, occupational training and re-training and medical care. My refugee and migration unit at the US Mission in Geneva was responsible for monitoring and auditing expenditures under the agreement.

Co-ordinated action on behalf of Ugandan refugees

In a surprise development in the autumn of 1972 President Idi Amin ordered the expulsion from Uganda of all Asians save those with Ugandan citizenship and a limited number of professional workers of particular value to the country. This expulsion order, which was to be met by 8 November 1972, created a crisis of international proportions and one which I was obliged to follow closely through contacts with the head-quarters in Geneva of UNHCR, ICEM and ICRC.

The United Kingdom Government assumed full responsibility for the 27 000 Asians with British passports and they were transported within the time limit to the United Kingdom. A number of others were nationals of India, Pakistan or other Asian countries and became the responsibility of their respective embassies in Kampala. However, those of undetermined nationality (some 4000), who did not enjoy the protection of any government, presented a particular problem, especially in view of the 8 November deadline. A variety of needs had to be met swiftly – exit permits, travel documentation, transportation and, of course, areas of temporary or permanent resettlement.

In a remarkable display of co-operation among organizations of the United Nations system, ICRC, ICEM, voluntary agencies and interested governments, the problem was faced and dealt with in a highly efficient way. During the period 28 October to 9 November 1972 a total of 4379 Asians of undetermined nationality were moved from Uganda, 3650 of them being admitted to transit centers in Austria, Belgium, Italy, Malta and Spain before being processed for permanent resettlement overseas.

ICEM played a particularly significant role in the Uganda operation, which prompted the following message to the Director at that time, John Thomas, from the Secretary-General of the United Nations:

I am personally grateful for the support and co-operation the United Nations and its family of organizations – especially the Office of the United Nations High Commissioner for Refugees – have received over the years from the Intergovernmental Committee for European Migration. I have long been aware of the valuable contributions of ICEM to the welfare of thousands of persons who have been displaced over the years, and I wish to thank member governments for their active support for the important contributions of ICEM.

During the past weeks, the United Nations has had the chance to intensify its relations with ICEM in the effort to evacuate several thousand Asians of undetermined nationality from Uganda. This successful operation, which was conducted under the umbrella of the United Nations, involved several weeks of around-the-clock work by ICEM staff and volunteers. The efforts of ICEM, the UN family, the ICRC and other organizations were enormously successful. ICEM is now working with the UNHCR to find sites for the resettlement of those Asians who are now in temporary transit centres.

This is but one of many examples of the ability and effectiveness of the Intergovernmental Committee for European Migration in humanitarian activities of international concern. We of the United Nations value the close association with ICEM and look forward to our continued work together in attempting to solve humanitarian problems confronting the international community.

Assistance effort in Southern Sudan

After the signing of the Addis Ababa Agreement of 1972, which brought peace to Southern Sudan after many years of civil strife, the UNHCR initiated an assistance program for the provision of shelter and food in the region and the supplying of equipment to permit the construction of roads, hospitals and schools. This timely assistance effort facilitated the repatriation and reintegration of some 180 000 Sudanese refugees from neighboring countries, as well as the re-establishment of some 500 000 Sudanese who had been displaced within their own country.

Two-way repatriation between Bangladesh and Pakistan

Following the so-called Delhi Agreement of August 1973 a program was organized under the auspices of UNHCR for two-way repatriation between Bangladesh and Pakistan. As a result of this program 108 000 persons were moved by air from Bangladesh to Pakistan and 121 600 from Pakistan to Bangladesh.

The extrication operation from Chile, including ICEM's special program for resettlement abroad

Following events in Chile in the autumn of 1973 the new governing *junta*, headed by General Augusto Pinochet, authorized the establishment of a National Committee for Aid to Refugees (CONAR). At the outset, when particular attention was being directed to the foreign refugees in Chile, the UNHCR played a leading role in the activities of CONAR, which also benefited from the operational participation of ICEM, ICRC and various Chilean church groups.

The refugees were practically all from rightist political régimes in other Latin American countries and upon the accession to power of Salvador Allende, they had made their way to Chile to participate in the building there of a democratic and socialist régime. Some were academics and students who had found themselves at odds with the political régimes in their homelands, and who sought more propitious conditions for their teaching and studies in Chile. Some were Marxist union leaders whose concern was the lot of the working classes. The others, the majority, were laborers and technicians who, while not necessarily having been active politically, were obliged to leave their homelands because they had supported trade union leaders.

After President Allende's death and General Pinochet's take-over these refugees – given their leftist political commitment – felt threatened; consequently, they either sought asylum in embassies in Santiago or refuge in shelters established by church groups – or otherwise went into hiding.

There was an urgent need for resettlement opportunities abroad for such refugees, and there were many prompt and positive responses to a UNHCR appeal, notably from Mexico and also from several European countries. Taking full advantage of any and all resettlement schemes ICEM, working in close conjunction with the church groups, played a key operational role in facilitating the processing and movement out of Chile of individual refugee cases – a most delicate and difficult task.

Additionally, and perhaps of even greater sensitivity, there was the problem of the thousands of Chilean nationals who had been associated somehow or another with the Allende régime. They too felt threatened and, like the refugees, many of them – the ones, that is, who were not already imprisoned – sought asylum in various embassies in Santiago.

Whereas the Office of the UNHCR had considered the foreign refugees in Chile to be *prima facie* eligible for assistance and protection under the UNHCR's mandate, the Chilean refuge seekers, being in their own country, were considered not to come within the scope of the activities of UNHCR. Since many of these people were nonetheless in jeopardy, there was great concern on an international scale for their welfare – and again many countries around the world agreed to open their doors and offer resettlement opportunities to them.

ICEM, not being restricted by a legalistic definition of a refugee, as was the case with UNHCR, moved swiftly, in concert with CONAR, ICRC and the church groups, to facilitate the resettlement of these needy Chileans. Their processing was, if anything, even more difficult and challenging than that of the foreign refugees. The promise of an entry visa from a country of resettlement was a primary requisite. Once that was to hand, an expulsion order from the Chilean Government could be sought. As soon as these two basic conditions were met, ICEM could finalize the processing and arrange for the movement of the person concerned to the receiving country.

As regards Chileans who had been indicted and sentenced to imprisonment under the new régime's security laws, such prisoners could apply for their sentence to be commuted into exile, provided they had obtained a visa for entry into another country. On their behalf ICEM conducted personal interviews in the jails and prisons throughout Chile, prepared individual dossiers and presented their case to potential countries of resettlement.

For all of the cases being processed by ICEM for resettlement abroad, whether they were foreign refugees or Chilean nationals, whether they were imprisoned, in asylum or in hiding, it was essential for ICEM, at the final stage of the processing and before actual physical movement of the person concerned, to secure from the Chilean authorities a *salvo-conducto* (a document valid for 48 hours guaranteeing safe conduct to the airport in Santiago).

Under ICEM's Special Program for Resettlement from Chile, which

The Refugee Connection

began in October 1973 and continued until the middle of 1978, a total of 18 368 persons were processed and moved, as shown in the following breakdown in Table 6.1.

Table 6.1   Movements effected between 6 October 1973 and 30 June 1978 by the Intergovernmental Committee for European Migration under the Special Program for Resettlement from Chile

Country of resettlement	Number of persons
Algeria	22
Argentina	915
Australia	272
Austria	394
Belgium	496
Bolivia	77
Canada	294
Colombia	195
Costa Rica	118
Cuba	463
Denmark	575
Ecuador	63
Finland	153
France	1 851
German Democratic Republic	467
Federal Republic of Germany	1 262
Honduras	102
Hungary	118
Ireland	89
Israel	13
Italy	827
Luxembourg	41
Mexico	868
Netherlands	786
New Zealand	57
Norway	358
Panama	278
Peru	37
Portugal	3
Romania	541
Spain	99
Sweden	2 458
Switzerland	487
USSR	62
United Kingdom	1 687
United States	1 297
Venezuela	363
Yugoslavia	61
Other destinations	119
Total	18 368

Humanitarian assistance to Cyprus

The invasion of Cyprus by Turkey in the summer of 1974 resulted in a *de facto* partitioning of the country and caused the displacement of some 200 000 Cypriots, the Greek Cypriots moving to the government-controlled area in the South and the Turkish Cypriots moving to the Turkish-occupied area in the North.

As soon as hostilities ceased the United Nations Peace-Keeping Force and the ICRC responded to the emergency needs of the Cypriot people. Subsequently, in August 1974, in response to an appeal from the Government of Cyprus, the Secretary-General of the United Nations designated the UNHCR to co-ordinate humanitarian assistance to Cyprus. After making an on the spot assessment of requirements for food, shelter, medical supplies, etc., the UNHCR appealed to the international community for contributions. The target for the remaining months of 1974 was $22 million, toward which the United States Government donated $7.8 million. In a second appeal for the early months of 1975 the UNHCR set a target of $9.3 million, toward which the United States Government. donated $3.1 million.

A significant aspect of the aid thus provided to Cyprus was that the beneficiaries were persons displaced within their own country rather than refugees, as defined in the mandate of the UNHCR. As a consequence of this state of affairs, the propriety of the UNHCR's involvement in Cyprus was questioned in certain international quarters.

To help ease the pressures resulting from the dislocations within Cyprus, the Cypriot Government requested ICEM assistance in connection with the emigration of Cypriots who were interested in re-establishing themselves abroad, putting an official of the Ministry of Interior at ICEM's disposal to facilitate the recruitment and placement of qualified candidates. It also requested ICEM to help with the resettlement of some 6000 refugees from the Lebanon for whom it was obliged to provide care and maintenance assistance.

During the period 1974–76 ICEM arranged the processing and movement of some 600 Cypriots and about 1500 refugees (mainly Lebanese) from Cyprus – mostly to Australia, Canada, the United States and various Latin American countries.

Simultaneously, at the urging of the Secretary-General of the United Nations, the Office of the UNHCR continued its assistance program in Cyprus, though aware of the fact (as indicated above) that the task went somewhat beyond its mandate and fearful that the situation of the displaced persons in Cyprus might evolve into a long-term care and maintenance program similar to that for the Palestinian refugees in the Middle East – the wrong way to attempt to resolve any refugee problem.

Further assistance to Africa concerning, in particular, Guinea-Bissau and Mozambique

The year 1975 also marked the UNHCR's involvement in certain new refugee situations in Africa. Following its attainment of independence the Government of Guinea-Bissau requested assistance in the return and re-integration of some 150 000 nationals who either had sought refuge in neighboring countries or were displaced within the country. By way of response the UNHCR helped to arrange the transport of the refugees and displaced persons to their villages, providing them with food as well as with seeds and tools for planting. At the request of the transitional Government of Mozambique the UNHCR provided relief assistance to about 25 000 displaced persons and/or refugees who were voluntarily repatriated.

Events in Indochina and international emergency relief operations

Then, of course, events in Indochina at the end of 1974 and early in 1975 gave rise to massive dislocations of persons. In the People's Democratic Republic of Laos some 700 000 persons were displaced or uprooted and the Office of the UNHCR provided $6 million for food supplies, as well as basic tools and agricultural equipment to stimulate the resumption of food production. In conjunction with UNICEF it launched a $14 million emergency relief operation to procure and deliver food and clothing and to provide shelter and medical supplies for the civilian population of the Republic of Vietnam.

Moreover, during 1975 the flow of Indochinese refugees to various asylum countries in South-east Asia began. About 88 000 entered Thailand, including 57 000 Lao, 26 000 Cambodians and 5000 Vietnamese from South Vietnam. Additionally an estimated 235 000 Cambodians, Lao and Vietnamese moved to various countries in South-east Asia other than Thailand. There was widespread concern for the welfare of these refugees, and special contributions exceeding $5 million were made available to the UNHCR to help meet their needs.

It was quickly realized that permanent resettlement in third countries would be required for many of them and already in 1975 several Western European countries, as well as Australia, Canada and the United States, opened their doors to considerable numbers of them. The operational expertise of ICEM was essential in this connection and ICEM proved itself equal to the task. Having moved swiftly to establish operational units in all of the asylum countries in South-east Asia, during the period April 1975 to June 1976 it handled the resettlement of 30 049 Indochinese refugees, of whom 17 287 went to the United States and 12 762 to 29 other receiving countries.

Also included in the initial exodus were about 110 000 persons (mostly Vietnamese) who were evacuated to the island of Guam. By mid-June 1975 the majority of these refugees had been processed and moved to the United States under a scheme known as 'Operation New Life'.

7 Transfer to Washington DC to Become Deputy Assistant Secretary of State in Charge of Refugee and Migration Affairs

In mid-1975 I was transferred from my post at the US Mission in Geneva to the State Department in Washington DC, where I was to become the Deputy Assistant Secretary of State in Charge of Refugee and Migration Affairs. This assignment placed me, for the first time in my career, in the realm of policy making as well as overall program management in the field of refugees and migration.

NEW RESPONSIBILITIES

My new responsibilities included

- formulating policy and exercising direction and operational control of US refugee and migration programs – and ensuring appropriate consideration of refugee and migration matters in foreign policy decisions;
- participating in the formulation and presentation of budgetary requirements and fiscal policies for refugee and migration programs;
- representing the United States Government in, and maintaining liaison with, United Nations agencies, intergovernmental organizations, voluntary agencies and other entities concerned with refugee and migration affairs;
- functioning as the State Department's focal point on refugee and migration matters as they related to the United States Congress and the public; and
- exercising policy direction and operational control over requests for political asylum in the United States and in US entities abroad from persons fleeing from authoritarian régimes.

My transfer to Washington came on the heels of the US withdrawal from Vietnam and the hasty intake into the United States of the tens of thousands of Indochinese refugees who had been evacuated from Vietnam to Guam. Such a massive influx together with the prospect of a continuing heavy flow of Indochinese refugees attracted widespread interest in refugee matters – and signalled the need for an orderly process of refugee admissions into the United States as well as for improved administrative and management capability on the part of both the public and private agencies involved.

ACTION LEADING TO THE ADOPTION OF THE REFUGEE ACT OF 1980

With refugee and migration problems assuming such significant proportions, it was suddenly realized, both in the Administration and in the Congress, that practically since the Second World War the United States Government had reacted merely on an ad hoc basis to specific situations (political and military) which had generated refugee flows. Thus either Congress had passed special legislation to meet those situations, such as the Displaced Persons Act of 1948 and the Refugee Relief Act of 1953, or the Attorney-General had exercised his authority under section 212 *(d)* (5) of the US Immigration and Nationality Act to parole persons into the United States, as had been the case for Hungarians in 1956 and was now the case for the Indochinese, or again recourse was had to the conditional entry provision of that Act, under which up to 17 400 persons from communist dominated countries or from the general area of the Middle East could be admitted to the United States each year.

With the aim of updating US policy concerning refugees and regularizing procedures for the admission of refugees into the United States, I promptly established and maintained close contact with the appropriate congressional committees and more particularly with the interested staff members of the judiciary committees, namely Dale De Haan and Jerry Tinker on the Senate side and Garner J. Cline and Arthur P. ('Skip') Endres in the House.

Garner J. Cline took a leading role in seeking such reform and I spent considerable time with him and his colleagues, Skip Endres and Peter Regis, evolving ways and means to bring about improvements and regularity in the United States Government's refugee policies and programs. A significant outcome of this frequent, but rather informal, contact was a hearing, under the chairmanship of the Honorable Joshua Eilberg, on 'policy and procedures for the admission of refugees into the United States' before the House of Representatives Committee on the Judiciary (Subcommittee on Immigration, Citizenship and International Law) on 24 February 1977. I was the principal witness at that hearing, a part of the proceedings of which, including, in particular, my in-depth statement, is reproduced below.

Mr. Eilberg   The subcommittee will come to order. This is the first in a series of hearings which will be held by this subcommittee in order to examine U.S. refugee policies, programs, and procedures. We will also consider a bill which I have sponsored to revise, or I should say to establish, a legislative policy governing the admission of refugees into the United States.

When we consider that the vast majority of refugees entering the United States each year do so at the discretion of the Attorney General, rather than under the regular refugee provisions of the Immigration and Nationality Act, it is clear that Congress has abdicated its responsibility in this area.

While there is some consultation with the Congress when the Attorney General exercises his ambiguous parole power, there is little if any meaningful input by the Congress or by members of the judiciary committees.

While I agree that some administrative flexibility is certainly required, I do not feel that it is reasonable or proper for the Congress to delegate to the executive branch its constitutional obligation to enact laws establishing this nation's refugee policy. I do not believe the Attorney General should be the sole decision-maker on this subject, particularly since there are no legislative guidelines or administrative criteria to assist him in exercising his parole authority.

In this regard, I requested the former Attorney General and the Commissioner of the Immigration Service to promulgate such criteria for general guidelines over one year ago. Despite many assurances that this would be done, they have never been issued.

For these reasons, I have introduced legislation, H.R. 3056, designed to establish a uniform refugee policy, which at the same time will preserve a certain amount of flexibility. Such flexibility is particularly essential if this country is to respond to emergent refugee situations which may arise at any time around the world.

My bill proposes numerical limitations for normal refugee flows, and for extraordinary situations such as we have experienced in the past with Hungary, Cuba, and more recently in Indochina. In my judgment, the American people have every right to expect their elected officials to enact humane and reasonable laws in this sensitive area.

Our witness this morning will be Mr. James Carlin, Deputy Assistant Secretary of State for Refugee and Migration Affairs, Department of State, who has been asked to provide the subcommittee with background information concerning both past and current U.S. refugee programs. I am sure that I and my colleagues will find this information particularly helpful and timely.

A detailed analysis of existing policies and procedures is essential in developing appropriate remedial legislation. Before hearing from our good friend, Mr. Carlin, I yield to the gentleman, Mr. Fish, for any statement he wishes to make.

Mr. Fish   Thank you, Mr. Chairman. I am pleased to join with you in opening these first hearings of the subcommittee in the 95th Congress. I think it is most appropriate that we begin our efforts this year by dealing with the important subject of refugees.

Our subcommittee very ably handled the grave problems encountered after the end of the tragic war in Southeast Asia by the Indochina Migration Refugee Assistance Act in the last Congress. Of course, we are now faced with the additional problems of enacting appropriate legislation to allow these refugees to regularize their status, which is not provided for in the Immigration and Nationality Act.

You and I have also been concerned with the movement of Jewish refugees from the Soviet Union. As international crises develop, more persons will come under the broad definition of 'refugee'. It is clear that our Government must share the international responsibility for dealing with this most human problem.

Therefore, I commend you, Mr. Chairman, for convening this hearing, which I understand will be the first of several dealing with this problem and for your bill, which will provide the mechanism for this country to deal with the continuing programs for refugee assistance.

Mr. Eilberg Thank you, Mr. Fish. I will be happy to hear from you now, Mr. Carlin.

Mr. Carlin Thank you very much, Mr. Chairman. With me here this morning are two of my colleagues. On my left, George Warren, Jr., Senior Adviser on International Organizations, and on the right, Mr. Shepard Lowman, Director of the Program and Asylum Division of the Office of Refugee and Migration Affairs.

Mr. Chairman and members of the committee, I am very pleased to appear before this committee today to review our government's role in refugee and migration activities.

I understand that today's hearing is a forerunner to hearings on Bill H.R. 3056, which is designed to amend the Immigration and Nationality Act to revise the procedures for the admission of refugees into the United States.

I further understand that with such hearings in view the committee at this time wishes to have an updating on our policy with respect to refugees and a general review of our involvement in refugee and migration activities over the years.

At the outset, Mr. Chairman, I wish to say how very much the Department of State appreciates this committee's keen interest in refugee activities and we very much welcome this opportunity to review the matter with you today. In doing so, I submit that we all must recognize the tragic truth that refugee problems are likely to be with us for an indefinite period into the future.

Some refugee problems are resolved relatively quickly. Others remain with us persistently. There is a steady flow of refugees from communist countries everywhere, punctuated at intervals, as history will attest, by massive flows of refugees resulting from particular political developments within communist countries. And then there are other refugee problems – in Europe, the Middle East, Asia, Africa, and Latin America. We cannot and do not ignore any of them.

Since World War II, the United States Congress has been generous in its appropriation of refugee assistance funds for use throughout the world, and has enacted a series of special refugee immigration measures. Every President during that period has requested substantial funds from Congress for refugee assistance purposes, and has taken special administrative measures within the Immigration and Nationality Act to enable us to accept additional refugee immigrants.

All told, since 1945 the United States Government has expended an estimated $5 billion for refugee assistance purposes, and has accepted some 1.8 million refugees for permanent resettlement in this country. During fiscal year 1976, our Government expended some $475 million on refugee assistance and we accepted about 31,000 refugees for permanent resettlement in the United States. Now what are the reasons for such unprecedented generosity?

In the first place, I think we should remember that the United States is a land of immigrants, and since the founding of the republic we have had a special national heritage of concern for the uprooted and persecuted.

This traditional concern is expressed by the American people to the Congress and, of course, the American voluntary agencies, representing the principal religious, ethnic and non-sectarian groups in our country, are the heart and soul of this concern. They are the appointed and recognized agent of the American people for carrying on the national tradition of compassion for the refugees.

But, Mr. Chairman, beyond our national ethos of humanitarian concern for the uprooted and persecuted, there are solid foreign policy reasons why we should involve ourselves substantially and regularly in resolving refugee problems. In the first instance, it is decidedly in our foreign policy interest to project in countries around the world the image of U.S. humanitarian assistance for refugees. Such assistance serves as a glowing example of the purposes and processes of the free democracy which we are, and of the free society which makes such assistance possible.

The flight of refugees into countries of first asylum places economic and political burdens upon such countries. This is particularly true in the case of underdeveloped countries and, as often happens when large numbers of refugees are involved, the economic burden alone is severely oppressive, and this tends to threaten the stability of the host country.

The political factors inherent in refugee problems frequently lead to controversy and problems for the asylum countries, especially with respect to the governments of the countries from which the refugees have fled.

Our efforts coupled with the broader efforts of the international community to resolve refugee problems thus contribute to the political as well as the economic stability of countries of first asylum.

Mr. Chairman, refugee problems can be and frequently are a threat to the peace. Such problems cannot be divorced from the strife, tensions, and oppressions which are so detrimental to the well-being of nations and peoples. Refugee problems if left unattended can quickly bring human deterioration fostering local frictions, ferment, political tensions, and even terrorism.

On the other hand, the provision of timely refugee assistance can lead to just and lasting solutions to refugee problems. Such solutions in turn can help promote the reduction of tensions, the solution of broader issues and the preservation of peace itself.

So much, Mr. Chairman, for the importance of the policy content of our refugee assistance. What is our structure and how do we operate in this field of concern for and assistance to refugees?

Mr. Chairman, within the Department of State, the entity which has major responsibility for carrying out the provisions and purposes of the Migration and Refugee Assistance Act of 1962 is the Office of Refugee and Migration Affairs – ORM.

This office also serves as a focal point for information and action for refugee and migration affairs as they relate to Congress, voluntary agencies and the public.

ORM develops an annual budget for carrying out the programs which it operates directly and for contributions, as appropriate, to international organizations engaged in refugee and migration activity. The programs covered by the budget authorized in large part by the Migration and Refugee Assistance Act of 1962, are submitted to the Congress within the context of the Foreign Assistance and Related Programs appropriation.

Apart from our regular budgets and programs, experience has proven it necessary to have a responsible system for meeting unforeseen, urgent requirements for humanitarian assistance to refugees and migrants. Pursuant to this need, the Foreign Relations Authorization Act, Fiscal Year 1976, P.L. 94–141, amended Section 2(c) of the Migration and Refugee Assistance Act of 1962 to establish the United States Emergency Refugee and Migration Assistance Fund. This Fund, with up to $25 million in appropriations, is to meet unexpected and urgent refugee and migration needs whenever the President determines it to be important to the national interest to do so. Budgeting for the Fund and recommendations for its use originate in ORM.

ORM works in close coordination with other concerned elements of the Department of State and the U.S. Government in general to ensure that its policies and programs in the field of assistance to refugees adequately reflect United States interests in all respects.

ORM is directly responsible, among other things, for carrying out the United States Refugee Program – USRP – which operates in behalf of refugees from communist-dominated countries in Eastern Europe and China. USRP is a people-to-people program with the objective of insuring adequate reception, care, and maintenance and prompt resettlement of the refugee asylum-seekers.

USRP operates through a network of voluntary agencies, namely: The American Fund for Czechoslovak Refugees, AFCR; The American Joint Distribution Committee, AJDC; The International Catholic Migration Commission, ICMC; The International Rescue Committee, IRC; The Polish American Immigration and Relief Committee, PAIRC; The Tolstoy Foundation, TF; The United HIAS Service, UHS; and The World Council of Churches, WCC.

In the area of assistance to Soviet Jewish refugees proceeding to Israel, ORM also contracts with the United Israel Appeal, UIA, to facilitate the reception and absorption of these refugees within Israel.

Mr. Chairman, these agencies collectively represent the concern of the American people for the homeless and persecuted refugees.

ORM is also charged with representing U.S. interests in the programs of the United Nations High Commissioner for Refugees, UNHCR, and the Intergovernmental Committee for European Migration, ICEM. These two international agencies are the principal outlets for our multilateral activities in behalf of refugees, over and beyond our continued support of the United Nations Relief and Works Agency for Palestinian Refugees in the Near East.

The close relationship at the policy and operational level existing between ORM and the voluntary agencies, UNHCR and ICEM, ensures coordinated support for refugee and migration programs.

Let me mention at this juncture, Mr. Chairman, that all refugee assistance is not material or financial in nature. The international protection of refugees is one of the most important and fundamental kinds of refugee assistance, and it is carried out under the aegis of the UNHCR. It consists of securing guarantees against the forcible repatriation, or refoulement, of the refugees to any country where they would face persecution; and also of securing for refugees those legal, economic, and social rights in asylum countries which are essential to the refugees if they are ever to cease being refugees and have the opportunity to live in dignity with self-respect and self-support. These include such rights as access to the courts of law, the right to hold gainful employment, freedom of religion, and freedom of movement.

These rights are set forth in the UN Convention and Protocol relating to the Status of Refugees, and the UNHCR works ceaselessly toward promoting more accessions to these international treaties and toward securing more effective implementation of the treaties by countries which are already parties to them.

Certainly, without the effective international protection of refugees, the safety of many would be in jeopardy, and material assistance programs for refugees would be far less effective, and, in some cases, would merely commit the recipients to refugee status on an indefinite basis.

The importance of this protection function is currently highlighted by the plight of Indochinese refugees who have left Vietnam in small boats and who are desperately seeking asylum and resettlement assistance.

Apart from the legal protection function, UNHCR's value lies in its ability to internationalize refugee problems and thus spread the burden of meeting the needs of the refugees among the international community. While the United States Government is, of course, a principal contributor to UNHCR, some 80 other governments also contribute to the regular program of that organization under which assistance is currently being provided to hundreds of thousands of refugees in Africa, Asia, and Latin America.

The utility of the UNHCR also assumes notable significance in the area of special activities – activities which transcend the basic mandate of his office.

For example, at the request of the Secretary General of the United Nations, the UNHCR has responsibility for coordinating assistance efforts for the benefit of displaced persons in Cyprus, a program of interest to the United States and one to which we are a major financial contributor. Similarly, the UNHCR is currently developing plans to coordinate assistance activities for the benefit of displaced persons within Angola as well as Lebanon.

Mr. Chairman, we also attach great importance to the activities of ICEM, and to our membership in that organization. Membership in ICEM, by terms of its constitution, is restricted to nations which support the principle of freedom of movement, a concern of great significance and importance to the United States.

ICEM has proven to be an immensely versatile instrument, undertaking special refugee processing and movement activities in many parts of the world, while maintaining its traditional refugee and national migrant functions in the European context. Since its inception in 1952, ICEM has moved in excess of two million persons, mostly refugees, for permanent resettlement.

Mr. Chairman, speaking of ICEM, it may be of interest to note here that in pursuance of the proposal which you yourself made at the 49th Session of ICEM's Executive Committee last May, ICEM has been endeavoring within the context of the Conference on Security and Cooperation in Europe – CSCE – to gather basic data on individual cases and serve as the focal point for purposes of family reunification. In this regard, ICEM is seeking to develop the practical measures needed to give real meaning to this very human aspect of the Helsinki Accords.

Mr. Chairman, there is another notable form of assistance to refugees carried out by the United States: namely, the consideration of requests for asylum made to United States Government personnel throughout the world. Such requests, when made in foreign areas, are relayed by priority cable to the Department of State, where they are dealt with on an urgent basis by ORM and the country desk officers for the geographic areas concerned.

We treat these matters with great urgency, because frequently the person requesting asylum is in physical danger of being forcibly repatriated if he falls within control of the diplomatic authorities of his country of origin.

For example, in Eastern European communist countries the criminal codes contain provisions calling for imprisonment from six months to five years or longer and in some cases, even more severe punishment, for persons who depart illegally or who overstay their leave abroad or refuse to return to their country.

Here in the United States, sizeable numbers of persons request asylum from U.S. Immigration and Naturalization Service officers. Over 2,000 such cases per year are referred by INS officials to our office for the advisory opinions of the State Department. Many of these persons are found qualified for asylum.

Mr. Chairman, the management of U.S. refugee activities since World War II has followed a long and uneven course. There have been periods when it was viewed as an unwelcome stepchild. It has suffered periods when the policy function was separated from the operational responsibility. Its activities have been attached to five different bureaus in the State Department over the past 25 years.

In times of crisis, special structures have been created to deal with the problem: the Displaced Persons Commission, the Refugee Relief Act Administration, the President's Hungarian Refugee Commission, and the Indochina Task Force.

There have been regular appropriations to the State Department and special withdrawals of Foreign Assistance funds.

Special arrangements were required to deal with emergency situations such as those involving Hungarians, Czechs and Indochinese. Special action has been taken to assist Soviet Jews to Israel, and other Soviet refugees not going to Israel. In short, Mr. Chairman, the management of refugee affairs has had to be quite flexible over the years.

None the less, the U.S. record of assistance to refugees is a good one. While I would hasten to admit there remains room for further improvement, particularly in the area of coordination among the various U.S. Government entities involved, the organizational structure now exists to meet any refugee emergency. The resources required for this year and next year have been identified, and we are currently in the process of seeking the necessary appropriations.

In concluding this overview of refugee problems and the existing policy and machinery to deal with them, I should like to emphasize the solid conviction within the Administration of the importance of dealing constructively, efficiently, and promptly with refugee problems.

I believe that the Government, the voluntary agencies and the American people are being true to the sacred American heritage of concern for the uprooted and persecuted. Mr. Chairman, the very initiative taken by your committee to hold this hearing here today attests to the vitality of the concern in America for refugees.

That concludes my statement, Mr. Chairman. I shall now endeavor to answer any questions that you or other members of the committee might have.

Mr. Eilberg Mr. Carlin, we wish to thank you for a very fine statement regarding the situation today, and before we ask you any questions, I would – consistent with the fact that we have a new Administration and there are problems of reorganization and it's difficult to move sometimes as quickly as we would like – I would like to stress, as I am sure you agree, the importance of moving formally into the refugee area and the principle perhaps established by H.R. 3056.

And for you and all those within hearing of my voice, try to do what you can to see that we get the departmental reports as quickly as we can.

Mr. Carlin You have our assurance on that point, Mr. Chairman.

My statement gave rise to an extensive and informative discussion, the essence of which, in view of the wealth of insights provided into US attitudes to the problem of refugees and migrants, and to the international organizations concerned with that problem, is contained in an appendix to this account.

In fact the brainstorming efforts in which I had engaged with the mentioned staff members of the judiciary committees, together with hearings such as the one reproduced in part above (and in the appendix to this volume), represented the genesis for the Refugee Act of 1980 which, once it entered into force, provided the first permanent legislative authority under which decisions about the admission of refugees into the United States could be taken and implemented.

Significant provisions of the Act

A salient feature of the Act is the inclusion in it of the international definition of a 'refugee', thereby removing the ideological and geographical limitations of previous legislation. According to the Act the term 'refugee' means a) any person who is outside the country of such person's nationality or, in the case of a person having no nationality, is outside the country in which such person last habitually resided, and is unable or unwilling to return to, and is unable or unwilling to avail himself or herself of the protection of, that country because of persecution, or a well-founded fear of persecution, on account of race, religion, nationality, membership in a particular social group, or political opinion; or b) in such special circumstances as the President, after appropriate consultation, may specify, any person who is within the country of such person's nationality or, in the case of a person having no nationality, within the country in which such person is habitually residing, and has a well-founded fear of persecution on account of race, religion, nationality, membership in a particular social group, or political opinion.

While limiting the use of the Attorney-General's parole authority, the Act does provide a permanent and systematic procedure for the admission into the United States of refugees of special humanitarian concern. Thus under the terms of the Act the President can request the admission of numbers amounting to a 'normal flow' of 50 000 per year without consulting Congress; he can request the admission of numbers over the 'normal flow' by having recourse to a congressional consultation; and he can request still additional refugee admissions through an emergency consultation in situations judged to be of 'grave humanitarian concern' or in the national interest. The Act requires information to be provided at congressional consultations on the nature of refugee situations abroad, foreign policy and humanitarian concerns, together with an analysis of the anticipated social, economic and demographic impact of the proposed admissions.

For purposes of implementing the Refugee Act the priorities applied are generally as follows:

1) Compelling concern/interest: exceptional cases of *(a)* refugees in immediate danger of loss of life and for whom there appears to be no alternative to resettlement in the United States, or *(b)* refugees of compelling concern to the United States, such as former or present political prisoners and dissidents.

2) Former US government employees: refugees employed by the US Government for at least one year prior to the claim for refugee status. This category also includes persons who were not official US government employees, but who for at least one year were so integrated into US government offices as to have been in effect and appearance US government employees.

3) Family reunification: refugees who are spouses, sons, daughters, parents, grandparents, unmarried siblings or ummarried minor grandchildren of persons in the United States. (The status of the anchor relative in the United States must be one of the following: US citizen, lawful permanent resident alien, refugee, asylee.)

4) Other ties to the United States: *(a)* refugees employed by US foundations, US voluntary agencies or US business firms for at least one year prior to the claim for refugee status; and *(b)* refugees trained or educated in the United States or abroad under US auspices.

5) Additional family reunification: refugees who are married siblings, unmarried grandchildren who have reached their majority, or married grandchildren of persons in the United States; also more distantly related individuals who are part of the family group and dependent on the family for support. (The status of the anchor relative in the United States must be one of the following: US citizen, lawful permanent resident alien, refugee, asylee.)

6) Otherwise of national interest: other refugees in specified regional groups whose admission is in the national interest.

STRENGTHENING POLICY AND PROCEDURES FOR DEALING WITH ASYLUM SEEKERS

As indicated earlier one of the responsibilities of my Washington assignment was to exercise policy direction and operational control, in so far as the State Department was concerned, over requests for political asylum in the United States or in entities under US jurisdiction from persons fleeing from authoritarian régimes.

From my long experience of refugee and migration affairs I was, of course, aware that US policy toward refugees was deeply founded on concern for the uprooted and persecuted – persons who, for fear of various forms of oppression, choose to flee from their country of nationality. For more than three decades the United States had taken the lead in the free world in translating this humanitarian concern into a variety of actions through programs of refugee assistance. In keeping with this policy I well knew that the United States Government and the American people strongly believed that refugees must be treated humanely, that their basic and urgent material needs must be met and that they should be accorded the same rights and protection as other citizens.

Equally I knew that the United States Government, being a signatory to the Protocol relating to the Status of Refugees, had an international treaty obligation to implement the provisions of that Protocol, including the explicit prohibition of the forcible return of refugees to conditions of persecution, within areas subject to the jurisdiction of the United States.

Learning from the lessons of the past

Aware as I was of the soundness of the United States Government's attitude to the handling of asylum seekers, I was nonetheless mindful, on taking up my new post in mid-1975, of the inglorious episode of the attempted defection by Lithuanian seaman, Simas Kudirka, on 23 November 1970.

Kudirka was a crewman on a Soviet vessel which had been temporarily moored to a US Coastguard cutter in US territorial waters off Martha's Vineyard. The Soviet vessel was in the area for purposes of a joint meeting between representatives of the US and Soviet fishing industries. At the end of the meeting, and shortly before the Soviet vessel broke mooring from the Coastguard cutter, Kudirka jumped to the cutter and declared his determination not to return to the Soviet vessel. Actually his intention to defect had been signalled earlier in the day and over a period of several hours there had been a flurry of communications between various echelons of the Coastguard and the State Department.

Despite the ample warnings, and due more particularly to bureaucratic ineptness and confusion, especially on the part of the Coastguard, Kudirka's attempt to seek asylum in the United States was rejected. Strange as it may seem, several crew members from the Soviet vessel were permitted to board the Coastguard cutter. They bound Kudirka in a blanket, forced him into a small boat (a boat, moreover, belonging to the Coastguard) and transferred him to the Soviet vessel. This rejection of Kudirka's bid for freedom was in flagrant disregard of the long-established American principle of granting asylum.

The US media gave wide coverage to the incident; concerned citizens across the country poured letters and telegrams into congressional offices; President Nixon took a personal interest in the matter and ordered immediate reports from the Departments of Transportation (to which the Coastguard belongs) and State; and congressional hearings were held. Following a full investigation of the incident, heads rolled; several senior-level Coastguard officers were either suspended from duty or permitted to resign from the Service.

A certain measure of blame also fell on the State Department and, while little or nothing could be done to rectify the Kudirka case, the Department hastened to update its policy and procedures for dealing with asylum seekers. The depth and urgency of the US commitment with respect to asylum was impressed upon all entities of the US Government (within the continental limits and abroad) which could possibly become involved with persons seeking asylum or wishing to defect and they were provided with updated detailed instructions and guidelines for dealing with asylum seekers.

Being determined to prevent a recurrence of the Kudirka case, at least during my tour of duty in Washington, I at once made a special effort to become fully conversant with the existing policy and procedures for dealing with asylum seekers. I then went on to seek ways and means of further strengthening them.

It was generally established, both within the United States and abroad, that any foreign nationals seeking asylum from the United States Government owing to persecution, or fear of persecution, should be given the opportunity to have their requests duly considered. Notwithstanding this broad position, it was the policy of the Government not to grant asylum at its installations abroad to persons under foreign jurisdiction. In exceptional circumstances, when the life or safety of a person was in danger, as in the case of pursuit by a mob, temporary refuge could be granted by the embassy or consular post concerned. However, in such rare cases standard procedure required that the Department of State be duly notified by an immediate precedence message. Protection would be terminated in such cases as soon as the danger was over and on the authority of the Department of State. Normally, this would occur only after the post concerned had received a satisfactory assurance from the host government that the asylum seeker's personal safety was guaranteed against lawless or arbitrary actions – and that he or she would be accorded due process of law.

As for cases within the continental limits of the United States, the Attorney-General has the discretionary authority to grant asylum to any alien regarded as a 'refugee' under the 1951 Convention and 1967 Protocol relating to the Status of Refugees. To come within the definition of a 'refugee', the alien must establish that he or she is unable or unwilling to return to his or her country of nationality because of 'persecution or a well-founded fear of persecution on account of race, religion, nationality, membership in a particular social group, or political opinion'.

In accordance with this discretionary authority of the Attorney-General, the actual processing of applications for asylum is handled by the Immigration and Naturalization Service of the Justice Department (INS). INS's implementing regulations have preserved for the Department of State the role of providing an advisory opinion in practically all cases of application for asylum. To establish such advisory opinions the Department draws on relevant information from the regional bureaus, from the Legal Adviser's office and, in some instances, from the US embassy in the asylum seeker's country of origin. An INS district director may approve or deny any asylum application at his discretion. Where an application for asylum is denied by a district director, the applicant may renew his/her request for asylum before an immigration judge in exclusion or deportation proceedings.

A role for the UNHCR

In addition to these established procedures I introduced, during my tour of duty in Washington, one further measure, providing a role for the UNHCR.

There was no question that the United States Government had every right, indeed obligation, to make its sovereign decision concerning each application for asylum – and, as indicated above, responsibility in this respect was vested in the Immigration and Naturalization Service of the Justice Department, albeit after it had received and duly considered an advisory opinion in each case from my office in the State Department. Being mindful of UNHCR's global concern for the protection of refugees, I reasoned that it would be useful also to have an advisory opinion in each case from the Office of the UNHCR. Despite some resistance from the INS to involving the UNHCR, this procedure was adopted – and arrangements were made for a UNHCR official (usually a protection officer with legal experience) to visit the Department of State periodically to review the dossiers of applicants for asylum on which the Department had developed advisory opinions. On occasion, when circumstances warranted it, arrangements were made for the UNHCR official to conduct a personal interview with the applicant.

Almost without exception the advisory opinion of the UNHCR official squared with that of the State Department, thus serving to neutralize criticism or suggestions from any quarter that the US Government was not being fair and objective in terms of granting asylum. Indeed the procedure worked very satisfactorily for all parties concerned throughout the time I was in Washington – and for a year or so afterwards. However, the UNHCR's involvement was subsequently abandoned when the volume of asylum seekers in the United States increased appreciably.

Judging from the poignant criticism in recent years from groups such as the voluntary agencies and sanctuary movements of the Administration's handling of asylum procedures, and the resultant congressional hearings, court actions, etc., it appears in retrospect that the Department of State might have been well advised to keep UNHCR in the act. Allowing for the increased case-load and the consequent obvious difficulty of establishing joint State Department/UNHCR advisory opinions in every case, UNHCR might nevertheless have been kept involved in respect of special individual cases and an effort made to develop the concept of statutory safe haven for national groups in certain situations or to hand down collective opinions on given groups of asylum seekers. Such an approach might have gone far toward heading off the acrimonious debate about the US Government's handling of asylum matters in recent years. After all, protection of refugees is the *raison d'être* of the UNHCR and the US Government is a signatory to the Protocol relating to the Status of Refugees.

BRIEFING US DELEGATIONS ATTENDING MEETINGS OF ICEM AND UNHCR

An important part of my work at the United States Mission in Geneva and, more particularly, at the Department of State in Washington was to provide an input for position papers for US delegations attending meetings of the governing bodies of ICEM and UNHCR, and to draft statements for delivery at those meetings.

In the case of ICEM this was done bearing in mind the fact that the United States Government had been instrumental in its creation and was a major supporter of the organization, so that it fell upon US delegations at ICEM meetings to play a leadership role, especially in encouraging ICEM to be adaptable and responsive with regard to the resettlement of refugees and displaced persons, as well as in promoting the formulation by ICEM of special migration programs for the benefit of developing countries, particularly in Latin America. Every effort was made to ensure that this role was fulfilled effectively.

In preparing for sessions of the UNHCR's Executive Committee I never failed to stress the importance of the protection of refugees – the *raison d'être* of the Office – and to encourage the UNHCR to exercise to the utmost the moral influence of his Office to ensure that the status and rights of refugees, wherever they might find themselves, were duly protected.

Proposal for a handbook to guide governments in the handling of asylum seekers

I had been at the State Department for about two years when the time came to prepare for the 28th Session of the UNHCR Executive Committee (October 1977) – and by that time I had gained, as will be appreciated from what was said earlier, a fair measure of experience of the US Government's handling of applications from individual asylum seekers.

Knowing the complexities of asylum procedures and the difficulty the US Government encountered, despite the extensive information resources available to it, in arriving at fair and objective decisions with regard to individual cases, I assumed that other governments, many of which would have less pertinent information available, would be experiencing the same or even greater difficulties in this respect. Thus I worked into the position paper for the US delegation at the UNHCR Executive Committee's 28th Session the notion that the Office of the UNHCR should prepare and issue a handbook to guide governments in their handling of asylum seekers. When the Executive Committee took up the agenda item 'protection' I took the floor and made a formal proposal to this effect. Following a meaningful discussion of the matter the Executive Committee requested the UNHCR to develop and issue for the guidance of governments a handbook relating to procedures and criteria for determining refugee status and – with due regard for the confidential nature of individual requests and particular situations involved – reproducing significant decisions on the determination of refugee status. In response to this request the UNHCR did in fact produce a *Handbook on Procedures and Criteria for Determining Refugee Status under the 1951 Convention and the 1967 Protocol relating to the Status of Refugees* – an excellent publication which serves governments well in wrestling with the complex questions of asylum and refugee status. The table of contents, reproduced below, gives a good idea of the broad range of problems covered by the handbook:

TABLE OF CONTENTS

CONCLUSIONS

Annexes

INDEX

8 Election as Director of the Intergovernmental Committee for European Migration

In October 1978 the then Director of ICEM, John F. Thomas, informed the ICEM member governments, through the Chairman of the ICEM Council, of his intention to resign, thus giving the Council the responsibility of electing a new Director at its 42nd Session the following month.

In the light of this development it was decided within the State Department, after consultation of certain key members of the congressional committees concerned, that my candidature for the directorship would be put forward to the ICEM member governments. Accordingly a telegram was dispatched from the Secretary of State (Cyrus Vance) to the United States embassies in all ICEM member countries requesting them to seek support for my election. The telegram read in part as follows:

Subject: New Director for the Intergovernmental Committee for European Migration (ICEM)
1. The ICEM Director, Mr. John Thomas, has informed the ICEM member governments through the Chairman of the ICEM Council of his intention to resign. Thus, the ICEM Council at its Forty-second session November 14–16, 1978, will have the responsibility of electing a new director. The United States has an excellent and well-qualified candidate for that position, namely, James L. Carlin, Deputy Assistant Secretary of State for Refugee and Migration Affairs. . . .
2. Election of a new Director comes at a time when ICEM faces a critical financial situation, and strong leadership will be needed if the organization is to survive. The United States Government is convinced that ICEM continues to play a key role in the important task of refugee/migrant resettlement and hopes that all its member governments will join in an effort to make it more efficient and financially sound. In our judgement, ICEM's structure and program require careful review, and the organization's financial situation requires a comprehensive audit as a basis for sound financial planning. This can be accomplished under a new Director.
3. Carlin, the US candidate for Director, has had many years of experience in the field of refugees and migration and understands ICEM's operations and problems. He has the full support of the Administration and has been selected because of his qualifications as an expert in the field. Moreover, Carlin is highly regarded by key Congressional members whose support for ICEM's continuation will be badly needed. Carlin is also known favorably to member government delegations to ICEM governing bodies.

4. Therefore, action addressees, drawing on the foregoing, are requested to approach host governments at appropriately high level and seek support for Carlin's candidacy. Meanwhile the Department and US Mission, Geneva, will be making separate approaches to key individuals in governments especially concerned with ICEM activities. (We will advise of these approaches by septels.) In the event any member government raises the question of an alternate candidate, it should be pointed out that the United States Government, as the principal contributor to ICEM's budget, considers it extremely important that the position of Director be held by an American national. Addressee posts should report host government reactions ASAP.

Vance

Diplomatic efforts having been successful, the ICEM Council, during its 42nd Session, adopted on 14 November 1978 Resolution No. 589 appointing me as Director of ICEM for a period of five years as from 1 March 1979.

This decision was notified to the United States Congress in the following statement by Peter W. Rodino, Jr., on 14 March 1979:

INTERGOVERNMENTAL COMMITTEE FOR EUROPEAN MIGRATION

Hon. Peter W. Rodino, Jr. of New Jersey
in the House of Representatives
Wednesday, March 14, 1979

Mr. Speaker, I would like to invite the attention of my colleagues to the changes which took place in Geneva, Switzerland, on March 1, 1979, in the directorship of the Intergovernmental Committee for European Migration.

On that date, after 10 years of dedicated service as Director of this 33-nation organization, John F. Thomas turned over the stewardship of this unique agency to James L. Carlin, recently retired Deputy Assistant Secretary of State for Refugee and Migration Affairs.

Over the many years of my service as a member and chairman of the Immigration Subcommittee and more recently as chairman of the Committee on the Judiciary, I have come to know the organization and these two dedicated public servants very well.

The creation of the Intergovernmental Committee for European Migration was the fruition of a concept nurtured by a former distinguished chairman of the subcommittee, the Honorable Francis E. Walter. His high resolve to eliminate the refugee camps in Western Europe, to promote family reunification in the aftermath of a long war, and to relieve unemployment and underemployment of the suffering populations of the Western European countries involved in the conflict led him to seek and obtain international cooperation in these goals. Although some of the original objectives of the Intergovernmental Committee for European Migration have changed over the years, it lives today as a viable international organization ready to lend its support in emergency operations in response to specific requests for assistance by its member governments.

I have had the honor of attending many meetings of the governing bodies of ICEM as a congressional adviser to the US delegation and as chairman of the ICEM Council in 1971 and 1972.

ICEM has faced many challenges in the past and no doubt will do so in the future. Over the years it has had its budgetary problems, but with the goodwill, understanding and support of all its members, the organization can continue to perform an essential and vital operational role in the migration and refugee field.

In wishing John Thomas a fruitful and happy retirement, I would like to commend him for his long dedication and devotion to the cause of refugees. He has actively participated in most of the major refugee situations since 1945 from the displaced persons camps in Germany to the evacuation of Indochinese refugees in Vietnam in 1975. President Johnson twice called on him in emergency refugee programs, once to head the US Cuban refugee program in HEW in Washington and again to AID in Saigon to coordinate the mass displacement of refugees occasioned by military operations.

It can truly be said that John Thomas has dedicated his life to the cause of refugees.

As to his successor, I can think of no other man who could fill John Thomas' shoes better than James Carlin. He too has devoted more than 30 years to the refugee and migration field. His experience as the refugee and migration chief in the US Mission in Geneva for many years and his active participation as a US representative to the ICEM and UNHCR governing bodies' meetings make him eminently qualified to lead the organization into the challenging years ahead.

In 1978, ICEM organized and carried out the migration movement of an over-all total of 91,118 persons, the biggest number since the organization handled the major influx of refugees from Hungary in 1956.

For 1979, ICEM forecasts the movement of 110,000 to 120,000 persons including at least some 70,000 Indochinese refugees and 35,000 from Eastern Europe.

I am sure you all join me in wishing James Carlin and ICEM great success in the coming years.

With my important new job in view I had resigned from the United States foreign service at the end of 1978 to prepare myself for the challenging responsibilities awaiting me at ICEM. Upon leaving the Department of State one of the 'powers that be' there gave me the ominous warning that I had 'one year to turn ICEM around, or the United States Government's continued membership in and support for the organization would be problematic'.

While recognizing that the challenges would be formidable, my close association with the organization practically from its inception, both as an ICEM official and as US Government delegate to sessions of ICEM's governing bodies, made me well aware of the organization's unique characteristics and great potential. Thus while accepting the warnings of my colleague at State, I was not intimidated. Indeed I approached my new tasks and responsibilities with confidence and optimism.

BALANCING THE BUDGET AND MAKING ICEM BETTER KNOWN AND APPRECIATED

Upon assuming the directorship of ICEM in March 1979 it became abundantly clear to me that priority would have to be devoted to restructuring and streamlining if there was to be any chance of my placing the organization on a sound financial basis by the year's end. To meet this objective I promptly established an in-house task force and, as a result of its efforts, economies in excess of one million dollars were effected. Moreover, through extensive adjustments in staffing operational efficiency was improved. Thus when the organization's books were closed at the end of 1979, the budget was fully-funded.

It was also evident that there was a necessity to establish closer ties with governments, both ICEM members and others, and to explain to well-placed officials in those governments not only ICEM's on-going programs, which were well worth while, but also the organization's potential for doing more in regard to refugee resettlement and migration for development – fields in which governments were showing increasing interest and experiencing growing needs and in which ICEM's expertise could be applied to greater advantage.

ICEM and its activities were not well-known – not even among member governments – and this was handicapping due recognition of the organization's achievements and limiting its development. In an effort to correct this state of affairs considerable official travel was undertaken by myself and senior colleagues, a series of meetings were staged with appropriate representatives of member governments and measures were initiated to establish and maintain a regular flow of information about all aspects of ICEM to governments and other interested entities.

Success in this publicity effort did not come easily, due in no small part to ICEM's basic nature and characteristics – and indeed the organization's somewhat misleading name. For while ICEM was constituted as an international, albeit intergovernmental, organization with a sound concept and purpose, it was created outside the framework of the United Nations. Although this feature has proved in practice to be one of the organization's greatest strengths – sparing it from rigid and constraining eligibility definitions and from crippling politicization, as well as enabling it to achieve an unparalleled operational performance – ICEM nevertheless does not have the *prima facie* appeal and apparent glamour – or the availability of a large public information budget and of an organized network of pressure groups – enjoyed by a United Nations body. Despite the fact that ICEM has always been heavily and effectively involved in the processing and movement of refugees, it is not exclusively a refugee organization and thus has not readily received the recognition accorded to an agency such as UNHCR.

While making a significant contribution through selective migration and other development-related movements to the economic and social advancement of developing countries, especially in Africa and Latin America, ICEM had not been perceived by the public at large primarily as a development agency like the United Nations Development Program

(UNDP). Even though ICEM had taken a lead role in staging problem-solving seminars and providing a forum in which governments, international organizations, voluntary agencies and interested individuals could meet and discuss migration in all its aspects, such events had not won formal recognition comparable to that given to similar fora of the International Labour Organization (ILO) or the United Nations Fund for Population Activities (UNFPA).

All in all – and particularly because of the need for it to perform discreetly in crisis situations and extrication operations – ICEM had been viewed and treated as something of a stepchild in the family of international organizations, but a stepchild with unique capabilities – capabilities which seemed ripe for further adjustment and development, especially bearing in mind that it has remained one of the few multilateral operational agencies in which representative parliamentary democracies have retained a decisive influence.

SPECIAL SESSION OF THE ICEM COUNCIL IN 1979 AND FOLLOW-UP ACTION

To gain support for my efforts to restructure ICEM, improve operational efficiency and, at the same time, secure a better appreciation of the organization's achievements and potential, I arranged for a special session of the ICEM Council (the organization's principal governing body) to be held in May 1979. This session, which was well attended by senior-level representatives of governments, international organizations and voluntary agencies, focused on the growing trend toward refugee resettlement activity, plans for improving ICEM's migration for development programs and attendant budgetary matters.

Particular attention was devoted to the resettlement aspect of the Indochinese refugee problem. Dramatic pleas for increased resettlement opportunities were voiced by the representatives of the South-east Asian countries of first asylum and a film illustrating the desperate plight of the 'boat people' was shown. The Council adopted a resolution expressing its 'grave concern' about the plight of the Indochinese refugees and called upon the international community to act swiftly to accelerate the resettlement of more of them from the first asylum countries in South-east Asia. In response Argentina, Australia, Belgium, Colombia, Denmark, Ecuador, the Federal Republic of Germany, Norway, Switzerland and the United States announced either new or enlarged programs for the resettlement of Indochinese refugees. Moreover, in response to my appeal for extra help to place ICEM on a sounder financial basis, the Governments of Belgium, Denmark, the Federal Republic of Germany, Israel, the Netherlands, Norway, Switzerland and the United States announced special contributions.

The Council's deliberations on the problem of Indochinese refugees in South-east Asia and ICEM's important operational role therein pointed up the fact that ICEM had evolved beyond its merely European image and indeed was acting more and more on a global basis. I highlighted this fact when addressing the Council and suggested that the time had come to consider eliminating the restrictive designation 'European' from the organization's name. The government delegates who spoke to this notion were generally supportive and the Council authorized me to present to a subsequent session an official proposal for such a change.

This special session of the Council (my first as Director of ICEM) was regarded as generally successful. Above all the member governments indicated their willingness to back up the organization and to develop and utilize more fully its potential. To give practical effect to this attitude the Council, through its then Chairman, Dr Oscar Schurch, of Switzerland, appealed in writing to several governments considered to believe in the basic purposes and principles of ICEM to join (or re-join) the organization and thus increase its capacity to fulfil its important humanitarian task. With such positive signals of encouragement I and my colleagues in the ICEM administration were spurred to renew our efforts to place ICEM on a sound basis – both financially and operationally – and to be alert to possibilities for the organization to undertake new projects and programs which would serve the interests of the international community.

Co-operation agreement between ICEM and Georgetown University, DC

One innovation was the conclusion in the autumn of 1979 of a co-operation agreement between ICEM and Georgetown University in Washington DC, providing for groups of Georgetown interns (mostly juniors or seniors) to be assigned to ICEM (usually for periods of six months) for practical work experience in the field of refugee resettlement and migration. Started on an experimental basis, this arrangement proved highly satisfactory and beneficial to all parties concerned, certainly to the individual interns. It has been a continuing success, with some 200 interns having participated in ICEM's field operations up to the time of writing.

The following verbatim record of an interview conducted in late 1984 with the Reverend Father Harold Bradley, Director of the Georgetown University Center for Immigration Policy and Refugee Assistance, on the ICEM/Georgetown University relationship, speaks for itself:

Q What was the basis for establishing the co-operative internship program between students of Georgetown's international program and ICEM?

Father Bradley: In 1977 immigration policy was selected by the university as an issue warranting heightened attention. Subsequently in 1979 an academic center for providing focus to the issue was formally established as CIPRA, the Center for Immigration Policy and Refugee Assistance. This coincided with the then developing massive exodus of refugees resulting from the aftermath of the Indochina conflict and the related urgent need to organize world-wide relief efforts to ease the plight of those refugees. This situation gave rise to the co-operative internship program between CIPRA and ICEM.

Q Do you consider the results of this internship program to be satisfactory both from the standpoint of the University and from the point of view of the students?

Father Bradley: Yes indeed. Now completing its fifth year, the six-month program provides practical learning experience for the participants in dealing with a major world problem while they contribute support to professional staff, primarily field officers, of an organization deeply committed to this field. Roughly 100 students have participated so far, including the current group of seven. Results have been highly satisfactory to Georgetown University, to the participating students and to ICEM. The internships afford unique opportunities for combining humanitarian service, in the context of different cultures, with related academic research in one of the most pressing problem areas of our time. Interest in the program by students and the university continues to be high. There have been considerably more applicants than available appointments for the new teams, notwithstanding the postponement in graduation which an internship usually entails, which testifies to the results as perceived by the students. All levels of university leadership and staff continue to give their utmost support.

Q What are the types of benefits that have been drawn from this experience, both by your department and by the students?

Father Bradley: Georgetown University's participation, through CIPRA, in internship programs with ICEM and other organizations, affords direct feedback for helping to meet its objectives of research and training, being an institution devoted to improved understanding of the phenomenon of mass migration as well as assisting in the alleviation of its consequences as a major cause of human suffering and political and economic instability. Returned interns provide a valuable group of resource persons for various aspects of CIPRA's activities not only while still on campus, but also later as university alumni.
To the students the internships have provided a consciousness-raising experience with active hands-on involvement in one of the major dramas of our day. As a consequence they are benefiting through becoming better informed about the humanitarian and political dimensions of important events taking place around the world. Their continuing interest is demonstrated by their willingness to volunteer, upon their return, for service at relief shelters, for tutoring and for other social services. Additionally, for many, the experience has given direction to academic/career plans.

Q With the students having participated in this program, have any contacts been maintained by the University, and to what extent has the experience played a role in shaping their post-graduate plans?

Father Bradley: At the end of July this year, a letter was sent to each returned intern seeking suggestions for program improvement as well as information on the influence of the experience on academic and/or career plans. The responses have only just begun to come in, but the preliminary results confirm what we have believed. Lives and careers are being importantly and constructively influenced. From the 15 responses received thus far we find:
– all have completed undergraduate studies;

- six went on to graduate study: four in international affairs, one in religious studies and one in medicine;
- nine are now employed: two in the US Foreign Service, one as a vocational English teacher for recent immigrants, one is a commissioned officer in the US Army, two work for ICEM, one is a program co-ordinator for an international journalist exchange program, one works for the Pearl Buck Foundation and the last teaches philosophy at a university.

Results of the follow-up enquiry will be documented when they are available.

Q   Is there anything else you can say about the program?

Father Bradley: Without reservation, the continuing program of internships is more than fulfilling the hopes and expectations of its founders. As was originally envisioned, it is, first and foremost, providing an enriched liberal arts education for the intern through an academic as well as a practical learning experience in refugee issues. CIPRA, in turn, is benefited by the availability of resource persons for various aspects of its other programs. Furthermore, a pool of enthusiastic, energetic, young people with first-hand experience is being developed for possible recruitment by organizations involved in refugees and international development work – a need which, as history dramatically shows, will continue.

Close of a banner year

As it turned out, 1979 was a banner year for ICEM, with refugee/migrant movements reaching 248 000 – an annual record in the organization's 28-year history. This substantially increased movement activity reflected ICEM's handling of more of the Indochinese refugees, increased emigration of Jews from the Soviet Union, which in that year exceeded 54 000, and the expansion of migration for development programming for the Latin American region.

9 ICM in the 1980s

DIVERSIFICATION AND ADAPTATION

The 1980s emerged as a period not only of intensification of effort but also of diversification on a global scale. The first year of the decade – 1980 – itself set another new record for the organization's operational activity, with 290 000 persons processed and moved for final resettlement.

The variety of often unforeseen situations faced and handled called for skilful adaptation. Glimpses of these situations and of ICEM's reaction to them in terms both of policy decisions and of operational measures are given in the following pages by way of illustration of the organization's sustained momentum and indeed rapid expansion.

1980

The Cuban emergency

Following events in Cuba in April 1980, as a result of which about 10 000 Cubans sought refuge in and around the Peruvian Embassy in Havana, ICEM received an urgent request from the Government of Peru to take all possible measures to facilitate the international resettlement of these persons. I immediately dispatched telegrams to 37 governments appealing for either temporary or permanent resettlement opportunities for them and for financial contributions to cover the cost of their resettlement. The Governments of Argentina, Austria, Canada, Costa Rica, Ecuador, the Federal Republic of Germany, Peru, Spain, and the United States responded promptly with resettlement offers, and the Governments of Chile, Denmark, the Dominican Republic, the Federal Republic of Germany, Israel, Italy, the Netherlands, Norway, Peru, Switzerland and the United States pledged financial contributions. The Costa Rican Government, following an initial offer to accept 300 of these Cubans for permanent resettlement, then offered to accept any or all of the 10 000 for either temporary or permanent residence.

The Council of Europe's Committee on Migration, Refugees and Demography met in special session to consider the humanitarian aspect of the situation in Cuba. The Committee passed a resolution welcoming the initiative of those governments which had already undertaken to receive Cubans, expressing appreciation of ICEM's action toward resolving the problem, and appealing to member governments of the Council of Europe to support ICEM's action by financial contributions and/or by receiving Cubans wishing to emigrate to Europe.

119

At the outset of the emergency ICEM established a task force of experienced staff members in San José, Costa Rica, to handle resettlement operations, and the organization also promptly contracted for three aircraft which were placed on a stand-by basis at San José airport. During the next few days the three aircraft completed six flights between Havana and San José, lifting out about 800 Cubans from the Peruvian Embassy compound. In addition some 300 were flown to Lima, Peru.

On 24 April, however, the Cuban authorities suspended this airlift. Soon thereafter Cubans desirous of leaving their homeland, including many of those in the Peruvian Embassy compound, were directed to the Cuban port of Mariel, from which a flotilla of small boats conducted a shuttle operation to Key West, Florida – an operation which lifted about 126 000 Cubans to the United States in the space of a few weeks. To cope with this heavy and rapid influx of Cubans into the country, the US Government established transit facilities in various military installations, the principal ones being Eglin Air Force Base in Florida, Fort Chaffee in Arkansas and Camp Indiantown Gap in Pennsylvania, and at the Government's request ICEM set up operational offices in each of those installations to co-ordinate the processing and movement of the Cubans to their final destinations in the United States and abroad.

The changing trend in refugee migration

During the meetings of ICEM's governing bodies in 1980 I invited the attention of member governments to the changing trend in refugee migration. I stressed that, although the definition of a refugee according to the Geneva Convention of 1951 remained valid in a legal sense, in practical terms there was a new phenomenon whereby increasing numbers of would-be refugees, instead of escaping illegally, were being permitted to depart legally from their homeland but, once across the frontier, found themselves in critical need of migration assistance. I further stressed that this change could have a significant bearing on the work of the international entities concerned. While in the past ICEM had been very closely involved in providing resettlement assistance to persons regarded as refugees in the traditional sense, at present and in the foreseeable future considerable numbers of the type of persons described above could be and were regarded in practical terms as legitimate refugee migrants for purposes of migration resettlement under ICEM auspices. My views were duly endorsed by the ICEM governing bodies and there was a consensus that the international community should be mindful of the change and supportive of ICEM programs aimed at facilitating the resettlement of refugee migrants regardless of the traditional designation of refugee status.

The Federal Republic of Germany was one of the principal countries experiencing a heavy influx of this type of asylum-seeker – their number having reached some 80 000 during the period January to September 1980. To cope with this problem, which was to be an on-going one, ICEM, at the request of the Federal German Government, initiated a special program there to facilitate the return to their home country of those persons willing to return and to assist in the emigration of those choosing to be resettled in a third country. A similar program was subsequently initiated in Belgium, and both have been notably successful.

Broadening of the criteria for refugee intake by the United States

With the enactment of the United States Refugee Act of 1980, a matter touched upon in an earlier part of this account, the criteria for refugee intake by the United States were broadened, and consequently in September 1980 ICEM moved the first African refugees (Ethiopians) to the United States – 182 from the Sudan and 131 from Djibouti.

In the context of US immigration policy in the 1980s, the Honorable Peter Rodino, Chairman of the House Judiciary Committee of the US Congress, referred to the role of international organizations in general and ICEM in particular, in a lecture delivered on 12 November 1980 at Georgetown University in Washington DC. He said, inter alia

> The need for international machinery to respond to refugee and migration problems is obvious. An international mechanism ... could develop adequate contingency plans [and] thereby reduce sometimes fatal delays in responding to refugee emergencies. It would also explore more aggressively the alternative of voluntary repatriation.
> ... the only operational international entity dealing with refugees and migrants is ICEM ... I have long valued the expertise of ICEM and we must promote the increased use of that expertise.
> We must also vigorously pursue the creation of a permanent international fund to finance special projects for resettlement in developing countries. These projects should include the identification of particular areas or regions which are underpopulated and susceptible to resettlement programs.

Assistance to Bolivians

In the autumn of 1980, following a coup in Bolivia that abruptly overthrew the democratic government of President Lydia Gueiler and brought General García Mesa to power, a large number of Bolivians who had been active supporters of democratic reform in their country found themselves at odds with the new régime; many were imprisoned and many others sought refuge in consulates and/or embassies in La Paz or went into hiding.

With encouragement from various governments and with the tacit consent of the new authorities in La Paz, ICEM initiated a special program in September 1980 for the resettlement of the victims of the political events in Bolivia – a role similar to that played by ICEM in Chile following the end of the Allende régime. Between September 1980 and October 1981 ICEM processed and moved from Bolivia 1787 persons – 215 political detainees from jails and prisons; 305 persons who had sought asylum in consulates and embassies; 403 persons who had been in hiding; and 864 family members of these various categories. The receiving countries were Andorra (1), Belgium (70), Brazil (5), Canada (5), Colombia (31), Costa Rica (1), Denmark (10), Dominican Republic (3), Ecuador (47), Finland (3), France (22), Federal Republic of Germany (5), Mexico (394), Netherlands (12), Norway (34), Panama (6), Peru (28), Spain (1), Sweden (919), Switzerland (135), United States (7) and Venezuela (48).

This program, which required delicate and discreet handling, was financed outside ICEM's regular budget with special financial contributions coming from Denmark, Italy, Sweden, Switzerland and the United States.

Changing the designation of ICEM to ICM

Reacting to the proposal I had made at the special session of the ICEM Council in May 1979, the Council, at its 45th regular session in November 1980, dealt with the matter of changing the designation of ICEM by adopting the following resolution:

> Recognizing the substantial contribution the Committee has made by its vastly increased refugee resettlement efforts and its international co-operation in the transfer of technology through the movement of specialized human resources,
> Recalling its Resolution No. 610 (XLIV) of 20 November 1979 in which, after recognizing that both the need for and the impressive development of ICEM's services outside Europe had increased as a result of the recent unforeseen and dramatic expansion of the refugee phenomenon, it concluded that circumstances would compel the Committee to continue to provide them on a global basis,
> Resolves that, for purely practical purposes, the Committee shall, as from the date of this resolution, be designated as the Intergovernmental Committee for Migration (ICM), it being understood that such change of designation shall in no way be regarded as modifying the Constitution of the Committee and shall be without prejudice to any resolutions hitherto adopted by the Council, to any existing agreements and contracts to which the Committee is a party, or to any national laws concerning the Committee.

Permanent new headquarters for ICM

A further notable development during 1980 was the conclusion of successful negotiations between the ICM Administration and the Government of Switzerland to have erected in Geneva a suitable building to serve as a permanent headquarters of ICM. The plan for this construction was approved by ICM's governing bodies in 1980.

A balanced budget

When ICM's accounts for 1980 were closed and audited, the organization's budget for the year, totalling some $166 million, was again in balance – a favorable state of affairs which had resulted in part from generous and timely contributions from governments toward ICM's expanding activities and in part from the Administration's having exercised strict budgetary discipline and continuing efforts to effect economies through improved operational efficiency.

1981

Program activity, including the departure of the three millionth migrant

ICM's program activity continued at a relatively high level in 1981 notwithstanding the fact that the emigration of Soviet Jews was at a reduced rate with a total of 9460 for the year as compared with 21 470 in 1980 and 51 330 in 1979. Altogether 205 000 refugees and migrants were processed and moved under ICM auspices during the year – the third consecutive year that the organization's movements topped the 200 000 mark.

The year 1981 also marked the departure of ICM's three millionth migrant – a Colombian physician who was moved from the Federal Republic of Germany to Colombia under ICEM's return of talent program.

Seminar on the situation of refugee and migrant women

In April 1981 ICM organized in Geneva a seminar on the situation of refugee and migrant women. The seminar, which was chaired by Mrs Anita Gradin (Sweden), Chairwoman of the Committee on Migration, Refugees and Demography of the Council of Europe, was attended by 190 representatives of 39 governments and 42 international governmental and non-governmental organizations, including Mrs Karin Anderson, Swedish Minister of Immigration and Equality between Men and Women; Mrs Jeane Kirkpatrick, then US Ambassador to the United Nations, US Congresswoman Mrs Patricia Schroeder and Dr Elizabeth Winkler, Secretary-General of the International Catholic Migration Commission.

The participants had available to them 14 expert papers and 23 information documents – material which reflected the concerns and positions of governments, international organizations and voluntary agencies on the problems of refugee and migrant women. The discussions revealed that migrant and refugee women were subject to threefold discrimination – first as women, second as foreigners and third as members of the lowest socio-economic group.

The participants called upon all governments to reaffirm and implement the fundamental principles of international law ensuring women's equal protection under the law, the universal right to preservation of the family unit and the universal right to health care. They also called for greater public awareness of the positive contributions made by migrant and refugee women to the economy, culture and society at large.

ICM was commended for staging a seminar on such a vital subject and was urged to promote increased attention to the needs of migrant and refugee women and to stimulate programs and projects for them, as well as to carry out further research into the problem. One concrete outcome of the seminar was a development project, funded by the Asia and Ford Foundations, for the benefit of Indochinese refugee women in camps in South-east Asia. The project was designed to identify the needs of refugee women, to ensure the preparation and implementation of programs to meet those needs and thus to upgrade the role and active participation of these women in development activities in local communities.

New influx of asylum seekers into Austria

The year 1981 also produced a heavy new influx of Eastern European asylum seekers, especially Poles, into Austria. The backlog in mid-1981 exceeded 13 000 and the influx during the year exceeded 30 000. This development prompted Austria's Minister of Interior, Mr Erwin Lanc, to attend the special session of the ICM Council held in July 1981 and to seek ICM's help in facilitating the rapid resettlement processing and movement of these asylum seekers from his country, which would enable Austria to maintain its liberal asylum policy. The appeal of the Austrian Minister was met with understanding and sympathy by the ICM member governments, and several delegates praised Austria for its unabated generous asylum policy over many years.

With encouragement from the Council the Administration was duly responsive to Austria's new emergency. The ICM mission in Austria was once again reinforced and all possible measures were taken to speed up the resettlement processing of the backlog of asylum seekers and to keep pace with the on-going influx.

Invigorated efforts for the benefit of developing countries

At that same special session the Council also focused on the organization's invigorated efforts for the benefit of developing countries, especially in Latin America, through the transfer of qualified human resources. The Council was generally appreciative of the Administration's action in this respect. The delegates of Latin American countries, in particular, praised the dynamism of ICM, characterized by the diversification of its programs for the transfer of technology through human resources and the Administration's readiness to adapt the organization's structure to changing circumstances.

A series of conclusions were reached at the special session, the principal ones being that:

● ICM should continue to strengthen its co-operation with developing countries;
● priority should be given to the return of talent program;
● more governments should arrange for the initiation of integrated experts programs similar to those already undertaken by ICM in close co-operation with the Governments of the Federal Republic of Germany and of Italy;
● new programs for co-operation between developing countries (horizontal migration) should be promoted by ICM;
● ICM should explore the possibility of establishing an information center (data bank) to serve the interests of migration in the Latin American region;
● special attention should be paid to the needs of Central American and Caribbean countries; and
● ICM should explore all possibilities for extending its migration for development activities to developing countries in other parts of the world, especially in Africa and Asia.

Conference of African Ministers responsible for human resources planning, development and utilization

In October 1981 ICM participated in a Conference of African Ministers responsible for human resources planning, development and utilization organized by the United Nations Economic Commission for Africa (ECA) in Monrovia, Liberia, and attended by delegates from 23 African countries as well as by representatives of several international organizations. The conference focused, inter alia, on the gravity of the brain drain from Africa, and in this context ICM was afforded the opportunity to report on its action for the transfer of technology through human resources including, of course, its innovative return of talent program. The conference adopted a resolution calling for measures to facilitate the return of technically/professionally qualified persons to Africa and the establishment of close co-operation to this end between African governments and ICM, thereby paving the way for ICM's subsequent introduction of its return of talent program in that continent. This program in practice reverses the brain drain. It is also widely seen as a useful contribution to structural adjustment, which in turn is increasingly being considered as essential to genuine development.

1982

Overall movements in 1982: changing acceptance trends

ICM's overall program for 1982 involved the processing and movement of 140 500 refugees and national migrants.

In this context it may be noted that, after some seven years (1975–81) of ICM action on behalf of Indochinese refugees, during which 700 000 persons (including some 350 000 boat people) were processed in the asylum countries of South-east Asia and resettled abroad, there was a marked change in 1982 when 'compassion fatigue' seemingly affected the attitude of the traditional refugee receiving countries. As a result, their acceptances of Indochinese for permanent resettlement declined to about 86 000 compared to 158 000 in the previous year.

There was also a sharp decrease in emigration from the Soviet Union, with the flow of Soviet Jews down from 9500 in 1981 to about 2700 in 1982, and a reduction during the same period of family-reunion cases (mainly Armenians) from 2500 to 400.

Conversely ICM's other programs for refugee migrants increased appreciably, with movements of Poles, for example, amounting to 50 000 in 1982. This made it possible not only to reduce the backlogs in Austria and Italy but also to keep pace with the on-going influx. Similarly the organization's migration programs for the benefit of developing countries, especially in Latin America, showed significant gains.

Council of Europe support for ICM

ICM received useful support from the Council of Europe in these efforts. The Assembly of that organization adopted in 1982 a resolution which

- expressed the Assembly's deep appreciation of the work of ICM;
- urged ICM to continue carrying out its regular programs, intensifying and developing its essential contribution to the assistance and transport of migrants and refugees;
- invited ICM to continue its policy of co-operation with developing countries in the field of the transfer of technology through human resources; and
- called upon the governments of European member states of ICM to continue affording ICM strong political and financial support, and upon member governments of the Council of Europe not members of ICM to consider joining the organization.

Special efforts for the resettlement processing of Poles

Apart from the above-mentioned resolution the Assembly appealed to Council of Europe member states and the main non-European immigration countries to 'give ICM political and material assistance in order to increase its means of intervention concerning the reception and resettlement of Polish refugees'.

In the early summer of 1982, in order to assist in the resettlement processing of Poles being released from detention in Poland so that they might emigrate (mostly members of the trade union organization known as Solidarity and their families), ICM established a special facility at Bad Soden near Frankfurt in the Federal Republic of Germany. The persons concerned were provided at this facility with temporary housing as well as language and cultural orientation training pending their processing for resettlement. The facility has been kept in existence ever since, and up to the time of writing some 3000 such Poles had been processed therein and finally resettled, mostly in the United States.

Typical of the cases passing through the Bad Soden facility was that of a young man whom ICM has referred to as Jerzy. His story, as recounted by Lena Lee, ICM's Cultural Orientation Instructor, is as follows:

For Jerzy, growing up in Wroclaw, Poland, not much thought was given to politics. Little did he know that one day his life would turn dramatically on the issue of political dissent, bringing him to the United States as a refugee.

When Jerzy was nineteen he was imprisoned for participating in a strike called by the Solidarity union. In 1982, after nine months and five appeals, he was freed. During the next four years he experienced frequent harassment by the authorities and was jailed several times. From 1984 through 1986, when he was closely associated with Solidarity in Wroclaw, he was kept under surveillance by the police.

It was while working for Solidarity that Jerzy met a girl whom ICM has called Anna and they were soon married. Jerzy then applied through the United States Embassy in Warsaw to emigrate under the US program for Polish ex-detainees. While still in Poland the couple was approved for emigration as refugees to the United States and they made their way to Bad Soden, where they were cared for and assisted by ICM.

While at Bad Soden a baby boy was born to them. The baby was baptized at a local church and, soon after, the family was informed that they would be leaving for the United States. While Jerzy and Anna had been awaiting the baby's birth, and wondering where they would all be going, a Polish refugee friend had been trying hard to find a sponsor for them in America. He himself had been sponsored by a church group in the Middle West and his particular sponsor was willing to sponsor Jerzy's family as well.

The day of departure finally arrived for Jerzy and Anna. On 14 September they flew out from Frankfurt and later the same day were met at the Oklahoma City Airport by their sponsor and a group of Polish refugee migrants from the Oklahoma City area. Also on hand was Lena Lee herself, who had been their teacher in the cultural orientation program at Bad Soden. Two of the refugees who met them had participated in the Bad Soden program, and another had attended ICM's classes at Maria Schutz, Austria.

Jerzy's sponsor and the church congregation had a furnished apartment waiting for them. Jerzy's friend and former classmate told Lena Lee that he hoped that more refugees would come to the southern and central regions of the United States. He said that life in America was hard, but that he would not trade it for life in any other place. There was a sense of freedom in America which he had felt "when my feet first touched the ground". He and the other former ICM students felt that they had benefited greatly from the cultural orientation program and had been better prepared than other refugees to begin their new lives in America.

Private audience with His Holiness Pope John Paul II

Taking account of ICM's Bad Soden operation, it seems relevant to refer to my official visit to Rome in the summer of 1982, during which it was my distinct privilege and pleasure to have been granted a private audience with His Holiness Pope John Paul II. His Holiness displayed a keen interest in ICM's work with respect to both refugee resettlement and migration schemes for the benefit of developing countries. Indeed it may be recalled that already on 1 December 1981, when the thirtieth anniversary of the establishment of ICM was commemorated by the Council, a message was received from the Vatican's Secretary of State, Cardinal Casaroli, which stated that

> Mindful of ICM's collaboration in international efforts which have helped millions of refugees to reach a new homeland and there to begin to construct a new life, His Holiness prays for the continued success of this vital work of justice and charity and he invokes God's blessings of joy and peace upon all associated in these praiseworthy endeavors.

During my audience the Pope, in his halting but otherwise precise English, expressed his deep anxiety about the plight of refugees and the events which produce them, and commended ICM for being effectively responsive to the resettlement needs of refugees and migrants. At the same time, however, alluding to the prevailing situation in his own country, Poland, His Holiness gently implied that emigration should not be unduly encouraged for those bravely engaged in waging the struggle for social and democratic reform in their homeland. I was able to assure His Holiness that indeed it was not ICM's constitutional purpose to take any initiatives aimed at stimulating emigration in such situations; its established policy was to assist interested governments, on humanitarian grounds, in refugee resettlement and development related movements.

Evacuation of members of the Palestine Liberation Organization (PLO) from Lebanon

ICM's unique capability to react to and perform swiftly in emergency

situations was again put to the test in August 1982. In the late afternoon of
20 August I was invited to attend an urgent meeting at the United States
Mission in Geneva. Upon my arrival the Chief of Mission, Ambassador
Geoffrey Swaebe, hastened to explain the purpose of the meeting, which
concerned essentially how to arrange the evacuation of members of the
Palestine Liberation Organization (PLO) from Lebanon under a plan
developed by Ambassador Philip Habib in the course of his shuttle
diplomacy in the Middle East aimed at reducing tension in Lebanon
and enabling Israel to withdraw its forces from that country. The
evacuation of PLO members from Lebanon was considered a key element
of the plan and one which had won agreement of all parties concerned,
including the leader of the PLO Yasser Arafat. It was due to start on
Sunday 22 August, and all systems were at 'go' until the morning of
20 August when Yasser Arafat, having learned that the evacuation was
to be effected under the umbrella of the International Committee of the
Red Cross (ICRC), balked and declared that he would not permit his
'fighters' to leave looking like prisoners of war (POWs) in the care of the
Red Cross. Thus a role for the ICRC had to be ruled out. What, then, was
to be done?

After a flurry of top priority cables and telephone calls between
Washington and the various diplomatic posts concerned, Ambassador
Swaebe's Mission in Geneva was instructed to contact me and determine
whether ICM would be willing to tackle the operation. Yasser Arafat had
not raised any objection to ICM's involvement.

While being somewhat nonplussed by such a striking challenge, especially
in view of the tight time frame, I nevertheless agreed in principle to ICM's
taking on the task and, after receiving further detailed briefing on the
planned operation, I returned to ICM headquarters to set the wheels in
motion. An in-house task force was formed, the ICM missions in Athens
and Nicosia were alerted, three planes were immediately chartered by ICM
from Middle Eastern Airlines and on Sunday morning 22 August, the
originally planned starting time for the evacuation, three ICM charter
flights lifted off the first 392 members of the PLO – 131 to Baghdad and
261 to Amman via Larnaca, Cyprus. This broke the ice for the full
evacuation operation and the remaining members of the PLO force were
moved from Lebanon in somewhat less dramatic circumstances by surface
carriers.

As a footnote to this operation it is interesting to observe that whereas
the PLO evacuees were permitted to bear their weapons (automatic rifles
and grenades) in the process of their departure from the Beirut area, all
such arms were placed in the cargo section of the planes for the flights from
Larnaca to Amman and Baghdad.

I was honored, upon the successful conclusion of this emergency operation, to receive from United States Secretary of State George P. Shultz the following letter:

23 September 1982

Dear Mr. Carlin:

The departure of the PLO forces from Beirut marks the completion of the first major stage of the long and difficult process toward solving the complex problems in Lebanon. The evacuation could not have succeeded without the co-operative efforts of a number of governments and organizations.

I would like to express my great appreciation for the role the ICM played in making this historic operation a success. Without your assistance in arranging for air transport on extremely short notice, the entire effort would have been far more difficult.

I believe that our joint success in resolving the Beirut crisis through diplomatic means marks an important beginning to the achievement of a just and durable peace in the Middle East. Thank you once again for your effort.

Sincerely yours,

(Signed)   George P. Shultz

Afghan refugees

In the early autumn of 1982 ICM was engaged in another somewhat unusual operation when it was called upon to airlift some 3800 Afghan refugees from Pakistan to Turkey, the largest group of Afghan refugees moved from Pakistan to a single resettlement country in one operation. All members of the group were Afghans of Turkish ethnic origin (Uzbeks, Kirghiz, Turkmen and Kazakhs) and they were destined for permanent resettlement in Turkey. Twelve charter flights were involved – five from Rawalpindi and seven from Karachi, all landing in Adana. Subsequently in August 1983 an additional group of 330 Afghans of Turkish ethnic origin were moved by ICM from Islamabad to Adana.

In addition, from 1981 up to the time of writing some 30 000 other Afghan refugees had been moved under ICM auspices for permanent resettlement, mainly to Australia, Canada and the United States, with limited numbers to Western European countries.

Assistance to Costa Rica, the Dominican Republic, Honduras and Panama regarding the transfer of technology through human resources

In mid-1982 I received official requests from the Presidents of Costa Rica, the Dominican Republic, Honduras and Panama for co-operation in their national development projects by means of ICM's programs for the transfer of technology through human resources. ICM dispatched to each of the four countries a survey team of experts which, working in close conjunction with the national authorities, identified some 600 positions in priority sectors for which qualified human resources from abroad would be required. Details of these positions were promptly signalled to ICM's various missions in industrialized countries and served as a basis for recruitment action.

To complement this effort, the European Community in Brussels reacted positively to an ICM project proposal by providing ICM with $1.3 million to finance the selection, transport and reintegration in the Central American and Caribbean regions of 70 qualified Latin American nationals.

Extension of ICM's return of talent program to Africa, with financial assistance from the European Community and the United States Government

Moreover, to enable ICM to introduce its return of talent program to Africa, a matter which had been discussed at the October 1981 Conference of African Ministers responsible for human resources planning, development and utilization in Monrovia (mentioned earlier) and was subsequently carefully explored by the organization during the early months of 1982, financing (approximately $3 million) for a pilot project was approved by the European Community in September 1982. The project proposal which ICM had submitted to the Community in this connection was designed to cover the return of 200 African nationals (mainly Kenyans, Somalians and Zimbabweans together with their families) who had received professional training and/or work experience in industrialized countries but who wished to go back and be part of the process of economic and social development of their homeland.

As a supplement to this European Community sponsored program, the Government of the United States agreed to contribute $700 000 to ICM to finance the processing and return of African nationals who had acquired professional qualifications and experience in the United States. In the first year this contribution was intended to cover 50 cases returning to either Botswana, Kenya, Lesotho, Malawi, Somalia, Sudan, Swaziland, Tanzania, the United Republic of Cameroon, Zambia or Zimbabwe.

The implementation of these pilot projects was successful beyond expectation – surprising sceptics in certain quarters – and by way of illustration one of them is described in greater detail further on. Suffice it to note here that the introduction of return of talent programming to Africa was significant for two reasons: it constituted on the one hand a potentially valuable contribution to Africa's economic and social development and on the other a vital new operational dimension to ICM's work.

1983

Seminar on undocumented migrants and migrants in an irregular situation

In April 1983 ICM staged in Geneva the sixth in a series of migration seminars – this one being devoted to the problems of undocumented migrants and migrants in an irregular situation. The seminar, which was attended by some 200 participants representing 54 governments and 47 international governmental and non-governmental organizations, discussed in depth the motivations and underlying causes of undocumented migration; the rights and obligations of undocumented migrants in receiving countries; the protection of their human rights and the regularization of their status; and possible remedies for undocumented migration.

The seminar had before it comprehensive working papers prepared by 14 experts and some 30 information papers reflecting research into and practical experience of the problem of undocumented migrants presented by various governments and interested organizations.

The conclusions of the seminar indicated general agreement on the need to intensify study with a view to achieving a better understanding of the complexities of the problem. Moreover the seminar made a number of recommendations

● encouraging governments to use the good offices of ICM and other international organizations and to take advantage of various means, including bilateral and multilateral agreements, to ensure orderly and legal migration;
● urging countries of origin and receiving countries to combat illegal migration by seeing to it that migrants had the necessary documents and exercising greater control over the hiring of migrant labor by employers;
● inviting governments to collect more adequate data, undertake further research into irregular migration and to make the information available to international organizations such as ICM, which act as a clearing-house for documentation and statistics on international migration;
● encouraging action to ensure that migrants in an irregular situation enjoy fundamental human rights;
● inviting ICM to develop appropriate programs, at the request of the governments concerned, for the resettlement in a humanitarian manner of undocumented migrants, and to provide technical and other assistance to ensure their smooth integration; and
● calling for regional conferences to be organized with the collaboration of universities and specialized organizations in order to achieve a better knowledge of the complexities of the problem of undocumented migration in various parts of the world and possibly to pave the way for an international conference to examine the phenomenon globally. (In his address to the seminar, US Congressman Peter Rodino proposed such a conference because of the increased pressure for migration world-wide. He stressed that long-term, carefully planned international approaches were imperative with a view to solving the problem of irregular migration.)

Special migration program for Salvadorans

In the summer of 1983 the Government of El Salvador requested ICM to undertake a special migration program for Salvadorans covered by its recent Amnesty Law (*Ley de amnistia y rehabilitación ciudadana*) who wished to leave El Salvador. ICM promptly made available in San Salvador the necessary staff and facilities, and by the time the Amnesty Law expired on 15 August 1983 ICM, working in close co-operation with the immigration officers of Australia and Canada, as well as the embassies of certain Western European countries, had arranged the processing and movement of about 500 amnestied Salvadorans to resettlement countries abroad.

Subsequently, however, Salvadorans continued to seek resettlement, many on compelling grounds of family reunification or as economic migrants, and some still for motives related to their security in El Salvador. The ICM mission in San Salvador maintained and indeed further developed its migration services – services including the initial screening of applicants, the preparation of individual resettlement dossiers, arrangements for interviews with visiting selection missions, medical examinations, obtaining exit permits and 'safe conducts' and finally transportation arrangements to the resettlement country abroad. Since the initial Amnesty Program, ICM assisted some 4000 Salvadorans in their emigration thus enabling them to achieve self-fulfilment in a new life abroad.

Establishment in Santiago de Chile of a Center for Information on Migration to Latin America (CIMAL)

Following a recommendation made at a special session of the ICM Council held in July 1981 ICM established in Santiago de Chile during 1983 an information center to collect, computerize and disseminate information on all aspects of migration in Latin America, so as to make available to governments in the region data required for their research as well as for the planning and formulation of migration policies and programs. As part of this work the center issues three times a year a journal presenting indexed abstracts of published and unpublished documents (books, articles, conference papers, reports, etc.) concerning migration in the Latin American and Caribbean regions.

Apart from being a source of information, the center can serve to facilitate horizontal co-operation through the exchange and development of human resources in the region, thereby contributing to the economic advancement of individual countries and the social well-being of their people. In other words it is a new instrument for giving concrete form to new ideas aimed at serving the best interests of the governments and people of Latin America.

Joint ICM/Georgetown University Hemispheric Migration Project (HMP), financed by the United States Government

Also within the framework of its mandate to deal with migration problems in the Latin American region ICM, working in conjunction with Georgetown University, Washington DC, submitted to the United States Government (Department of State) in the spring of 1983 a proposal for financing a two-year research project on the causes of migration in the Western Hemisphere, known as the Hemispheric Migration Project (HMP), with the following objectives:

● to increase knowledge about the determinants and consequences of migration in countries of origin;
● to contribute to policies that incorporate the migration dimension in national, bilateral, regional and hemispheric contexts;
● to establish links among research institutions to carry out comparative studies of the influence of migration on sending societies; and
● to disseminate research results in a variety of formats in order to reach a wide audience.

The project, which was approved by the US State Department in the autumn of 1983 with $1.2 million to be made available for its implementation, actually got underway in December 1983 when ICM independently initiated priority research in various Central American countries. This comprised the following items:

● a comprehensive census of displaced persons in El Salvador, giving age and sex data as well as the location of camps and concentrations;
● estimated numbers of Salvadorans fleeing poor economic conditions as opposed to those fleeing civil strife;
● numbers of Salvadorans in Guatemala;
● numbers of Guatemalan and Salvadoran refugees in Mexico;
● numbers of Central American refugees in Costa Rica and Honduras;
● the burdens and hidden costs being borne by first asylum countries, principally Costa Rica, Honduras and Mexico;
● the influence of underemployment and unemployment on movements out of El Salvador, Guatemala and Nicaragua;
● the basic socio-demographic and economic characteristics of Central American refugees in Nicaragua; and
● identification of potential receiving countries in Latin America which would accept for permanent resettlement refugee migrants from Central America, their self-interest in receiving them or the obstacles to their doing so.

Detailed reports on each of these items were prepared and submitted to the US State Department in June 1984 and copies were made available to ICM's information center and data base at Santiago de Chile.

The other, broader aspects of HMP were organized jointly by ICM and Georgetown University in the spring of 1984. Regional co-ordinators were appointed and an experts review group, composed of several of the foremost authorities on migration in the Americas, was established.

In keeping with the project's overall objectives it was decided that the research should focus, inter alia, on the impact of migration on countries of origin and that proposals for study topics should be sought from social scientists in Latin America and the Caribbean. Among the topics given priority were the following:

- the impact of emigration on local labor markets;
- return migration;
- the impact of remittances; and
- the socio-economic integration of refugees in countries of first asylum.

It was further decided that a 'state of the art' paper on migration issues and policy options for each sub-region would be prepared by the regional co-ordinators.

To facilitate this research two workshops were organized – one in San José, Costa Rica, and one in Bogotá, Colombia – enabling some 20 researchers who had been recruited by the regional co-ordinators to present their plans and benefit from the comments and suggestions of their fellow researchers. The discussions focused on themes in the research, methodological approaches, areas of compatibility among projects and policy issues. These workshops marked the first time that such a large group of scholars on migration from Spanish-speaking countries in Latin America were able to exchange useful ideas with their colleagues from the English-speaking Caribbean region and it was clear that the seeds for future useful collaborative research were sown there.

The final research reports together with five 'state of the art' papers were disseminated to the US Government (the funder) and to all the other member governments of ICM and copies were, of course, provided to ICM's information center and data base at Santiago de Chile.

Provision for ICM assistance in relation to priority development sectors in Nicaragua

Following an official request in 1979 from the Government of Nicaragua, a memorandum of understanding between the entities concerned was signed in September 1983 as a result of which ICM, working in close conjunction with Nicaragua's Fondo Internacional para la Reconstrucción (FIR) and the Economic System for Latin America (SELA), recruited and placed in Nicaragua for permanent resettlement during the ensuing years some 300 persons in highly skilled and professional categories. Included in this selective migration program were returning Nicaraguans, other Latin Americans and Europeans with expertise in the fields of agriculture, education, energy, mining, natural resources, telecommunications and transport.

Re-election in December 1983 as Director of ICM and progress report to the ICM Council on that occasion

At its 49th Session in December 1983 the ICM Council unanimously re-elected me to the directorship of ICM for a second five-year term starting on 1 March 1984. In accepting re-election I used the occasion to update the Council on highlights of ICM's development and activities during my stewardship. The substance of my statement is reproduced below.

It is indeed an honor and privilege to address the Council as I near the completion of one term as Director and look forward to another. The statements in support of my continuing in this office were extremely generous and encouraging and ... inspire re-dedication to the work ahead. I wish to express my sincere gratitude to the representative of the United States for having nominated me for a second term, and equally my appreciation to those delegates who spoke in support of the nomination. I am, indeed, grateful to the entire Council for having given me this opportunity once again.

With the renewed mandate, I wish to inform the Council that I accept this task and challenge without reservation. The confidence and trust you have shown today greatly encourage me to continue my efforts to strengthen ICM, to broaden its activities, and to serve the interests of the member governments wherever those interests lie. I pledge also to continue the highest standards of financial and managerial responsibility.

... I should like ... to join with ... members of the Council in welcoming the Governments of Belize and Mexico as observers at this Council. I would only add the hope that this development may lead in due course to the full membership of those governments in ICM.

... It would seem appropriate on this occasion to take a few moments to reflect on our organization – its recent past, its present and prospects for its future.

When I assumed the directorship in the spring of 1979 I informed the Council that I intended to give due consideration to old as well as new ideas, but not to be mastered by either. I opined at that time that ICM, by its very operational nature, must be dynamic, it must be adaptable, and it must be responsive to a changing world. Migration, it was noted, is a world-wide phenomenon made up of many currents. It responds to many varying stimuli – economic, social, and political – and thus it is subject to continually changing patterns ... I continue to be guided by these notions – firmly convinced that a specialized migration organization is probably more necessary today than it has ever been.

Now, on reflection, I believe the Council can take a measure of satisfaction from the fact that many of the goals set five years ago have been achieved. And I would hasten to add that these were accomplished in the most active period in

ICM's history – a period in which some 988,000 persons were processed and moved under the organization's auspices, and a period during which the organization assumed a global character – in name as well as in functions.

It is also significant ... that there is now a much broader awareness of ICM's potential and of the necessity of making the organization an even closer partner of governments and of the modern world community. It is ... increasingly recognized that, just as other people, migrants have rights and should benefit from the over-all principle of the free movement of people, so that their journey to foreign shores will be less risky and better guided than in the past. Again progress in this direction has been made.

In the period under review ICM's administrative procedures have been developed and refined. New operational techniques have been devised. Procedures for internal audit and inspection were reinforced and this, I might add, has produced additional revenue to finance operations. Agreements for very favorable rates have been negotiated with most of the international airlines, resulting in substantial savings to the organization.

ICM now maintains the ability to handle almost routinely such regular flows of refugees as those from Eastern Europe and from Indochina. Yet the organization retains the capacity to respond as a fire brigade – able to move swiftly in emergency situations. For example in 1980 ICM assisted in the resettlement of Cubans who sought asylum at the Peruvian Embassy in Havana ... [and] was involved with those arriving in the United States from Mariel Bay. In 1981 an emergency program for resettlement from Bolivia was implemented. In 1982 ICM assisted at very short notice in the movement of members of the Palestine Liberation Organization (PLO) from Lebanon to various countries. In 1983 ICM undertook special efforts for the resettlement of refugees from NW-82, a camp on the border between Thailand and Kampuchea...

With respect to national migration – one of the pillars of ICM's program – the organization can readily adjust to meet manpower needs in the developing countries, to assist in relieving population pressures in certain countries, and, indeed, to cope with other push and pull factors which influence migratory movements.

We have continued during the period under review our major operation for the processing and movement of Indochinese refugees from South-east Asian countries of first asylum to countries of final resettlement. While the rate of resettlement under this program has decreased somewhat during the past year or so, we have intensified other assistance measures. To ensure the most effective treatment of refugees prior to their movement, ICM provides the requisite immunization services, treatment for infectious diseases, and documentation necessary for adequate medical care upon arrival in the receiving country. We have also introduced special escort services for serious medical cases, not only as a humanitarian responsibility, but as a practical measure to reduce the potential social service costs for the receiving countries. In an attempt to counteract the build-up in first asylum countries of physically or mentally disabled refugees, a special ICM team compiles comprehensive dossiers to facilitate the resettlement of such handicapped refugees. These dossiers contain specific recommendations for the rehabilitation of the handicapped individuals and their integration. This I regard as an important humanitarian contribution to help relieve the problem as a whole.

ICM has become increasingly involved in the orderly departure program from the Socialist Republic of Vietnam. Medical procedures for this program have been further developed in close collaboration with the Vietnamese authorities in order to respond to the requirements of the receiving countries. Medical supplies are being sent by ICM to Vietnam, and our regional medical co-ordinator holds regular meetings with the competent Vietnamese authorities. The steadily increasing volume of this regularized migration reflects the determination of the international community to stem the irregular flow of Vietnamese refugees, thereby saving lives and hardship for the "boat people".

Equally noteworthy is ICM's special effort for the benefit of Polish former detainees and their families. Since the beginning of this operation in June 1982, over 2,000 Poles have been processed through our special transit facility near Frankfurt in the Federal Republic of Germany.

We have further strengthened our language training activities and more recently have started implementing special programs in Western European countries for the cultural orientation of refugees being processed for resettlement. These activities are a result of today's general recognition that refugees and migrants should be more fully prepared to meet the problems and challenges which they will have to face in their new homeland. The positive aspects of this concept are evident.

We have also increased ICM's activities in an area which has become one of the most troubled parts of the world today – Central America. While it is recognized that the majority of the victims of the upheaval in this region will have to be resettled locally, a more durable solution for a certain number of them can only be attained through resettlement abroad. This year ICM has responded to the requests of various governments to assist in the processing and moving of nearly 5,000 such refugees. More recently we have also undertaken, at the request of the governments concerned, to set up a special program for the processing and movement of Salvadorans benefiting from the political amnesty declared by the Salvadoran Government. Some 500 former detainees and their families have been assisted by ICM.

I mention these matters ... not to draw credit or praise but rather to remind members of the Council of ICM's unique capability to lend international authority and to defuse situations where bilateral contacts may be difficult to achieve – and to assist a broad variety of persons in need of resettlement assistance, ranging from national migrants to legally recognized refugees and the various categories in the grey area in between. As all of us are aware, the international political and economic situation continues to generate heavy flows of displaced persons, refugees, persons in quest of asylum, and migrants throughout the world. Few countries have been spared the multiple effects of these influxes, whether countries of the industrialized world or of that part of the globe where underdevelopment and poverty still remain the norm of everyday life.

With the continuing heavy flow of refugees and persons in refugee-like situations, the burden imposed on countries of asylum remains extremely heavy. In this regard we listened with interest to the remarks made by the United Nations High Commissioner for Refugees in October, when he expressed his perception that the problem of refugees and displaced persons will not be solved within the short- or even medium-term, but that it will remain an issue of international concern for many years to come. ICM, having dealt with the resettlement of refugees since its creation in 1951, can only share this view.

... I should like to revert now to ICM's activities for the benefit of Latin America. It may be recalled that, when taking office in 1979, I expressed my determination to intensify co-operation between ICM and its Latin American member governments and to revitalize programs for the Latin American region. In so doing I was fully aware of the importance and the necessity of meeting more specifically the needs and interests of the Latin American governments. I realized that this could only be achieved through vigorous efforts to broaden the policy, operational and financial bases of these programs.

When reflecting on ICM's efforts for the benefit of the Latin American region I can say with satisfaction that, based on our continuing dialogue with Latin American member governments – individually and collectively – it has been possible to adjust our programs to the specific and varying needs of individual countries and to the interests of the sub-regions and the area as a whole.

Furthermore I believe that all member governments appreciate the expanded services ICM has been able to render to the Latin American region, as reflected in their active participation in and growing support for our Latin American activities. There is now a much greater mutual understanding between member governments of industrialized countries and those of the developing countries in Latin America. This has made it possible to obtain support for Latin American programs from governmental and international organizations which had not directly participated in these activities in the past.

As a result our programs for the transfer of specialized human resources have been improved, certainly in qualitative terms, and ICM's role in the field of technical co-operation has expanded significantly.

Permit me to cite a few events which, I submit, are outstanding examples of the evolution of these programs.

I have recently returned from the Latin American Regional Seminar held in Cartagena, Colombia. Representatives of 17 Latin American member and observer governments participated in the five-day discussion.

ICM's new technical co-operation projects in the field of migration and horizontal human resources transfers were examined in all their aspects by the participants in the seminar.

As a result of the discussions ... the delegates formulated conclusions and recommendations which reflect the importance attached to the action taken by ICM in these new fields.

The participants welcomed the establishment of a Center for Information on Migration in Latin America (CIMAL). They considered this to be an excellent example of co-operation between ICM and regional organizations such as the United Nations Economic Commission for Latin America.

The tasks and functions of this center will be of importance in furthering the accumulation of knowledge on migration and will be of service to governments in the formulation of migration policies and as a source of data on which to base measures to regulate and control migration flows. Here I would like to mention that the first issue of the *Latin American Migration Journal*, which was published by CIMAL and distributed during the Cartagena seminar, was greeted with enthusiasm by the participants. This *Journal*, which will be published three times a year, contains indexed abstracts of published and unpublished documents concerning migration in the region.

Equally important and far-reaching are the measures proposed to further horizontal co-operation among Latin American countries in the field of transfer of qualified human resources. In their recommendations the delegates agreed that ICM should assist in establishing and, where necessary, in strengthening existing national information systems on qualified human resources and, concurrently, continue its newly introduced operational program for the exchange of qualified personnel and experts between the countries of the region.

Another development on which I am pleased to report is that the Government of the United States has pledged a special contribution of $1.2 million in support of a hemispheric migration project, which will cover, over a two-year period, research activities in the field of migration in Latin America, the Caribbean and the United States. This grant will make it possible for ICM to focus intensively on the causes and consequences of migration, with particular emphasis on its effects in countries of origin. The research, to be conducted by internationally recognized experts, should contribute to the eventual formulation of migration policies aimed at eliminating the adverse effects of unregulated emigration. ICM will have responsibility for the implementation and administration of this project, which will be carried out in close co-operation with Georgetown University in Washington. Then . . . I should like to refer to actions taken and progress made in response to the appeals to ICM by the Presidents of Costa Rica, the Dominican Republic, Honduras and Panama.

It will be recalled that ICM was asked to develop an assistance program to provide these countries with additional specialized manpower critically needed in priority sectors of their national development plans. During the last Council session it was suggested that the first step to meet these requests would be a systematic manpower survey carried out in the four countries to determine priority manpower needs. The Government of the Netherlands agreed to put an expert at the disposal of ICM for this purpose and, in addition, three Italian experts were provided under an agreement between ICM and the Italian-Latin American Institute (IILA).

As a result of this three-month survey over 600 priority positions which cannot be filled locally have been identified. In following up on this survey ICM missions in the Central American region have thus far received over 160 specific job offers which are currently being processed in our offices in Europe, the United States and Latin America. The initial response to my first appeal to member and observer governments was based on a program target of 100 qualified personnel at a cost estimate of $3.2 million.

May I take this opportunity to thank those governments which have already responded to my appeal.

The Government of Belgium pledged approximately $120,000 to cover the cost of the assignment of five Belgian experts to the countries concerned.

The Government of the Federal Republic of Germany has agreed to intensify its Latin American reintegration assistance program (LARAP) and integrated experts programs. The Government of the United States has made an amount of $250,000 available for the ICM program.

The Governments of Greece and Israel have each expressed willingness to make available experts and specialists without, however, being in a position to provide financing.

We have continued to intensify our liaison and co-operation with the European Community in Brussels. A project was submitted by ICM under which 75 qualified Latin Americans would return to Costa Rica, the Dominican Republic, Honduras, Panama and Nicaragua. The project was approved recently and funds provided in an amount of approximately $1.3 million.

Nevertheless further funding to meet project requirements and the expectations expressed by the Presidents of the countries concerned is still required, and I must therefore renew my appeal to member and observer governments to give favorable consideration to the matter and make maximum efforts to enable ICM to carry out the program successfully.

Turning now to other new horizons, I am pleased to inform the Council that in April 1983 the Commission of the European Community made available to ICM a special contribution of approximately $3 million to permit the transfer from the industrialized countries of Western Europe of skilled Africans residing in those countries to four developing countries in Africa, namely Kenya, Somalia, the Sudan and Zimbabwe.

In addition the United States Government, encouraged by the success of ICM's return of talent program, has made an initial special contribution of $714,000 to extend [that] program to seven additional countries in Africa, namely Botswana, Cameroon, Lesotho, Malawi, Swaziland, Tanzania and Zambia. Thus, with some working capital available, we are now making special efforts to establish the necessary operational machinery in order to carry out a successful program for the benefit of much of the African Continent.

But in speaking about the African program a word of caution is in order. We are breaking new ground in the African region and in general it is not easy to counteract the brain drain. Our experience has been that some countries will take back only their own nationals, thus excluding some return of talent candidates who otherwise meet job qualifications.

Also, many skilled Africans residing in industrialized countries are well paid and are aware that the salary gap between Africa and the industrialized countries is wide. For this reason much of this valuable human capital will not be avilable to us. But for others there is an incentive to return in the support ICM offers at the receiving end; and then there is the intangible yearning in all of us to go home to the family, the old language and the culture of the homeland.

Thus development of this return of talent program will be a step by step process for a period, but I am convinced that we are on the right track and that in the long run ICM can aid the African countries to achieve economic progress.

I should here like to say a few words about co-operation with other international organizations. Co-operation with those within the United Nations system has always been considered essential to the accomplishment of ICM's main tasks. Permit me to stress the importance of our close day-to-day working relationship with the Office of the United Nations High Commissioner for Refugees (UNHCR). Ever since ICM's inception the movement of mandated refugees has been the subject of joint planning and often of joint financing. In the 1983 budget alone $10 million of ICM's operational budget represents reimbursements from UNHCR.

ICM has carried out joint projects which have led to or influenced the development of migration programs with other United Nations specialized agencies. To cite one example, since 1967 ICM has assisted 10,000 students from third world countries, who benefit from the International Labour Organization's vocational and technical training scholarships, to travel to the ILO's training centre in Turin. The savings the ILO makes on transport costs enable it to admit increased numbers of students.

Noteworthy also are our co-operative relationships with the United Nations regional economic commissions, the International Committee of the Red Cross, the Organization of American States, the Organization of African Unity, the Council of Europe, and many others, with respect to migration matters. Close contact is maintained with the Council of Europe. In this connexion I wish particularly to mention ICM's participation in the second Conference of European Ministers responsible for Migration Affairs, which was held in Rome in October 1983. It focused on the integration of migrant workers and their families in the economy and the social life of the receiving countries and considered various aspects of clandestine migration.

ICM's partnerships with voluntary agencies are of inestimable value ... because the agencies' network extends to the grass roots. They are able to reach the individual in need of emigration assistance and help him on his way. In the receiving countries they assist immigrants in the process of orientation and integration. It is difficult to envisage how we could operate some of our programs, especially those involving refugees, without the skilled and caring assistance of the voluntary agencies.

I should like now ... to say a few words about conferences and seminars.

In today's world, being an intergovernmental organization concerned with migration implies providing governments with a wide range of technical services and advice to improve the economic, social and humanitarian aspects of planned or assisted migration.

It is important for governments and international organizations and agencies to discuss the implementation of appropriate measures to promote the welfare, security and successful integration of migrants and refugees in their new homeland.

In recent years ICM has been called upon increasingly to contribute its expertise to conferences and seminars dealing with international migration issues.

At such meetings policy recommendations are made and agreements discussed concerning organized manpower movements, migrants' rights, family reunification and other related topics. ICM cannot remain isolated from such activities. On the contrary, at the suggestion of member governments ICM has taken the lead in organizing seminars on adaptation and integration of permanent immigrants. Our seminars are technical in nature and provide a forum for those directly involved in migration work to take an active part in airing migration problems openly and without restraint.

The most recent ICM seminar, the sixth, was convened in Geneva in April of this year and dealt with undocumented migrants or migrants in an irregular situation. The participation of 54 governments and 47 international organizations, a total of some 200 persons from all over the world, revealed how much the problem of irregular migration is presently of concern at national and international levels. We receive clear indications from government departments, international agencies and migration research centres that the results of our seminars are taken account of and the recommendations stemming from them are being applied, studied or quoted to good effect. Our working group on the preparation of seminars has just begun consultations on the content of a seventh seminar to be held in 1985.

And now, ... turning to the financial situation of our organization, I am pleased to inform the Council that we will have a fully funded budget for the current year – the fifth consecutive year for this satisfactory state of affairs. As with previous years, it is difficult to predict advance budgets, which are influenced by exchange rates, inflation and other unknown factors. However, our present judgment is that the organization's financial position in 1984 will be manageable.

... The positive record which I have been able to outline is due, I believe, to ICM's institutional strength, which in turn is the result of a conscious and intended convergence of factors. In concluding my remarks permit me to cite these notable factors.

● First and foremost ICM's motivation is exclusively humanitarian.
● Second, although the refugee and refugee-like situations which the organization deals with and alleviates often result from international tensions and conflicts, ICM scrupulously avoids making value judgments on circumstances generating the outflows of the unfortunate persons concerned.
● Third this Council is in a position to determine, usually on the basis of consensus, when and in what circumstances ICM's operational assistance is warranted and should be given.
● Fourth this assistance, which is of an operational, technical nature and involves movements and related migration support services, is provided at the highest possible level of efficiency and discretion. This impartial behavior has enabled the Administration to keep international channels open and to operate in otherwise sensitive conditions.

- Fifth, by making ICM's operational mechanism available, when and where humanitarian needs justify it, for refugee resettlement, national migration and development-oriented movements and services, ICM governments have linked two mutually reinforcing factors. I submit that this unique linkage accounts to a large extent for ICM's vigor and promising outlook.
- Sixth, by having a relatively small assessed administrative budget, as distinct from a flexible operational budget based on voluntary contributions which can be earmarked by donors for specific purposes, member governments have given ICM a resilience, viability and broad-gauged operational capability virtually unmatched in the field of international organization endeavors.

These six considerations justify, I believe, confidence in ICM as an effective and practical tool of multilateral humanitarian diplomacy.
As I look forward to a new term as Director of this unique international organization, which has affected the lives of millions of people, I have a very good feeling about the future, confidence in an effective and efficient staff ... and enthusiasm for the work ahead. I can assure you ... that the continuity the Council has just agreed to will enable ICM, without a pause, to pursue the goals that still find their origin in the Constitution.

1984 AND BEYOND

New challenges and further opportunites for ICM to be of service to the international community

With the Council's vote of confidence, as affirmed by its having re-elected me, I approached my second term of office in 1984 with renewed vigor, convinced that ICM had not only proved itself as a vital member of the family of international organizations, but also, owing to its unique characteristics, shown the potential to be of ever greater service to the international community. This was particularly important in view of the disquieting fact that in many parts of the world economic and political pressures to emigrate were intensifying just at a time when hospitality toward all types of migrants appeared to be lessening against a background of world economic difficulties and consequential social factors, including unemployment.
While the inherent challenges of the situation were formidable, ICM seemed well placed and indeed well equipped – as well as or better than any other international entity – to provide imaginative solutions and serve generally to ameliorate the situation.

The move to ICM's new permanent headquarters

In mid-1984 the ICM secretariat moved into its newly constructed permanent headquarters in the Grand Saconnex area of Geneva, close to the headquarters of the International Labour Office, the World Health Organization and the World Council of Churches. The building, which has been described as 'comfortable high-tech', has an indoor garage, two well-equipped conference rooms, a cafeteria and movable partitions with adapted main facilities which permit rational and efficient use of working space along with the possibility of modification according to the evolution of needs. The building has been good for staff morale partly because of its bright, airy and friendly atmosphere, but also because it tends to give the organization a more permanent character and image.

ICM/CIRED meeting on international migration research

In June 1984 ICM, working jointly with the Committee for International Cooperation in Research in Demography (CIRED), organized a meeting at ICM headquarters in Geneva to review and update research plans relating to given aspects of international migration. Forty research fellows representing national and international research institutions from developing and industrialized countries in various parts of the world presented reports on their current work and planned activities. The discussion concentrated on preparation of an outline for a research project on the impact of international migration on developing countries, including the analysis of the different kinds of migration involved such as temporary migration, clandestine migration, the brain drain, refugee resettlement and return migration. Dr T. Reginald Appleyard, Professor of Economic History, University of Western Australia, was designated co-ordinator of the project which, it was agreed, would be carried out with the participation of the various research institutions represented at the meeting.

Second Conference of African Ministers responsible for human resources planning, development and utilization

ICM participated in the Second Conference of African Ministers responsible for human resources planning, development and utilization held in Addis Ababa in October 1984. The Conference endorsed and reconfirmed the resolution adopted in Monrovia in October 1981, in which African governments were called upon to initiate appropriate national policies and programs to facilitate the return to the African Continent of qualified African personnel, thereby alleviating the effects of the brain drain, and to establish bilateral contacts with ICM to this end.

Processing and movements in 1984

In 1984 ICM assisted in the processing and movement of 139 000 refugees and national migrants for permanent resettlement. This figure included 88 000 Indochinese from the asylum countries of South-east Asia, 26 700

Europeans, some 9000 Latin Americans and about 9000 persons from Africa and the Near and Middle East.

The migration for development part of the program included the placement of some 1400 highly qualified persons in priority sectors in various Central and South American countries, 1050 of whom were processed under the return of talent program, and the return to their homelands from industrialized countries of 95 African professionals and technicians under ICM's equivalent new program for Africa. A wide variety of professions were represented among these migrants, who included university teachers, architects, engineers, agronomists, business administrators, computer scientists, medical practitioners and para-medical personnel.

Returning Salvadorans

At the request of the Governments of El Salvador, Honduras and the United States, ICM began in 1984 to assist Salvadorans returning, or being returned, to their homeland. For this purpose it established special reception and counselling facilities at the San Salvador airport and in the city of San Salvador. Depending upon his or her wishes the individual concerned could be channelled to existing camps for displaced persons or provided with transportation to his or her home or other destination within El Salvador. ICM assistance covered the provision of transportation, temporary accommodation, food and pocket-money. Moreover it stood ready to counsel and process those individuals seeking further emigration.

Change in two top officials' titles to Director General and Deputy Director General

At its 50th Session in November 1984 the ICM Council, recognizing the appropriateness of authorizing the organization's two top officials (the Director and the Deputy Director) to use titles similar to those applying to the heads of other international organizations, whether within or outside the United Nations system, adopted a resolution changing the titles of these two positions to Director General and Deputy Director General respectively.

ICM's involvement in the emigration of Africans, including the problem of the Falashas

Apart from the return of talent programming, the year 1984 marked a significant increase in ICM's involvement in the emigration of Africans, largely Ethiopians. Developments during the year resulted in considerable media attention being focused on one particular group, namely Ethiopian

Jews (Falashas) – persons thought to be the descendents of Solomon and the Queen of Sheba – who, particularly in the early months of 1984, had made the hazardous trek through the desert from the Gonder region of Ethiopia to the Gedaref area of Sudan. Many were in dire straits by the time they reached Sudan and, reportedly, many of them died of dehydration, disease or hunger en route while others died after their arrival. The problem, once it became known, aroused widespread sympathy and willingness on the part of governments and welfare agencies to assist in the care, rescue and resettlement of these desperate individuals.

In keeping with its traditional humanitarian role ICM, on being asked, took all possible measures to facilitate the prompt movement of those Falashas for whom the necessary visas or resettlement arrangements were assured. However, given the inordinate amount of public speculation and guesswork about this particular activity it is important to clarify that, to the extent that ICM was involved – and it is a fact that the organization played an active and useful part in the operation over a period of several months – its involvement conformed to normal operating procedures, including meeting the requirement of having official authorizations from the authorities of the host country, the receiving country and, where necessary, the countries of transit in respect of each individual moved.

In so far as ICM was concerned this was simply another case of the organization acting to the best of its ability to facilitate matters – albeit in this instance in delicate and taxing circumstances – in order to permit the resettlement of certain individuals in desperate straits, thus meeting a very special humanitarian need.

Return of talent to Africa: the case of Dr Ahmed Sidahmed

As indicated earlier, the objective of ICM's program for the return of talent to Africa and Latin America is to accomplish, through job identification and migration assistance, the transfer of qualified personnel and thereby contribute toward reversing the brain drain and to the economic and social development of those regions.

To illustrate the value of this program for Africa it may be worth describing the case of Dr Ahmed Sidahmed who, together with his family, was processed and placed in Kenya.

Dr Sidahmed was born in Sudan in 1946. He graduated from the University of Khartoum in 1969 with a degree of bachelor of science in agriculture. In 1974 he went to the United States for post-graduate study and obtained a degree of master of science and a doctorate from the University of California-Davis in 1981. During the period 1981–83 he engaged in research at the US Department of Agriculture's Meat and Animal Research Center at Clay, Nebraska.
A placement opportunity was found for Dr Sidahmed at a research center in Mazeno, Western Kenya. At that center Winrock International, and the

Government of Kenya operate a collaborative research support program aimed at demonstrating the potential use of sheep and goat products – especially milk – as a protein supplement to the daily diet of farm families whose small plots of land do not permit both crop growing and animal husbandry. Under this program a collective farming system was initiated to maximize the utility of the farms. This involved integration of traditional crop growing with cultivation of animal feeds, as well as the breeding of a goat producing a high yield of both meat and milk. To this end an animal breeder cross-bred goats from different parts of Kenya and subsequently a veterinarian's skills were needed to assess the newly bred goats' resistance to local diseases. Next came the identification of feeding régimes to achieve the goats' optimal production. Locally grown feeds were examined and, where possible, cultivation of feed crops as a supplement to the habitual crop growing was initiated. One result of this experiment was the use of crop wastage as feed for the goats, enabling the farmer to husband the goat without detracting from the use of his land for food crops. Rural sociologists played a critical role at the next stage. The acceptability of the goat and cropping system by local farmers was, and is, the key to the project's success. The sociologist's task was not only to promote the economic feasibility of the system but also to educate consumers regarding the nutritional benefits of including goat meat and milk products in their diet.

ICM's return of talent program for Africa – which, as already mentioned, is financed by the European Community and the US Government – enabled Dr Sidahmed and his family to travel to Kenya and to take with them their household goods and personal belongings. Subsequently ICM purchased two pieces of professional equipment which are of vital importance for Dr Sidahmed's research work and for the project itself, namely a freeze-dryer and a micro-computer. The freeze-dryer was essential for the accurate processing of forage samples for chemical analysis. The micro-computer, which also serves as a word-processor, was useful for modelling and simulation, thereby saving travel time and waiting for the results of statistical analyses. Simulation and modelling fulfil an important function, especially in developing countries hampered by lack of funds and by research restrictions.

The success of this entire effort was recognized by a senior member of Winrock when he stated that "ICM's actions demonstrate a success story where a modest amount of funds encouraged the return to Africa of a well-trained scientist who is now making a major contribution".

To date Dr Sidahmed has applied his expertise to 27 experimental farms. He has emphasized how the computer equipment has contributed to the project by saving money subsequently used to establish an on-site analysis laboratory. Now, he says, all experiments can be conducted in Maseno and results obtained much more quickly. The project supervisors hope to expand the operation to 300 farms within a year or so. Dr Sidahmed further reported that the computer, which also serves as a teaching tool for research fellows, is utilized ten hours a day storing data from the different research fields which are sent to the collaborative institutions.

Admission to membership in the organization of Kenya and re-admission of Australia in May 1985

The good results achieved with return of talent programming for Africa, as illustrated by the case of Dr Sidahmed, led Kenya to seek to join ICM and, indeed, at a special session of the ICM Council in May 1985 Kenya was accepted by acclamation as a full member of the organization. Addressing the Council on that occasion Mr B. A. Kiplagat, Permanent Secretary of Kenya's Ministry of Foreign Affairs, stressed that 'Kenya was the first African country to benefit from ICM's ... schemes ... for the return of skilled African nationals'. He added: 'In almost two-and-a-half years Kenya has received in total more than 130 Kenyan professionals and technicians who have returned home and are participating in our development projects in both the public and private sectors.' Mr Kiplagat expressed his government's gratitude for the implementation of these programs and called upon other countries sharing ICM's humanitarian concerns and objectives earnestly to consider the possibility of membership in the organization.

At the same special session Australia, which had withdrawn from membership in 1973, was re-accepted, again by acclamation, as a full member of the organization. The representative of Australia, Ambassador R. H. Robertson, drew the Council's attention to the fact that since 1973 Australia had embarked on the reassessment of its migration philosophy and in the twelve ensuing years 'a non-discriminatory approach has been repeatedly affirmed as a matter of national policy. Our migration operations now extend globally. As a result, Australian society comprises sizeable migrant communities from all parts of the world.' Ambassador Robertson added that ICM had also changed over the past twelve years and that 'these changes have fundamentally affected [its] role in world migration. The organization is now a body with a global structure. Furthermore it is one which is capable of facilitating movements and delivering services under demanding and at times dangerous circumstances prevailing in some parts of the world.'

This was indeed a most auspicious occasion for ICM and I observed to the Council that the acceptance of Kenya and Australia within ICM's membership was an important step in broadening ICM's base. I expressed the hope that this would provide an incentive to other governments which had the membership question under consideration to move toward a positive position. In highlighting the fact that Kenya was the first African nation to join ICM, I further expressed the hope that this would demonstrate to other African nations that ICM, although relatively new to the African region, did have a contribution to make to the development process there. Moreover, recalling that Australia was 'one of the major immigration countries in the world', I pointed out that it was no stranger to ICM, since in the past 'tens of thousands of migrants and refugees were processed and moved to Australia under ICM auspices'. I specified that 'the number has exceeded 600 000', adding that this substantial migration had had a significant impact on Australia's social, cultural and economic life.

Assistance in the repatriation of Argentine and Uruguayan nationals

In mid-1985, with the development of heightened interest among Argentine and Uruguayan nationals living abroad in industrialized countries to return home following the re-establishment of democratic governments in their countries, official requests for ICM assistance in this connection were received from the Governments of Argentina and Uruguay.

I responded positively to these requests and measures were promptly taken to develop plans and establish procedures for special return programs to the two countries. These included appeals to certain governments and institutions for special financial contributions to cover the cost of the repatriation and, to the extent possible, the re-integration and employment of the persons concerned.

Movements under the programs started almost immediately and up to the time of writing some 1200 persons had been repatriated – about 700 to Argentina and 500 to Uruguay.

Agreement between ICM and SITA for the use by ICM of SITA's international communications network

In July 1985 negotiations were successfully concluded between ICM and the Société Internationale de Télécommunications Aeronautiques (SITA), enabling ICM to utilize free of charge SITA's international communications network. This arrangement provided ICM with direct access to the international airlines and vice versa, and greatly facilitated the organization's operations, as well as resulting in substantial savings in costs for communications.

Inter-American course on labor migration

An Inter-American course on labor migration was organized in Buenos Aires in June–July 1985 under the co-sponsorship of the Organization of American States, the Government of Argentina and ICM with the following objectives:

- to increase knowledge of migration matters and of the relationship between migration and the labor market, linking migration policies with the goals of socio-economic development;
- to analyze the characteristics of migration in the countries of the region in the light of the most recent research on the topic and through the exchange of experiences among course participants;
- to emphasize the role migration plays in population growth and distribution, as well as the effects of migration on the rural/urban structure and the quality of life of the populations affected by it; and

● to give orientation to administrators on the design and organization of specific migration programs and on the formulation of migration policies.

The countries represented at the course were Argentina, Bolivia, Brazil, Costa Rica, Chile, Dominican Republic, El Salvador, Guatemala, Honduras, Mexico, Panama, Paraguay, Peru, Uruguay and Venezuela. All concerned, that is the national authorities, scholars and representatives of the sponsors, regarded the course as having been a marked success.

Seminar on the economic and social aspects of voluntary return migration

The seventh in ICM's series of migration seminars was held in Geneva from 9 to 13 December 1985 on the subject of the economic and social aspects of voluntary return migration and was attended by representatives of 42 governments and some 40 international governmental and non-governmental organizations.

The seminar, which was chaired by Mr Jonas Widgren, Under-Secretary of State in the Swedish Ministry of Labor, assisted by two vice-chairmen, Ambassador O. López Noguerol of Argentina and Dr W. Hoynck of the Federal Republic of Germany, had before it comprehensive working papers prepared by 13 experts, together with 18 information documents submitted by governments and organizations and based on their research and practical experience.

Guest speakers at the opening session included Mrs Anita Gradin, Minister of Migration Affairs and Equality between Women and Men (Sweden), Mrs Maria Manuela Aguiar, Secretary of State for the Portuguese Communities, Ministry of Foreign Affairs (Portugal), Mrs A. Kappeyne van de Coppello, Secretary of State for Social Affairs and Employment, Ministry of Social Affairs (Netherlands), Mr Victor Vaillant, President of the National Commission on Repatriation (Uruguay), Mr Learco Saporito, Member of the Commission of Constitutional Affairs in the Senate (Italy), Mr G. Adinolfe, Deputy Secretary-General, Council of Europe and Mr C. Grey Johnson, representative of the United Nations Economic Commission for Africa.

The conclusions and recommendations of the seminar reflected general agreement on the need to strengthen co-operation among governments and international organizations with a view to increasing research activities (including seminars), intensifying studies and achieving a better understanding of the various aspects of return migration.

Participants agreed that the problem of return migration called for co-operation between the host country and the country of origin and that all measures to facilitate the reintegration of return migrants should be conceived in a spirit of mutual understanding taking account of not only the needs of the migrants but also the interests and priorities of both the host country and the country of origin. They further expressed the view that return migration, which is to a great extent spontaneous, should be the result of a decision freely taken by the migrants, and emphasis was placed on the importance of counselling services to provide migrants with detailed information on all aspects of return.

Referring to the role of women in return migration and to the need for special attention to be paid to the problems of women and migrants' children, the participants stressed that action should be taken by the governments concerned to ensure the reincorporation of women in the activities of the country of origin and of children in the educational system.

Processing and movements completed during 1985

During 1985 ICM assisted in the processing and permanent resettlement of a total of 125 000 persons, including some 78 000 Indochinese, 25 000 Europeans, 8300 Latin Americans and 6500 persons from Africa and the Near and Middle East.

Admission to membership in the organization of Guatemala and Thailand

Given the nature of ICM's mandate and operational role, the work of the organization – showing, as it does, results that can be quite accurately measured on a week-to-week or month-to-month basis – provides a constant source of encouragement and satisfaction to those involved. But in terms of the long-range interests of the organization 1986 and 1987 must be regarded as having been exceptionally significant years.

Two additional countries, Guatemala and Thailand, joined ICM during this period, bringing the organization's membership to 33. Guatemala's action reflected solidarity among the Latin American governments in supporting the purposes and principles of ICM. That of Thailand marked a particular milestone in ICM's history, since as a result ICM for the first time includes member states from every continent. Addressing the ICM Council on the occasion Mr Charoenjit Na Songkhla, Deputy Permanent Secretary in the Thai Ministry of Interior, said: 'In signalling its acceptance of the ICM Constitution and obligations flowing from it, Thailand underscores its strong interest in migration as well as its commitment to work with like-minded members of the international community in this field.'

He drew the Council's attention to the fact that Thailand's association with ICM had already lasted more than a decade, having begun with the first outflow of refugees from neighboring countries in Indochina, and he observed that 'through these many years, sometimes in dramatic and even tragic circumstances, Thailand has provided temporary haven to hundreds of thousands of persons fleeing their homelands. My country also has facilitated arrangements for transit of its territory by persons leaving the

Socialist Republic of Vietnam under the orderly departure program.' He further stated that 'from the very beginning of this massive outflux, it was clear that third country resettlement was the only viable, durable solution for the vast majority of refugees on Thai soil.... As a result the international community undertook in South-east Asia one of the largest refugee resettlement programs in history. ICM's role in the processing and movement of persons leaving Thailand for receiving countries throughout the world has been one of the key elements in the smooth functioning of this resettlement effort.'

Amendment of the Constitution

The ICM Council at its 50th Session in November 1984 had approved my proposal to set up an internal task force to review the Constitution of the organization, drafted in 1953, and establish an updated version for submission to member governments. This phase having been completed, the Council at its 52nd Session in November 1985 approved in principle an updating of the Constitution and created an open working group of representatives of interested member governments to examine the amendments suggested by the ICM Administration together with those of member governments themselves, and to formulate recommendations for consideration by the Council. The guiding principles for this working group were:

● to maintain ICM's basic character, scope and organizational structure;
● to recognize the global mandate of the organization and preserve its flexibility in carrying out its tasks;
● to strengthen ICM's basic humanitarian objectives and orientation;
● to incorporate into the Constitution the substance of various resolutions approved by the Council in the course of the years, in particular those concerning the world-wide dimension of ICM, the changing of its designation, the policy concerning the Latin American program, the role of ICM in the organization of seminars, and its mandate with regard to special resettlement programs; and
● to reinforce the need for co-operation among international organizations on migration, refugee and human resource matters.

Meeting in closed session in May 1987 the Council adopted by consensus a series of amendments to the Constitution which reflect the evolution of the organization since the original mandate was drafted three decades earlier. Among the modifications approved by the Council was a change in the name of the organization from the Intergovernmental Committee for Migration (ICM) to the International Organization for Migration (IOM). Equally significant were those formally recognizing the applicability of

ICM's mandate world-wide; the organization's role in temporary and intra-regional migration as well as in migration for the benefit of nationals, refugees and displaced persons; the organization's utility in assisting individuals compelled to leave their homelands; the importance of ICM's providing a forum for discussion of migration issues; and the need for close co-operation among states and international governmental and non-governmental organizations in all aspects of migration and refugee matters.

All of these, along with other amendments, will enter into force once formal notification has been received from two-thirds of ICM's member states that they have ratified or otherwise accepted the amended Constitution in accordance with their national procedures.

Initiation of measures for the re-installation and labor re-insertion of less skilled return migrants

ICM's experience in recent years with return migration, especially to Southern Cone countries in Latin America (Argentina, Chile and Uruguay), pointed up the need for services beyond basic processing for movement and transportation. Since many, indeed most, of the exiles interested in return do not possess the level of skills or professional qualifications of the persons moved under ICM's return of talent program their placement in satisfactory employment presents a problem, particularly taking into account the relatively high level of unemployment in their countries of origin. Accordingly ICM, working in close co-operation with certain non-governmental organizations such as DIAKONIA of Sweden and HEKS (Swiss Inter-Church Aid) of Switzerland, as well as with local governmental authorities and institutions, has initiated special measures for the re-installation and labor re-insertion of this type of return migrant.

While the program is adapted to each country's needs and situation, its general objectives are:

● to facilitate labor re-insertion through the creation or development of small productive enterprises;
● to include among the beneficiaries not only return migrants but also persons who never left their country; and
● to bring together all the separate efforts developed by local and international institutions concerned with exile and return problems in order to achieve co-ordinated action.

This innovative approach to return migration usually implies establishing the beneficiary in a small, relatively inexpensive enterprise capable of making him self-supporting and assuring a livelihood for his family – and, in some cases, even providing an extra job or so for unemployed compatriots who have not left the country.

Although the program is relatively new, it can already be regarded as successful, with several hundred job-generating projects underway benefiting several thousand persons. Given the substantial on-going demand for return migration and/or repatriation, this approach may well serve as a promising example that could be followed in future in various other parts of the world.

ICM assistance in connection with the migration to Argentina and Uruguay of agriculturists with capital

At the request of the Governments of Argentina and Uruguay ICM has also initiated a campaign to promote the immigration to their respective countries of agriculturists with capital. Information material on the opportunities for agriculturists in the two countries was prepared in five languages and disseminated through farmers' associations in various Western European countries and the United States. To enable interested candidates to observe at first hand agricultural conditions and investment possibilities in Argentina and Uruguay, ICM organizes periodic group tours to the region.

Medical assistance program for seriously wounded Afghan refugees

In autumn 1986, at the request of the United States Government, ICM undertook a medical assistance program for seriously wounded Afghan refugees – men, women and children suffering, for example, from serious eye injuries, or requiring reconstructive or orthopaedic surgery – in Pakistan, where adequate specialized medical facilities were not locally available to them.

After one year 14 of the 28 countries which I had officially approached were participating actively in the program and at the time of writing some 600 cases had been dealt with. This special humanitarian action is being implemented with the co-operation of national Red Cross societies, voluntary agencies, Afghan committees, sponsoring groups or private individuals and, of course, governmental authorities.

ICM's role is first to seek out, on the basis of complete medical dossiers received from the field, cost-free medical treatment opportunities in Europe, the United States and elsewhere and, when this has been done, to make all the necessary arrangements for the transfer of the wounded to the medical installation in the receiving country and, once the treatment has been completed, for their return to Pakistan.

The Austrian newspaper *Kronenzeitung* reported on 9 February 1987 on one of these Afghan cases. It quoted 36-year old Allah Noor, at

St Pölten hospital in Lower Austria, as saying 'I can see again. I am so happy.' Referred to as 'the wonder of St Pölten', Allah Noor described how, on being wounded in July 1982, he found he was blind. However, when a team of US doctors examined a number of wounded Afghans, including Allah Noor, they concluded that his right eye might be saved through a special operation which, however, could not be performed in Pakistan. On 6 December 1986 30 wounded Afghans left Pakistan for medical treatment abroad, 20 of them going to various hospitals in the United States, 5 to the Federal Republic of Germany, 4 to Switzerland and Allah Noor to Austria. On 10 December he had already been operated on by Doctors Klemen and Todter. Today Allah Noor is back in Pakistan. Having been blind for four years he can, as he said, now see again. 'After the good experience we have had with this Afghan, we are prepared to accept others', declared Dr Todter.

Seminar to evaluate ICM's return of talent program for Africa

In December 1986 a seminar, co-sponsored by the Government of Kenya and ICM, was held in Nairobi, Kenya, for the purpose of evaluating ICM's return of talent program for Africa. The participants included representatives of the Governments of Ghana, Kenya, Somalia, Tanzania, Uganda, Zambia and Zimbabwe, as well as of the Economic Commission for Africa, the European Community, the Organization of African States and, of course, ICM. Observers from the Federal Republic of Germany and the United States were also present.

The documentation prepared for the seminar revealed that, out of a total of 1070 cases processed since the inception of the program in 1983, 445 highly qualified African nationals, including 157 women, had been placed in their homeland. As many as 83 per cent of the returnees considered their jobs to be commensurate with the professional training and experience they had acquired abroad and 69 per cent felt that they could impart useful knowledge and experience to their colleagues at work. There were 58 per cent employed in the public or semi-public sectors and 43 per cent in the private sector.

The participants recognized that ICM's return of talent program was serving to facilitate the implementation of the African priority program for economic recovery and the United Nations program of action for African economic recovery and development, both of which had identified the effective planning, development and productive utilization of human resources as a priority area. Accordingly ICM was encouraged to negotiate the extension and expansion of the program with the African governments concerned, the European Community and other potential donors.

At the specific request of the Government of Kenya the seminar explored the possibility of encouraging intra-regional migration of skilled personnel as a means of assisting the development process of the African Continent. It was felt that ICM experience in this connection, based on its horizontal migration program in Latin America, might usefully be applied in the African context.

After the Nairobi seminar the European Community, taking into account the substantial results achieved under the initial pilot project, approved ICM's proposal for extending its return of talent program for Africa and agreed to make available $8.7 million to enable ICM to facilitate the return and placement of 550 additional qualified African nationals over a four-year period.

10 ICM – an Instrument for Peace

In an early part of this account I paid tribute to the statesmen who met in Brussels in late 1951 to create the organization that is now known as ICM and that will soon become the IOM. Clearly they displayed both wisdom and vision in establishing outside the orbit of the United Nations a strictly non-political and exclusively humanitarian international operational mechanism for the orderly migration of various categories of needy persons, including victims of persecution and conflict, as well as a forum for contacts, discussions and co-operation among like-minded governments and other entities concerned. Clearly, through their far-sighted action in Brussels, they created an instrument that equally would serve the cause of peace by contributing toward stability in a troubled world.

That man aspires to peace – whether in the most personal sense within himself or in society at large – is amply demonstrated every day in the headlines one reads and the speeches one hears. It might even be suggested that there is a general understanding of what really constitutes peace. Where the problem lies is in devising practical means to prevent conditions which threaten peace or, if such conditions already exist, in arranging to move swiftly to reduce their impact and remove their causes. Since its creation almost four decades ago ICM has focused on pragmatic and effective humanitarian actions to promote stability and, by extension, peace.

Indeed, ICM's very *raison d'être* can be found in the search for peace and progress following the devastation caused by the Second World War. As one of the successors to the International Refugee Organization ICM was charged by its founding members with facilitating the processing and movement for resettlement of refugees and displaced persons, as well as of national migrants. The motivation was clear: the presence of a large uprooted population, combined with the difficult employment situation for nationals in the ravaged economies of post-war Europe, created an intolerable strain on the social and economic fabric of the societies in question and presented a clear threat to stability, progress and lasting peace. These same elements held the seeds of spontaneous, irregular migratory movements which could have broader destabilizing effects.

Over the years the wisdom of their thinking has been proved in circumstances that ICM's founders might never have imagined. For example, the influx of tens of thousands of Hungarians into Austria in 1956 – an event described in detail in an earlier part of this account – risked overwhelming a small neutral country which was willing to help but had a

limited capacity to do so. What were the choices? Forcible return of the
persons concerned, which in any case would have been anathema to the
Austrian people and Government, would have exacerbated the situation in
Hungary. At the same time the presence of such a large refugee population
so close to their homeland held the potential for confrontation at the
international level. Permanent integration of all those refugees in Austria
so soon after the Peace Treaty would have created internal pressures that
could have been highly disruptive for that country's social and economic
stability. The only way to ease the situation, avoid a potential threat to
peace and ensure the continued availability of a source of first asylum was
to provide for resettlement abroad. This was the first major instance in
which ICM was called upon to mount a rapid program of resettlement in an
emergency situation. Building upon the basic tenets of non-political action
embodied in its charter ICM demonstrated its capability to become
immediately operational – initiating the first movements from Austria
within days – and thereby helped to lower the tension created by the sheer
volume of arrivals.

In a refugee situation such as existed in Austria in 1956 the potential
threat to peace was, I believe, quite clear in both domestic and international terms. Sadly, since that time the world has witnessed many more
instances in which large numbers of refugees have fled into neighboring
countries – countries prepared to receive them on humanitarian grounds
while unable for a variety of political or economic reasons to absorb them
and to allow them to remain indefinitely. When their presence becomes a
cause of strained relations between the government of the country of origin
and that of the country of asylum, or when their numbers represent an
overwhelming burden and potential source of domestic ferment, migration
may become essential in the interest of stability. A more recent example of
this state of affairs, and certainly one of the most dramatic of our times, is
to be found in South-east Asia. There, largely for geopolitical reasons,
resettlement has to date constituted the only viable option for the vast
majority of Indochinese refugees. During the past decade ICM has assisted
in the processing and movement of more than one million of these persons
from the asylum countries of South-east Asia and by its action has
undoubtedly attenuated some of the tension in the region.

Just as resettlement contributes to alleviating pressure in refugee situations, migration can play an equally crucial role in other circumstances
where stability and ultimately peace are threatened. This was true, for
example, of ICM's early migration programs, which helped to solve the
surplus population problem existing in the post-war years in many European countries that were unable to provide their nationals with adequate
employment opportunities. Now, as then, in various others parts of the
world the existence of large pools of unemployed or underemployed
nationals represents a potential source of social unrest and instability. Yet

simultaneously opportunities may exist for the persons concerned to lead productive lives elsewhere, either in large-scale immigration countries or in countries where their particular skills are in demand and not otherwise available. Matching the two ICM has, over the years, assisted well over one million national migrants to find new homes and to contribute to progress and development, putting creative talent to use rather than allowing it to be under-utilized or ignored.

In the past decade ICM added a new dimension to this activity by fostering the return and placement of nationals of developing countries who have acquired abroad training and experience valuable in promoting development, growth and stability in their homeland, thus helping to alleviate the negative effects of the brain drain. Such redistribution of intellectual and technical resources for economic, social and cultural advancement is a direct contribution to the establishment of conditions conducive to social justice and peace.

In these two fields – refugee resettlement and trans-national migration – ICM's actions at first sight appear essentially as contributing to peace in a collective sense, through the resolution of large-scale problems which, if allowed to fester, would pose a threat to the stability of a given societal structure. But there is also the peace of the individual to be considered, and his desire to live at ease with himself and with the society around him. When he is prevented from doing so by oppressive official policy or by other adverse conditions, it is his peace that is threatened and it is the stability of his life which becomes the object of concern. This is especially true of persons persecuted or fearful of persecution on religious, ethnic, political or other grounds who, since they remain in their own country, cannot be considered as refugees in the strictly legal sense of the term but are nevertheless of broad humanitarian concern to the international community. Many wish to emigrate but do not comply with the criteria of programs which would allow them to do so. By remaining in their own country they are forced to live in fear, sometimes the objects of official rebuke or even the scapegoats for failed governmental policies. Released political detainees who are treated as pariahs, members of minorities who apply for emigration and consequently become non-persons in their own country, persons stripped of their citizenship who have nowhere to go – these are but some examples of man's inhumanity toward his fellow man and they represent very real cases with which ICM has dealt and continues to deal.

ICM's activities in this respect have been extremely varied over the years, ranging from mounting an airlift for Ugandan Asians expelled from their country by government order to assisting members of minority groups from the Soviet Union in their resettlement processing. Of particular interest as a contribution to the continued peaceful existence of individuals, however, is ICM's action on behalf of political detainees.

Following the overthrow of the Allende government in Chile in 1973, large numbers of persons were detained and many of them, after their release, sought resettlement outside the country. There were others who obtained release on condition that they depart from Chile. For some members of both groups emigration was seen as the only means of restoring their individual peace of mind and enabling them to pursue active, productive lives, and ICM assistance was unstintingly provided to this end. Subsequently similar ICM action was undertaken elsewhere on behalf of persons living in their own countries in fear of persecution, notably in Bolivia and in El Salvador.

In the preceding paragraphs I have dwelt upon the benefits of ICM intervention to individuals whose possibilities of leading a peaceful and self-fulfilling existence in their own country were in many cases non–existent. That emigration would contribute to their inner peace was clear, and it was for this reason that ICM undertook to assist them once they had made their own decision to seek resettlement abroad. If, as a side effect, their departure also lessened tensions within their own societies, this was an equally valuable contribution. To those who argue that it is undesirable for forces of change to distance themselves in this way from the center of action, I would only comment that ICM, given its non-political and humanitarian mandate, cannot take such considerations into account. The guiding principle of ICM member governments is to provide, through ICM, humanitarian-motivated operational assistance to persons who have decided, for whatever reason, to emigrate, for whom existing facilities are inadequate and who could not otherwise be moved. Indeed I would submit that the absence of ICM's means of action would, in practice, deny the individuals concerned the basic right to start a new self-fulfilling life, at peace with themselves, in the country and society of their choice. In short ICM remains a lifeline of hope for millions in need.

I have attempted to describe some of ICM's practical actions that have made a positive contribution to the peaceful defusion through migration of situations that are potentially conflict-producing. Yet the question might still be asked why an international organization's involvement is required in such cases. Could simple bilateral efforts not have achieved the same results?

In the particular instances cited I believe that any approach other than a multilateral one would have been doomed to failure or, at the very least, so slow as to dissipate the effectiveness of the planned action in relieving tension and avoiding conflict. The sheer size of the populations to be assisted in the first examples I mentioned required burden sharing within the international community on an operational scale which bilateral efforts, lacking the stand-by resources and overall co-ordination facilities of an international organization, would not have been able to achieve. In the other cases similar means of co-ordination were necessary to ensure rapid practical solutions and avoid duplication of effort. A single organization, familiar with the needs and desires of all the beneficiaries as well as of the sending and receiving countries, achieves economies of scale, efficient use of resources and orderly processing and movement which cannot be aspired to by disparate unco-ordinated efforts. ICM was created for precisely this reason.

If ICM still exists today – after 36 years of operations and the re-establishment of almost four million persons – it is in recognition of the fact that an international structure needs to be maintained by governments as a locus for discussion of such issues and co-operation in regard to them and, most importantly, as a means of providing the required movement and support services in an orderly and timely way. That ICM's membership is expanding at a time when support for international organizations is tending to diminish is, I believe, further evidence of the need for such a structure to which governments and individuals can turn to resolve problems through flexible, pragmatic and non-political action.

In concluding this account I have sought to develop the proposition that migration can and does contribute tangibly to peace. The examples I highlighted were intended to indicate what the alternatives might be in given situations if the migration option did not exist: in each case they would be sources of human suffering, heightened tension and threats to stability and peace.

How ICM can combine its forces with those of governments and other entities committed to the principle of free movement of persons provides a useful case study of what a humanitarian-motivated and non-political international organization can do to contribute to reducing tension in the world and promoting peace. In an ideal world there would be no refugees in need of resettlement, no unemployed populations in search of illusory jobs, no brain drain and no persons in fear of persecution in their own countries. ICM cannot claim to be able to eliminate on its own the root causes of such problems. But as long as the problems exist ICM can assist through migration in developing and bringing to fruition practical solutions to them.

A THOUGHT FOR THE FUTURE

Now, when migration issues throughout the world are ever more to the fore, now, when more and more individuals, whether refugees, displaced persons, political detainees or national migrants are in need of resettlement assistance, now, when the need for a multilateral forum for discussion and resolution of migration problems is ever more evident, above all now, when ICM's membership is expanding and its global mandate is enshrined in an updated Constitution, the international community could ill afford, for all of these reasons and more, to renege on a promise to future generations that they too will be able to count on the assistance that nearly four million persons around the world can thank ICM for today.

Without question the world is a better place because of ICM. If the organization did not exist, it would indeed have to be invented.

Geneva, September 1988

Epilogue

Shortly after completing this account I retired, on 30 September 1988, as Director General of ICM. In this connection I was presented, by Ambassador Joseph Petrone, Permanent Representative of the United States to the Office of the United Nations in Geneva, with a Tribute of Appreciation signed by the United States Secretary of State, George P. Shultz, on behalf of the US Government,

> for sustained exemplary dedication as Director General of the Intergovernmental Committee for Migration in providing leadership and imaginative direction to facilitate the movement of refugees and other migrants forced to flee their homelands in search of freedom and security. You have assured that the deep humanitarian concerns of the United States and the international community have been brought to bear in a practical and effective manner to alleviate the suffering of human beings.

This was indeed a gratifying formal recognition of my lifetime of running a lifeline.

Appendix

Questions and Answers at the US House of Representatives Hearing on
"POLICY AND PROCEDURES FOR THE
ADMISSION OF REFUGEES INTO THE UNITED STATES"
(Wednesday 24 February 1977)

Mr. Eilberg   Mr. Carlin, I realize that you perhaps cannot submit this now, but you indicated that since 1945, the U.S. Government has expended $5 billion for refugee assistance, and has accepted some 1.8 million refugees from – We would like a record. We would like a history of U.S. participation in refugee programs, citing the nature of the situation; U.S. legislation, if any; what it was; the amount of money expended on the program; and the number of refugees accepted under each program.

Mr. Carlin   Mr. Chairman, we would be very pleased to provide that information for the record. [See Annex 1]

Mr. Eilberg   You alluded to this in your statement, and as you know, I addressed the Executive Committee of ICEM last May and called upon that organization to promote family reunification within the context of the Helsinki declaration. Many of the speakers at that meeting actively supported our proposal, as did the ICEM Director himself.

I would be interested in knowing whether any positive results have been achieved by ICEM along these lines. Have there been any organizations within the structure of ICEM to handle this project, and how is the International Red Cross co-operating in this effort?

Mr. Carlin   Mr. Chairman, since your proposal last May, the Director of ICEM has dispatched a communication to all the signatory governments of the Helsinki Accord. He has had replies from most of the Western governments, several of which were positive and encouraging. He has had no replies from any of the Eastern bloc governments.

ICEM, working closely with the voluntary agencies, has developed substantial data on individual cases. They have established within the ICEM headquarters a special unit to deal with this family reunification activity. At the autumn sessions of the ICEM governing bodies in Geneva, the U.S. delegation encouraged the ICEM Director and his administration to pursue these efforts, and we received his assurance that they would do so.

Now, as to results: it is rather difficult to measure them precisely. However, I can tell the committee that with respect to family reunification cases from the Soviet Union, there were approximatly 2,400 (persons, that is) in 1976, which represented an increase of several hundred over 1975.

Whether or not these positive results can be traced back to the Helsinki accords cannot yet be determined, but we are observing this matter very closely.

Mr. Eilberg   On that point, are you suggesting that as a result of ICEM's efforts, there have been some 600 families that have been reunited from behind the Iron Curtain?

Mr. Carlin   That is generally correct. During 1976 there were 2,400 handled by the voluntary agencies and ICEM. They were moved from the Soviet Union to Rome for final processing, and then processed for immigration to this country.

Mr. Eilberg   Can you tell us further what ICEM has been doing, or any of the member countries specifically, particularly with regard to the Soviet Union? In other words, you have stated there have been possibly 600 cases since May rendered by ICEM. I am just wondering about the mechanics of communication.

Mr. Carlin Well, the mechanics of the communication: usually the American voluntary agency is aware of the split family. They work very closely with the ICEM administration. And then our embassy in Moscow becomes involved. When the individual concerned receives an exit permit to leave the Soviet Union, he is partially processed by our embassy in Moscow and then moves to Rome for final processing. The entire matter is co-ordinated very closely by ICEM with the voluntary agencies and the sponsors.

Mr. Eilberg In the question, also I refer to the International Red Cross. Do you have any expression on its activity?

Mr. Carlin The ICRC actually follows this matter in various Eastern European countries. They, for their own reasons, seem to prefer to operate independently, and I do not think that ICEM and the ICRC have a particularly close working relationship. But they are both seeking the same objective, as is, incidentally, the UNHCR. The UNHCR has repeatedly encouraged Eastern European governments to permit more family reunification.

Mr. Eilberg Could you briefly review for the subcommittee the background and current status of the Soviet refugee programs since 1973?

Mr. Carlin Mr. Chairman, the significant movements from the Soviet Union started in 1973. In that year, there were 35,200 movements out of the Soviet Union. 33,249 went to Israel; 1,951 went to destinations other than Israel. In 1974, there were 16,842 who went to Israel; 5,238 who went to destinations other than Israel for a total of 22,080. In 1975, 8,395 went to Israel; 7,195 went to destinations other than Israel for a total of 15,590. In 1976, 7,216 went to Israel; 8,545 went to destinations other than Israel for a total of 15,761.

We estimate in the current year, 1977, that there will be a total of 18,000; we further estimate that 7,000 of those will proceed to Israel and that 11,000 will go to destinations other than Israel.

Mr. Eilberg What is the current drop-out rate in Vienna of Soviet Jews, and what are the other countries that are receiving and resettling Soviet Jews, other than the U.S. and Israel?

Mr. Carlin The current drop-out rate is around the 50 per cent mark. It fluctuates from month to month, but that has been the mean average in recent months.

Mr. Hall Mr. Chairman, what do you mean by "drop-out rates"?

Mr. Eilberg By "drop-out rates" we mean that exit visas are applied for by Soviet Jewish citizens, and their announced destination is Israel. They arrive in Vienna, however; they indicate the desire not to go to Israel, but to the United States or some other country.

Mr. Carlin You asked, sir, what other countries were taking them?

Mr. Eilberg Yes.

Mr. Carlin As I indicated, by far the majority go either to Israel or to the United States. Limited numbers are being accepted by Canada, Australia, and a few go to Latin American countries.

Mr. Eilberg The granting of exit permits by the Soviets has fluctuated over the years. Do you have any idea what are the factors, or what were the factors, that prompted these fluctuations?

Mr. Carlin Mr. Chairman, I really do not consider myself qualified to speculate on the motivation of the Soviet authorities, so I cannot provide an answer to that question. I would repeat that we do expect an increase in 1977; a total of 18,000, as I mentioned a minute ago, which would be up from some 15,000 last year, principally reflecting an increase in the number of so-called "third country" cases – family reunion type cases.

Mr. Eilberg   What makes you feel that there may be that increase? What is the basis for that expectation?

Mr. Carlin   There has been a gradual increase in family reunification cases in recent months and during the past year.

Mr. Eilberg   What is the nature and status of the special U.S. program to assist in resettling the Soviet Jews in Israel?

Mr. Carlin   As you recall, sir, starting in 1973, the Congress appropriated special funds for assistance to Soviet refugees including projects for their absorption in Israel. The 1973 amount was $50 million; in '74, $36.5 million; in '75, $40 million; in '76, $15 million.

Mr. Eilberg   Excuse me. Are you referring to the calendar year or to the fiscal year?

Mr. Carlin   These are fiscal year appropriations. These funds were appropriated for a variety of services for those Soviet refugees going to Israel. First of all, their care and maintenance in Vienna, where they were in transit; their transportation from Vienna to Israel; and upon arrival in Israel, their care and maintenance in absorption centers, training and retraining, medical care, scholarships, and housing and rental payments – things of that nature.

Mr. Eilberg   Does the State Department closely review expenditures under this program? If not, do you believe there is a need for greater scrutiny of these expenditures?

Mr. Carlin   We do keep this matter closely under review. The staff of our mission in Geneva audit our contracts with UIA, and also during the past 18 months, the GAO has conducted an in-depth study of this matter, both at the European end and within Israel.

Mr. Eilberg   And do you believe there is a greater need for scrutiny of these expenditures?

Mr. Carlin   I think the matter is getting adequate attention, sir.

Mr. Eilberg   Mr. Hall, would you like to ask some questions?

Mr. Hall   Mr. Carlin, I notice you made a statement a moment ago about the greater portion of these refugees coming into the United States, and I thought I understood you to say that Canada had more or less of a restrictive policy toward admission of refugees. Is that a correct statement?

Mr. Carlin   I understand, Mr. Hall, that the Canadians have no particular program for accepting refugees. They have a broad immigration program, and they have migrant selection missions in the various Western European countries. They consider refugees along with other qualified migrants from Western European countries. I think they operate on what they refer to as a "point system" which reflects the individual's qualifications and various criteria. I'm not sure that in the asylum areas of Western Europe they give particular priority or attention to refugees.

However, in special situations, such as that involving the Ugandan Asians a few years back, Canada was very prompt in taking substantial numbers.

Mr. Hall   Of course, they'll accept draft-dodgers without any question, but that's beside the point. [In your basic statement] you said, "While I would hasten to admit there remains room for further improvement, particularly in the area of co-ordination among the various U.S. Government entities involved..." My question is: Is there any overlapping of agencies with reference to this refugee problem that's creating a problem for you and your organization?

Mr. Carlin   No, sir. I am not aware of any particular overlapping. There is obviously a need for us to work closely with our own colleagues in the Bureau of Security and Consular Affairs in the Department, and similarly with the Immigration and Naturalization Service. The one area where I think we probably need closer co-ordination and a better working relationship could be with the Department of Health, Education, and Welfare, in connection with such matters as reception and placement grants and the training or retraining of new refugee immigrants in this country.

Mr. Hall All right. Under your section 203(a)(7), speaking of the annual admissions to the United States of 290,000 quota immigrants, is that a figure different from those that the Attorney General may, on a discretionary basis, admit?

Mr. Carlin Yes. The 203(a)(7), I think, permits the acceptance by our country of some 17,000 refugees per year. That's part of the overall total of immigrants authorized annually.

Mr. Eilberg If the gentleman will yield, I think to amplify under immigration law, the seventh preference provides for admission of refugees in the seventh preference. Of the 290,000, 6 percent of those may enter and obtain visa numbers. However, our concern, I think, this morning as we deal with the subject, arises from the fact that the Attorney General in his discretion may parole individuals, and by practice, groups into the United States, and the numbers that have been admitted under that discretionary authority are of a proportion that one-third of those who legally enter the country do so by the personal discretion of the Attorney General. This is above and beyond the 290,000.

Mr. Hall What sort of screening process is used to seek to determine that no people come into this country that may have political leanings or practice doctrines contrary to the principles of Americanism?

Mr. Carlin In the process of dealing with a refugee applicant for admission to this country, apart from the interviewing of the individual by either a consular officer or an officer of our Immigration Service, data are compiled on the individual and background checks are run through our various national agencies. They also conduct checks as far as possible in the asylum areas where the refugee applicant resided. They do a thorough background check on each individual.

Mr. Hall Thank you. That's all I had.

Mr. Eilberg Mr. Carlin, will you describe the U.S. refugee program, and the types of assistance provided to refugees in these programs?

Mr. Carlin The United States refugee program is, as I indicated in my opening statement, a people-to-people type of program. To give you a general idea of how it operates, I'll take the situation of a refugee asylum-seeker in Italy.

He is first of all dealt with by the Italian authorities, probably apprehended and channeled up to the refugee reception center in Trieste. There, after the Italian authorities have completed their processing, he is referred to one of the voluntary agencies – one of USRP's working partners.

The voluntary agency would, first of all, register that refugee for USRP assistance, and from that point on, the agency would be able to administer various kinds of assistance to the individual; first of all, counseling with respect to his immigration or his future, whatever he may choose to do. The agency could also provide him supplemental care and maintenance assistance, resettlement documentation and probably arrange for the refugee to take language training, and eventually, through ICEM, arrange for transportation of the individual.

Mr. Eilberg How do we identify a person from Eastern Europe as a refugee?

Mr. Carlin I think the individual pretty well identifies himself. As I say, he's dealt with by the authorities of the asylum government. Usually the authorities of the asylum government, working jointly with the UNHCR, determine whether or not that individual is entitled to refugee status under the mandate of the UNHCR, so it's through a matter of interrogation and processing of the individual that determination is made.

Mr. Eilberg Are they all registered with the UNHCR or are they identified without UNHCR assistance?

Mr. Carlin They are not actually registered with the UNHCR. However, in the principal asylum areas of Western Europe, the UNHCR sits with authorities of those asylum governments and makes a determination, assists in the process of determining whether or not that individual is a refugee under the mandate of the UNHCR, and whether he is entitled to political asylum.

Mr. Eilberg How does the refugee get into the USRP channel?

Mr Carlin He is referred to one of the various voluntary agencies. There are eight which are contracting partners of USRP.

Mr. Eilberg And at what point does INS come into the picture?

Mr. Carlin INS comes into the picture when the voluntary agency registers a refugee. Among other things, they determine what the individual's wishes for immigration are, and if it happens to be the U.S., which is usually the case, the voluntary agency then assists the refugee to fill out his application for immigration to the U.S. The voluntary agency thus puts the refugee in contact with the Immigration and Naturalization Service.

Mr. Eilberg What are the respective roles of the host government, the voluntary agencies, UNHCR, and ICEM with regard to this program?

Mr. Carlin The entities that you have just mentioned really comprise a team. Obviously, the host government provides the asylum, and in the case of many of the refugees, the basic care and maintenance in the Refugee Reception and Resettlement Center. The voluntary agencies come along and provide the services which I just mentioned; the counseling, the supplemental care and maintenance, the resettlement documentation, the language training. They get the individual groomed and processed for resettlement. When he is movement-ready, the refugee is then referred to ICEM for transportation. The UNHCR's role in Western Europe is what I mentioned a minute ago: to work with the local host government authorities to determine whether or not the individual is a political refugee in terms of the mandate.

Mr. Eilberg Must all refugees ask for political asylum in the country they enter?

Mr. Carlin No, they must not; they need not. But the majority do. I would mention an exception, however: the Soviets who break off in Vienna and go to Rome. They would not seek asylum in Italy, because they are just in transit status there, as opposed to a refugee who enters Italy either legally or illegally, and seeks asylum.

Mr. Eilberg Are these refugees given any rights to stay, if they are accorded asylum rights?

Mr. Carlin Yes.

Mr. Eilberg Would you provide the subcommittee with a breakdown of the number of Eastern European refugees who were assisted over the last five years, including a breakdown of those from the Soviet Union, and from other Eastern European countries? And does the Department of State have any projects or projections as to how many such refugees are expected this year, 1977?

Mr. Carlin First of all, sir, we'd be very pleased to provide that material for the record. [See Annex 2]

With respect to the projection for this year, this involves a certain amount of crystal-ball-gazing. We estimate that there will be 18,000 refugees from the Soviet Union; in addition, we expect 6,000 refugees from other Eastern European countries; a total of 24,000.

Mr. Eilberg Is it possible for a person to come to the United States as a refugee, remain here for two or three years, and return to his home country?

Mr. Carlin Yes, sir.

Mr. Eilberg And to your knowledge, this has happened before?

Mr. Carlin Yes. I think that has happened in a very small number of cases.

Mr. Eilberg Is this not one justification for not providing permanent resident alien status to the refugee upon his arrival here? There is the possibility that he may return, or want to return, to his home country, or go elsewhere?

Mr. Carlin I understand that it is not the practice of INS to lift the passport of the individual asylum-seeker in this country. However, in many cases, I think the refugee on his own feels that he wishes to surrender it. The asylum-seekers who are granted asylum here, or admitted as refugees, can be issued, and frequently are issued, refugee convention travel documents, which our government is obliged to issue in keeping with our obligations under the protocol.

Mr. Eilberg But they're not eligible to become an immigrant or a permanent resident alien for two years after their entry?

Mr. Carlin That's right sir.

Mr. Eilberg How is the judgment made that a refugee is unwilling to return to his home country? Is this merely a statement, or does he have to prove it in one way or another?

Mr. Carlin Mr. Chairman, I think the refugee is obliged to provide significant evidence, substantial evidence, of his intentions in this regard to the authorities of the asylum government on the one hand and to either consular officers or INS officers on the other.

Mr. Eilberg How do most of these Eastern European refugees enter asylum countries? Do they still cross borders clandestinely, or are they mostly persons coming out with tourist visas or exit permits, who then decide not to return?

Mr. Carlin Mr. Chairman, I think the majority by far would be in the latter category: those who come out of their home countries legally, either as tourists, on business trips, to attend sports events, things of that nature, and then choose not to return, and seek asylum.

Mr. Eilberg Is that also true of those entering Yugoslavia, would you say?

Mr. Carlin In the case of those entering Yugoslavia, Eastern Europeans can travel fairly freely within the Eastern orbit without visas; many travel to Yugoslavia and because the Yugoslav-Italian border is a fairly easy one, there are the illegal arrivees in Italy.

Mr. Eilberg Without these individuals having tourist visas or exit permits, right?

Mr. Carlin That is right; yes.

Mr. Eilberg One of the basic theories underlying our refugee bill which is before us is that refugee situations should be internationalized; and I am aware that the UN, the United Nations High Commissioner for Refugees, is the primary mechanism for achieving this objective. Can you explain to the subcommittee how the UNHCR responds when an emergent refugee situation develops?

Mr. Carlin Mr. Chairman, if there is an emergent refugee situation in a given country, the usual pattern would be that the government being seized with the problem would turn to the UNHCR for help. The UNHCR then would normally visit the area, assess the problem, assess the needs of the refugees, and then consider courses of action. First of all, if it was an urgent problem, the UNHCR might make an emergency response. He has an emergency fund of $2 million, and might provide some measure of emergency relief. And then he would probably appeal to the international community for both financial funds and resettlement opportunities for the refugees. That would be the normal pattern of events.

Mr. Eilberg With regard to the pattern, can you be a little more specific as to what occasions the triggering of international action in these refugee situations?

Mr. Carlin I would cite the recent example of the tragic boat cases involving

Vietnamese individuals who leave Vietnam in small boats and seek asylum in one of the countries on the periphery of the South China Sea. The UNHCR has been seized with that problem and has appealed to governments first of all to admit those boat cases for temporary asylum, has appealed for funds to assist them, and has appealed to governments to open their doors and provide permanent resettlement opportunities to these refugees.

Mr. Hall What success have you had?

Mr. Carlin Mr. Hall, UNHCR has had fairly good responses, both in terms of financial support and the willingness of governments to take some of those boat cases. We urged the UNHCR to internationalize that effort before we ourselves made any commitments to take any of them, and the UNHCR satisfied us that he had placement opportunities for . . .

Mr. Lowman Well, about 50 percent have been taken by other countries to date, of those that have been resettled out of the Southeast Asian area; the boat cases that have been resettled out of the Southeast Asian area, about half have been taken by other countries; about half by ourselves, under existing programs.

Mr. Carlin So having been persuaded that a substantial number would be accepted by other governments, we made the commitment to accept 100 per month under our Conditional Entry program.

Mr. Eilberg What other countries are receiving those boat cases?

Mr. Carlin Certain of the Western European countries; Australia, Canada, New Zealand.

Mr. Lowman The major resettlement area is France. The Canadians, the Germans, the Australians, and the Dutch, and the Norwegians have all made smaller contributions.

Mr. Eilberg Do you have precise statistics available on those?

Mr. Lowman We can provide them for you, sir.

Mr. Eilberg We'd like to have them as part of the record. [See Annex 3]

Mr. Eilberg In some cases, such as Lebanon, the U.S. and UNHCR do not respond, even though a large number of people depart from one country for one particular reason or another. Therefore, can you explain how the UNHCR selects those refugee situations with which the UNHCR is involved?

Mr. Carlin Sir, in the case of the – case involving Lebanese following the recent conflict there, tens of thousands of Lebanese did, in fact, leave Lebanon for Greece, Cyprus and various other Western European countries. However, most of them had means; did not regard themselves as refugees; and thus did not represent a refugee problem. None of the host countries where these Lebanese found themselves sought international assistance.

The UNHCR sent its representative to many of the countries where the Lebanese were temporarily located, and they satisfied themselves that these Lebanese were not refugees; did not need international assistance. So that would explain the situation with respect to Lebanese generally. I'm sorry; I missed the other part of your question.

Mr. Eilberg Well, the other part was, how does the UNHCR decide when to get into a refugee situation, or not?

Mr. Carlin Well, for the reason I just mentioned they did not consider it necessary to deal with the Lebanese as refugees. In other situations, where they get an appeal from a host government seized with a refugee problem, they would then go in, assess that problem, assess the needs and concern themselves with it. An example – a current example of that would be in Southern Africa, where in recent months there have been substantial numbers of refugees from Angola, Rhodesia and South Africa.

Mr. Eilberg Mr. Carlin, in the Indochinese situation, when South Vietnam fell, this committee and I believe the Congress expected greater international participation; and evidently, that kind of participation was not present. We would like to know – and it's very much on our mind, as we consider this refugee bill – what countries do participate in taking refugees. Do you have that, those kinds of statistics, available?

Mr. Lowman Yes, sir.

Mr. Eilberg For the last couple of years, and perhaps provide them for the record. I'm talking about any refugees.

Mr. Carlin Right. [See Annex 4]

I think in that connection, Mr. Chairman, I might just make the observation that there are obviously certain refugee groups where the majority of the refugees themselves seek to come to the U.S., as in the case of the Soviets.

There are other refugee situations where the majority might seek to go to countries other than the U.S.; for example, the Chileans; I think out of some 20,000 Chileans moved by ICEM for resettlement, only about a thousand came here; the balance went to other countries.

Mr. Eilberg Now, in the refugee situation.

Mr. Hall Mr. Chairman, may I ask one question at this point?

Mr. Eilberg Surely.

Mr. Hall Does your organization – When you mentioned Chile, some went some place and some went other places. Do we participate in the cost of people settling from Chile to other countries, other than the United States?

Mr. Carlin First of all, Mr. Hall, we did respond to two appeals: one from the UNHCR for care and maintenance assistance to Latin American refugees – Chileans, Bolivians, Uruguayans in various parts of Latin America; so we responded with a financial contribution; we, along with other governments, for that purpose. Additionally, we responded to an appeal from ICEM, the Migration Committee, for funds for the transportation of Latin American refugees, Chileans and others, to overseas destinations.

Mr. Hall Well, is that same situation applicable to any other country where refugees may leave a country and go to another country, as far as the United States' financial participation is concerned?

Mr. Carlin We would deal with those appeals and requests individually and assess the problem, first of all; assess the various aspects of it, our own interests, domestic and foreign, things of that nature, before we would make a decision.

Mr. Hall Now where do we get the jurisdiction, under existing law, to do that?

Mr. Carlin Well, I think – I think the basic Migration and Refugee Assistance Act of 1962 authorizes the appropriation of funds for contributions to both the UNHCR and ICEM. There is also the Emergency Refugee and Migration Assistance Fund. It would be in that context, sir, that we would be assisting in such activity.

Mr. Hall I understand that part of it; but does that, in itself, authorize expenditures of funds to a Chilean who wants to go to Bolivia, or to a Bolivian who wants to go to France?

Mr. Carlin Our interpretation would be that it does; yes, sir.

Mr. Eilberg I think what you're saying, and correct me if I'm wrong, is that under the emergency appropriation that was made available by the Congress and by our government, the President then has the power to spend those monies, even though they are not coming – the refugees are not coming to the United States; but are participating in any movement from one country to another, even though they are outside the United States.

Mr. Carlin This is right; so as to respond to emergency situations. That's right.

Mr. Eilberg Getting back to the UNHCR, we're concerned with what efforts he makes to try to place refugees among member countries. What is the mechanism, or procedure for, say, consultation with member countries?

Mr. Carlin Usually it would be in response to a refugee situation in a given asylum area. After assessing the problem, the UNHCR would appeal to the international community to, apart from providing financial assistance, provide resettlement opportunities for the refugees. That would be the normal procedure.

Now, the UNHCR's activities in this area are reviewed periodically by his Executive Committee. The U.S. sits on that committee. They review his program proposals, his activities, and make judgments with respect to them. I might just cite, as an example of resettlement of refugees by other countries, that from among the 70–80,000 Indochinese refugees remaining in Thailand, France is currently accepting about 600 per month.

Mr. Eilberg But there is no specific mechanism that comes into play in a refugee situation, when a refugee situation evolves?

Mr. Carlin The mechanism, sir, would come into play after the UNHCR determines that a special refugee situation exists. UNHCR would then make a special appeal to the international community – to encourage refugee-receiving countries to open their doors to the refugees.

Mr. Eilberg Now, in connection with that decision to try to find countries for refugees to go to: Is this decision made personally by the UNHCR? Is it made by the Executive Committee? By whom is it made?

Mr. Carlin Well, I don't think the UNHCR decides where the refugees should go. The UNHCR makes the refugee problem known. He interprets the problem to governments, and encourages governments to open their doors to the refugees. Individual governments then decide what their responses might be.

Mr. Eilberg What factors are considered, and what is usually the determined criterion, with regard to the nature of our government's assistance to refugees; that is, the U.S. relationship with the asylum country, pressures from the asylum country, conditions and numbers of refugees in the asylum country, political pressures, foreign policy considerations?

Mr. Carlin In most refugee situations, we contribute to an international effort to provide both material assistance and protection to refugees. Whether or not the U.S. Government agrees to accept any of the refugees for permanent resettlement here would hinge on such considerations as the resettleability of the individuals, resettlement opportunities in other countries, the potential for local settlement in the asylum area, domestic and foreign policy interests, national security, and lastly, sir, whether or not the refugee himself would be interested in coming to our country.

Mr. Eilberg What actually determines whether we provide humanitarian assistance to refugees in asylum countries, as opposed to accepting such refugees for resettlement into the United States?

Mr. Carlin There again, I think we would be responding to an international appeal for assistance to the refugees in the asylum area, probably an appeal from the UNHCR. But then, whether or not we would decide to accept any of the refugees for permanent resettlement in this country would hinge on considerations such as those which I just mentioned.

Mr. Eilberg Now, we've been concerned with the ad hoc, helter-skelter appeal made to us as emergency situations develop, and that is why we have introduced the bill that is before us. Should guidelines or criteria be established, notwithstanding the fact that each refugee situation might be different and require a different approach?

Mr. Carlin I would say, sir, there is always, perhaps, room for improvement in our decision-making processes as to how we react, respond, to refugee situations.

They are varied in nature, and we usually try to make the most honest assessment of each that we can, and recommend action accordingly, whether it be just making financial contributions for material assistance to the refugees in the asylum area, or a recommendation to admit some for permanent resettlement in this country.

Mr. Eilberg I'm not sure that you have been quite responsive. We have before us H.R. 3056, which attempts to establish the guidelines or criteria. Recognizing that you are not authorized by the Administration at this moment to state an opinion on that bill or that approach, I am really asking for your opinion: do you feel that an approach is necessary to regularize or to provide that guidance, as far as it is possible to do so?

Mr. Carlin I think that my answer to that question, sir, would be clearly 'yes'. We are still studying your bill in the State Department, and will be formulating our position with respect to it. We think, first of all, there is a need for the broader definition of a 'refugee', as set out in your bill. We shall be providing our official reaction to other aspects of your bill very soon, sir.

Mr Eilberg Over the years, we have witnessed numerous population disruptions within countries where the U.S. responded by providing humanitarian assistance. These situations, such as Cyprus, did not involve moving to a third country; but then under the subcommittee – Can you, for the subcommittee, can you describe the legal distinction between 'refugees' and 'displaced persons'?

Mr. Carlin Mr. Chairman, a refugee is a person who finds himself outside his country, his homeland, his country of nationality and either cannot or does not choose to return for well-founded reasons of fear of persecution because of political opinion, race, religion, nationality or involvement in certain social groups – things of that nature.

A 'displaced person', on the other hand, is an individual displaced within the geographic boundaries of his country, usually owing to some sort of civil conflict. Cyprus is a current example of a displaced person problem, where there are some 200,000 individuals displaced within that island.

As for dealing with two different groups, we in the State Department have our programs to deal with refugees – refugees, that is, in the legal sense of the word. When there are problems involving displaced persons, funds for assistance programs are usually made available by AID. Frequently the programming for displaced persons gets into the field of development assistance and therefore becomes appropriately a function for AID, rather than for State. However, we do always keep a watching brief on displaced person situations, as well as refugee problems.

Mr. Eilberg With respect to the role of the voluntary agencies, do you believe there is a continued need for involving the voluntary agencies in the resettlement process?

Mr. Carlin Mr. Chairman, I have worked in the field of refugees and migration for approximately 30 years, and over that span of time, I have gained, I think, a good appreciation of the value of the voluntary agencies. I would say absolutely, 'Yes'. They have a vital and essential role to play in the refugee resettlement process, particularly in programs involving refugees from Eastern Europe, where it is essential for the voluntary agency to work with the refugee in the asylum area – to counsel him, to provide material assistance to him, to assist him with his resettlement documentation, to assist him in various ways. And then, more particularly, they have a vital role in locating sponsorships for the refugee in order to facilitate his permanent resettlement.

Mr. Eilberg What changes, if any, should be made in the relationship between the U.S. Government and the various voluntary agencies? In other words, should we continue to provide a per capita grant approach; money? Or should we adopt program grant approaches? Should the voluntary agencies be required to provide matching grants through their own contributions or resources?

Mr. Carlin I think that our present arrangement for providing aid to the refugees through the voluntary agencies in the asylum areas is satisfactory. Through that arrangement and through the U.S. refugee program, help such as counseling, care and maintenance, resettlement documentation, language training and transportation is made available to the refugee through the network of voluntary agencies in the asylum areas. Through that process, the refugee is efficiently cared for, processed and brought to the resettlement country.

A problem may then exist as to whether or not additional assistance is required by the voluntary agencies to facilitate the placement, the integration, the training or retraining of the refugee in this country.

During the past few years, since 1973 as a matter of fact, since Congress has taken the initiative to make special funds available for Soviet refugees, we have been able to draw down from the special appropriations to cover reception and placement grants for the voluntary agencies for those Soviet refugees coming to this country.

Last year, however, Congress restricted the use of that special appropriation to only those Soviet refugees going to Israel. Consequently, we did not have funds for such grants in the current year. We have never budgeted for this particular item. We recognize, however, the need for the voluntary agencies for this kind of help, and we agree in principle that they should have it. However, we feel quite strongly, sir, that if and when we are again financially able to cover such reception and placement grants, they should not be merely for the Soviet refugees, but for all nationality groups. In that connection, we have talks underway with HEW. We think, because this type of assistance gets into the domestic programming field, it might be more appropriately handled by HEW rather than the State Department.

But the matter is being pursued in the meantime. Both the House Appropriations Committee and the House International Relations Committee have cited this need, and they may be taking the initiative to provide funds for this purpose for this calendar year, giving us time to work out a satisfactory solution for the future.

Mr. Eilberg What is your opinion of the per capita grant approach; that we should change it to a program grant approach?

Mr. Carlin I think, sir, that our current means of handling the USRP program, which reimburses the agencies for actual costs for things like resettlement documentation, care and maintenance, language training, etc. – that system is working quite satisfactorily now. Your question might more appropriately fit if we were in a position to pay reception and placement grants in the U.S. Then it would be a question of whether or not it should be done on a grant basis, or on an actual cost basis.

I would think it would probably have to be on a grant basis because most of the agencies spend, by far, more money than we would ever be able to give them to actually effect the resettlement and absorption of the refugee.

Mr. Eilberg Should the voluntary agencies be required to provide matching grants, was another part of my question.

Mr. Carlin As a matter of fact, sir, they do. Since 1973, we have been paying a reception placement grant of $300 per capita for Soviet refugees resettled in the U.S., but many of the voluntary agencies participating in this activity have been spending considerably more than that. I think one or two of the agencies report that their expenditures for this service have been reaching $2,000 per capita; so they have been more than matching what we gave them.

Mr. Eilberg And you are – We are, in effect, reimbursing the voluntary agencies only for expenses which are actually incurred, as I understand it.

Mr. Carlin At the European end, sir, we reimburse them for actual expenses for care and maintenance, resettlement documentation, staff support costs, etc.

Mr. Eilberg Should the U.S. Government establish a formal agency or mechanism for assisting and resettling refugees in this country, similar to the Jewish agency in Israel?

Mr. Carlin To repeat, sir, I think the existing machinery is quite adequate. In fact, I think our teamwork involving the voluntary agencies, our own United States Refugee Program, ICEM and the UNHCR is working very smoothly and very effectively.

Mr. Eilberg What pressures does the UNHCR bring on countries to ensure their compliance with the refugee convention and protocol?

Mr. Carlin Well, I think that generally speaking, the UNHCR tries to exercise the moral influence of his office in dealing with governments to achieve this. The matter is reviewed at the periodic sessions of his Executive Committee, when the High Commissioner himself stresses the importance of the protection function. And I think on every occasion of an Executive Committee that I can recall, our own U.S. delegation has certainly stressed the importance of this function, and through such public statements, has encouraged governments to be more responsive in terms of meeting their obligations under the protocol and convention.

Mr. Eilberg I wonder if you could briefly describe for the record what is meant by 'the refugee convention and protocol'?

Mr. Carlin Well, it's a document, sir, which some 69 odd governments are signatories to, and it places certain obligations on a signatory government. While it does not, I should say, authorize the acceptance of an individual for immigration, it requires a government to grant asylum to an individual who makes a good case for basing his unwillingness to return to his home country on well-founded fear of persecution for reasons of race, religion, nationality, political opinion or involvement in particular social groups. It also obligates signatory governments to grant to refugees a broad range of legal, social and economic rights – such as the right to work and the right of access to the courts – which are essential to promote the successful assimilation of the refugees and to enable them to cease being refugees and to live in dignity and self-respect.

Mr. Eilberg Has the UNHCR ever criticized a country for refusing to live up to its obligations under the convention.

Mr. Carlin Well, he may not have named names with respect to countries. He has certainly been, in public statements, critical of countries and areas where refugees have been neglected or mistreated. For example, in the recent case of the Vietnamese boat cases, he has certainly been critical of those countries on the periphery of the South China Sea which have refused to admit the boat cases for temporary asylum to permit their resettlement processing. He has also conducted his own personal diplomacy in such situations.

I think there have been situations in Africa where he has directed publicly remarks aimed at certain governments that had returned refugees forcibly to their own countries. So while he perhaps does not name names of such countries, he actively pursues situations where the terms of the protocol or convention are violated.

Mr. Eilberg Do you have examples available in your records as to such cases, where UNHCR has criticized –

Mr. Carlin I think we could provide that for the records, sir. We don't have that information here at the moment.

Mr. Eilberg Would you please? [See Annex 5]

Mr. Eilberg To what extent does the U.S. urge other countries to adhere to the UN protocol and convention with regard to refugees who have sought asylum in that particular country?

Mr. Carlin Well, I think, again, at sessions of the UNHCR Executive Committee, we have encouraged that sort of thing. More than that, over a period of two or three years, we have promoted and supported a project through the World Peace Through Law movement to encourage not only further accessions to the refugee convention and protocol by additional governments, but more particularly to interpret the real meaning of those documents to governments, and to members of the legal profession in various countries around the world. So I think there have been actions of that nature taken, sir.

Mr. Eilberg Is there a need for international mechanisms or commissions to review the compliance by the various countries to the international agreements on refugees?

Mr. Carlin Well, I think, Mr. Chairman, that is the basic purpose of the UNHCR. The purpose of that Office is to provide international protection to refugees. That's what the Office was established for. In more recent years, UNHCR has gotten more and more into the area of material assistance to needy refugee groups, but the Office's basic reason for being is to provide international protection to refugees.

Mr. Eilberg Well, I think we understand and agree what the purpose is, but some of us at times doubt that the purposes are being carried out. That is what concerns me, having been through a number of these situations. I've seen activity – I have seen lack of activity on the part of the UNHCR, and that's the basis for the question: whether we need something more than the UNHCR. That may be an editorial comment on my part. That's why I'm...

Mr. Carlin I think we must continue urging the UNHCR to meet his responsibilities in the area of protection and assistance, encourage other friendly governments to support us in that effort.

Mr. Eilberg For the benefit of the subcommittee, can you give us a brief description of what ICEM does?

Mr. Carlin ICEM exists essentially to provide transportation to refugees and migrants who are processed and movement-ready. ICEM also assists in certain situations with the documentation and processing of refugees and migrants for movement; so their main function and purpose is to provide transportation to refugees and migrants.

However, more than that, ICEM has a special program for moving skilled and professional migrants to Latin America. It's called the 'Selective Migration Program for Latin America', under which they identify particular needs at the Latin American end and then recruit in Europe skilled or professional migrants to meet those needs.

This process is designed to enhance the economic development of Latin America. Under that program, ICEM is moving between 3 and 4 thousand highly skilled migrants per year. In the transportation field, of the 50 to 60 thousand persons moved by ICEM per year, a very high majority would be refugees.

Mr. Eilberg And the others would be the movement of nationals who simply want to relocate to a place where they may have better opportunities?

Mr. Carlin That is correct, sir. ICEM over the years has moved many thousands of national migrants to countries like Australia, Canada, New Zealand; and while the numbers have been less to Latin American countries, there it's been a select group of migrants.

Mr. Eilberg What is the level of ICEM's program for the current year?

Mr. Carlin For the current year, I think their program totals about $28 million.

Mr. Eilberg How much is the U.S. contributing toward the program?

Mr. Carlin About $7 million.

Mr. Eilberg How many persons, broken down into refugees and migrants, did ICEM move in '76? How many do they plan to move in '77?

Mr. Carlin In 1976, they moved about 65,000 persons. Of that total, some 4,800 would have been national migrants as opposed to refugees. I think in 1977 they project the movement of 57,000 persons; again, by far, mostly refugees.

Mr. Eilberg In your opinion, is the ICEM operation essential as an integral part of our processing of the refugees?

Mr. Carlin Yes. We feel that ICEM's services are extremely valuable, and represent an important part of the teamwork which I have already described to the committee.

Mr. Eilberg Do you see any room for improvement on what they're doing?

Mr. Carlin Again, sir, I think there's always room for improvement. By way of a general comment, I think ICEM is doing extremely well in the area of refugee resettlement – very responsive and very effective. I think there is room for improvement in the area of their Latin American program. They have not been successful in interpreting that program to governments. Consequently, over the years, it has been badly under-financed. I think that in concept it's a sound program, but it has had limited success; probably because governments don't thoroughly understand it.

Mr. Eilberg As I understand it, ICEM is the only international organization which has limited its membership to democratic governments. Is this membership qualification still valid and for what reasons?

Mr. Carlin I don't think that limitation necessarily exists. Of course there must be on the part of governments a willingness and interest to become a member of ICEM. There is a constitutional requirement, so far as ICEM is concerned, that member governments must support the principle of freedom of movement. And there are obviously countries in the world today who do not practice that principle; consequently they are not in ICEM.

Mr. Hall May I ask – Mr. Chairman, may I ask a question? How many governments are a part of this ICEM?

Mr. Carlin 33 governments.

Mr. Eilberg Are there any non-democratic governments included in those 33?

Mr. Carlin No, sir.

Mr. Hall You've got a budget of how much? We're paying – We're putting how much into it?

Mr. Carlin $6.9 million in the current year, sir, against a total budget of about $28 million.

Mr. Hall $28 million.

Mr. Eilberg How do you arrive at a budget allocation for ICEM?

Mr. Carlin We sit on all three governing bodies of ICEM. There is a Subcommittee on Budget and Finance, an Executive Committee, and a Council. And ICEM's programs, project proposals, etc., are reviewed by those three bodies, so that we have ample opportunity to see what they are proposing, what they think the needs are. And then we try to make a judgment in relation to those projected programs and needs in relation to our interests.

Mr. Eilberg Do you consider that we are giving adequate support to the organization, or should we fund to increase the support? What would you suggest?

Mr. Carlin I think, sir, comparatively speaking – and I mean comparing the U.S. government to the other member governments of ICEM – we are doing extremely well. There is no particular – There is no particular problem of financing ICEM's refugee settlement activity. They have had a rather chronic deficit in the area of Latin American programs probably for the reasons I have already mentioned, but to get back to your question; I think that we have been reasonably generous in supporting ICEM over the years. We think it's doing a very valuable job. We think other governments, other member governments of ICEM, should be doing more; and we repeatedly pursue that objective in the governing bodies of ICEM.

Mr. Eilberg   All right. I think the subcommittee will take a recess until we can – So we can go to a vote; and then we'll come back with just a few more questions.

(A brief recess was taken.)

Mr. Eilberg   The subcommittee will come to order. Mr. Carlin, just so that we may have a better understanding of the function of UNHCR and the other agency, ICEM, apparently the UNHCR renders protection to the refugee – legal protection – but then the refugee may be moved to a country, an asylum country, where there may not be any voluntary agency. And then ICEM has responsibility for moving them to resettlement countries. Is there a possible void or gap there at the point of the asylum country? Who looks after the refugees there?

Mr. Carlin   I think, Mr. Chairman, UNHCR maintains representation in most of the principal refugee asylum countries and while they have limited staff representation, I think they make a good effort to watch over the interests of the refugees, particularly in terms of providing protection.

So far as ICEM is concerned, ICEM's work obviously ends when they deliver the refugee to his resettlement country. The voluntary agencies, on the other hand, have the capability to follow up on the placement of the refugee and, on occasion, when there is a breakdown in that placement, to step in and find a second placement opportunity. So there is some follow-up, both on the part of the UNHCR in terms of protection, and on the part of the voluntary agencies in terms of follow-up work, to ensure satisfactory placement.

Mr. Eilberg   Do you believe that the present system for handling refugees, UNHCR, ICEM, the voluntary agencies, is adequate, or do you think the present system and procedures could be improved?

Mr. Carlin   I think by and large, the machinery that exists today involving the UNHCR, ICEM, the voluntary agencies, our own USRP program is adequate. We did touch earlier on one, perhaps one area of deficiency; and that would relate to the financial ability of the voluntary agencies to receive, place, train, retrain refugees in this country. But otherwise, I think the existing basic machinery is adequate, and functioning very efficiently; certainly insofar as European refugees are concerned.

Now, refugee problems are dealt with differently in different parts of the world depending upon the needs and wishes of the refugees. In Africa, for example, UNHCR will go in to deal with a refugee problem, provide immediate emergency assistance, and then take measures to provide the tools, utensils, agricultural implements and seeds to permit the refugees to become self-supporting in agricultural communities as rapidly as possible. That is the approach in many of the African refugee areas. It's something else in Europe; it's something else again in Latin America. By and large, sir, I think the machinery that exists is generally satisfactory.

Mr. Eilberg   Are you convinced that our support to the international refugee organizations, or the private voluntary agencies, is adequate, or should it be increased? If so, in which way?

Mr. Carlin   Taking first of all our supports to international agencies, like UNHCR and ICEM, comparatively speaking, I think we are doing very well. A number of other governments are not doing as much as we think they should. Apart from our regular support to the annual programs of ICEM and UNHCR, the U.S. frequently responds to special situations, and makes special financial contributions.

Turning to the voluntary agencies, I would again have to refer to the matter of reception and placement grants. We are exploring a long-term solution to that problem.

Mr. Eilberg   I understand your support to these organizations is subject to overall

State Department budget constraints. Do these constraints limit support where a determination has been made that the requirements are essential?

Mr. Carlin Well, that's absolutely true, sir, that we are subject to budget ceilings and constraints; and there have been occasions where things that we have recommended in the area of assistance to refugees and migrants have been disallowed or reduced. Reception placement grants and ICEM's Latin American program happen to be examples of that type of action, sir. However, I think by and large the measure of our assistance to the agencies, to the international organizations, has been reasonably generous and for the most part adequate.

Mr. Eilberg To what extent has, or will, the $25 million emergency fund alleviate some of the problems we have experienced in the past in providing timely assistance when an emergent refugee situation arises?

Mr. Carlin First of all, sir, we are very pleased that Congress has taken the initiative to establish this $25 million emergency fund. However, to date, only $15 million of the $25 million has been funded; and at the present time, we have just over $1 million remaining in the fund; so while that fund is extremely useful to meet emergency situations, we feel quite strongly that there's a need to have it fully funded and then to have prompt action on replenishment as draw-downs are effected.

Mr. Eilberg Some communications from the State Department and Justice indicate there is no yardstick available to really gauge the impact of past refugee programs on the economic, demographic, sociological and political situation in the United States. In your opinion, do you consider that these studies would be of value?

Mr. Carlin I would think, sir, for the long pull, particularly in terms of immigration policy and refugee immigration, that such a study would be of value, and perhaps provide useful data in terms of measuring our ability to continue accepting more and more migrants and refugees for permanent settlement. So I think my quick answer would be, 'Yes, sir'.

I am not sure we in the State Department have the staff and resources to carry out such a study. Perhaps it should be an interdepartmental exercise involving HEW, Labor, ourselves; perhaps it could be a joint effort.

Mr. Eilberg Is there really an overall refugee policy? Or do you think we ought only to react, rather than act?

Mr. Carlin Well, we like to think we do have a policy; and we try to be as responsive as possible to refugee situations. And on occasion, I think we have acted rather than reacted. To cite an example or two: the evacuation of the refugees from Vietnam; more recently, we have prompted the initiative to lift some 2700 Christian refugees out of Beirut during the conflict situation in Lebanon.

We are currently taking initiatives to have a new look at the emerging refugee situations in Southern Africa, and encouraging UNHCR and others to give the new problems in that area the careful attention they deserve. So I think we are acting as well as reacting, and I think we are trying to be as responsive as possible to emergent refugee problems and situations.

Mr. Eilberg Mr. Carlin, I don't want to disagree with you, but some of our most hectic moments in the last years that we've been here have been when we have considered parole by the Attorney General. And reflecting on those meetings that we've had, in which I have participated, frequently with the Attorney General and the Immigration Commissioner, the Commissioner for the Immigration and Naturalization Service present, there was really inadequate information: very little information, distorted information based upon further study, and so that about all that they were accomplishing at various points in these various programs was conveying to us their sense of emergency, but certainly no sense of refugee policies.

So I'm inclined to disagree with you, sir, based upon the trauma of these meetings. And hopefully, in this Congress we'll get some legislation through, perhaps on the basis of the bill which we've introduced, which will establish a more clear refugee policy. Do you know what the total budget for the UNHCR was last year?

Mr. Carlin I think in '76 UNHCR's budget was some $14 million; $14.8 million, yes, sir.

Mr. Eilberg And do you know what the funding level of UNHCR is for the current year, for its regular program?

Mr. Carlin Its regular program in the current year is at the $16.6 million level.

Mr. Eilberg And what percentage is the U.S. contributing to that program?

Mr. Carlin Approximately 10 percent, sir.

Mr. Eilberg Is that enough, or should it be increased, or decreased?

Mr. Carlin I think toward UNHCR's regular program that is sufficient, and compares favorably with contributions from other governments. However, apart from our contributions to that regular program, we do make a number of special contributions to UNHCR in response to special appeals for emergent refugee situations.

Mr. Eilberg Does the United States have any input into the decisions which are made by the UNHCR as they relate to priorities for his regular program, or the expenditure of funds under either its special program or its special activities?

Mr. Carlin We are a member of the UNHCR Executive Committee, and, of course, we attend all meetings of that body, so we are able to provide our input, judgments, recommendations as to what UNHCR programs should be, the financial level, etc. Through our mission in Geneva, we have contact with UNHCR practically on a day-to-day basis to discuss particular projects of interest to the U.S. Government, and to encourage the UNHCR to move in given areas. I think generally speaking, sir, we are well represented with respect to the activities of UNHCR.

Mr. Eilberg Has the United States delegation to the United Nations ever made its refugee priorities known, or have we ever requested the UN Secretary-General to respond to a particular emergency using the good offices of the UNHCR?

Mr. Carlin Yes, Mr. Chairman. I think we've done that on occasion. For example, we encouraged both the Secretary-General and the High Commissioner for Refugees to become involved with the problem of displaced persons in Cyprus.

We also encouraged UNHCR to take a more active role with respect to the boat cases, the Vietnamese boat cases, which are currently presenting a very tragic problem. We have recently encouraged UNHCR to be more responsive to the needs of a particular group of refugees in Africa.

Mr. Eilberg I wonder if we could ask you to go back and give us a more complete answer to that question. We're very interested in the role of the UN and UNHCR, and our curiosity never ends. And its activities frequently – are frequently unknown. What priorities it has; they're certainly unknown to us. And what we should know, what the U.S. Government is doing with the UN, UNHCR. So I'd appreciate it if you would give us a more complete report on that subject.

Mr. Carlin We'll develop that for the record, sir. [See Annex 6]

Mr. Eilberg Has the U.S. Government ever failed to respond to an appeal or special request by the UNHCR for funds or for providing resettlement opportunities in the United States for any group of refugees?

Mr. Carlin Yes, Mr. Chairman. For example, the UNHCR had a program to assist displaced persons within Vietnam, and a similar program in Laos. We did not respond to his request for financial support for either of those programs. In the case of Latin American refugees we have responded, but our response has been a limited one. In the case of Chileans, I think about 19,000 have gone to destinations other than the U.S. Approximately 1,000 have come here.

Mr. Eilberg I wonder if you could – Again, I think you have given us examples. We would like to have a more complete report for the record, if you could provide one.

Mr. Carlin We'd be pleased to, sir. [See Annex 7]

Mr. Eilberg What factors are considered by the Department of State in determining the nature of our response to these appeals that you referred to?

Mr. Carlin Well, I think we take a number of things into account – the humanitarian factors, to what extent is it an emergency. We consider our national security, the extent of our concern and interest in particular refugee groups, the interest or lack of interest among the refugees in coming to the United States, our capacity to absorb the refugees – that is, voluntary agency willingness and capacity to provide sponsorships; and, as I think I mentioned earlier in our deliberations this morning, the resettleability of the refugees in question. Those are some of the factors that are taken into account.

Mr. Eilberg Do we examine any of the responses or possible response of other countries?

Mr. Carlin Yes indeed, we do, sir. We watch very closely what other countries are doing, and frequently encourage UNHCR to press other countries to do more when we think we're getting too far out front in given situations.

Mr. Eilberg You may have answered this, but do we utilize a 'fair share' approach, or do we independently determine the nature of our response?

Mr. Carlin Generally speaking, we try to put our response on a fair share basis. The most recent example of that has been in relation to the Vietnamese boat cases. The UNHCR demonstrated to us that other countries were taking their fair share. We then made a commitment to take 100 per month under the Conditional Entry Program.

Mr. Eilberg Sir, I don't know that you answered the part of the question dealing with the fair share approach.

Mr. Carlin Well, as I say, we as far as possible endeavor to take our fair share, but we also like to see other refugee-receiving countries take their fair share, and we negotiate with the UNHCR with respect to that objective. I think, at least during the past year or so, we have met with some measures of success in this regard. Mr. Lowman would like to add something if he may.

Mr. Eilberg Yes.

Mr. Lowman In that connection, Mr. Chairman, our definition of 'fair share' as we have seen it has been not an automatic percentage, but rather a judgment of these individual cases; what other countries have interest in the refugees involved, what our own interests were. So we're back to the kind of situation where, indeed, our fair share, as we saw it, was a considerably higher percentage in the case of Vietnamese refugees and considerably lower in the case of, say, the recent Chilean program. But it is an endeavor to take a fair share within our perception of all the factors involved.

Mr. Eilberg Mr. Carlin, I wonder if you can, when the opportunity presents itself, express our concerns to the U.S. delegation to the UN and to the UNHCR, possibly even to the Secretary-General himself; and I'm stating for the record, now, that we expect to send a record of this hearing to the individuals that we've mentioned, but we are anxious for them to know our concerns as early as possible. I'd like – Will you agree to do that?

Mr. Carlin Yes, sir.

Mr. Eilberg I would like to place on the record at this point Presidential determinations of amounts contributed over the years following the '62 Migration

Act and including the sums contributed under the recent emergency fund, and make them part of the record without objection at this point. [See Annex 8]

Mr. Carlin, would you briefly describe the nature of the following refugee situations, and please indicate the types of assistance being provided by the United States in each of these cases. I have eight different situations. We have referred to a few of these, and you may want to amplify in those cases. First, refugees in Thailand.

Mr. Carlin Mr. Chairman, there are approximately 70 to 80 thousand Indochinese refugees remaining in Thailand today. The UNHCR has an ongoing program there for assistance to those refugees. I think it totals approximately $26 million for the current year. Toward that effort, we are providing $5 million plus for the care and maintenance in Thailand.

Mr. Lowman Also $2.5 million for resettlement outside Thailand, and another $1.8 million for care and maintenance of boat cases; not in Thailand but in other areas of Southeast Asia.

Mr. Eilberg Do you wish to amplify that, Mr. Carlin?

Mr. Carlin The nature of the UNHCR's program in Thailand is care and maintenance, and I think in this current year UNHCR has added the new dimension of trying to develop projects which are designed to make the refugees self-supporting.

Mr. Eilberg Is there anything further that you would add on the so-called 'boat cases'?

Mr. Carlin I think there are about 3,000 of them needing help at the present time.

Mr. Lowman To date, about – Between 800 and 900 have been resettled out of Southeast Asia, about half of those coming to the United States, under the old expanded parole, and we have identified and nominated by the host in the area about another 800 to 900 individuals who would qualify under old criteria for special attention by the United States.

Mr. Eilberg What kind of special attention?

Mr. Lowman Well, we had intended now to make available to – as a part of the commitment, responding to the UNHCR appeal, committed 100 conditional entry numbers per month to the acceptance of these refugees.

Mr. Eilberg Mr. Carlin, referring next to the Assyrian and Armenian refugees in Lebanon: What kind of assistance is being provided by the U.S. in these cases?

Mr. Carlin Mr. Chairman, we have made no particular contribution for those groups in Lebanon. During this past year we have made a contribution of $4 million to the ICRC, the International Committee of the Red Cross, mainly for medical assistance to victims of the conflict there, and some emergency relief assistance. Additionally, we have made a pledge of $1 million to the UN, $300,000 of which would go to UNHCR for activities within Lebanon for the benefit of the displaced Lebanese and victims of the conflict; but we have made no particular contribution to the two nationality groups you referred to, sir.

Mr. Eilberg And what about the Chilean refugees?

Mr. Carlin I'm sorry. I missed your question, sir.

Mr. Eilberg The Chilean refugees; the nature of the refugee situations and the type of assistance being provided by the U.S.

Mr. Carlin Well, we have been operating for the past year or so a scheme to accept 400 Chilean detainees from Chile, 400 cases. That program is just about completed now. Some 370 cases involving about 1100 persons have arrived in the U.S., and the remaining number of that 400 will shortly be arriving.

More recently, we have started a program for the benefit of Chilean and other

Latin American refugees in Argentina, and we've made a commitment to take 200 such cases from that country. That program has just recently been initiated. We have some 200 cases in processing down there at the present time, and movements should commence very shortly.

Mr. Eilberg What types of assistance are being granted to the Chilean refugees, wherever they may be?

Mr. Carlin Well, apart from what we're doing in terms of resettlement, many other countries have opened their doors to Chileans, and the total number having been resettled to other destinations, I think, is approximately 19,000. Quite apart from resettlement assistance, the UNHCR has had care and maintenance programs in Latin America, in Argentina, mainly, for the benefit of Latin American refugees.

Toward that effort, we have made a commitment of $1.2 million. $500,000 of that was for UNHCR care and maintenance programs in Argentina and elsewhere in Latin America. $500,000 was channeled to ICEM for transportation of Latin American refugees, and $200,000 was given to the International Committee of the Red Cross. They've had an active medical program in Latin America, a tracing action, and they, from time to time, administer emergency relief supplies to refugees and detainees.

Mr. Eilberg Are we doing anything for the Chilean refugees right now, here in the United States.

Mr. Carlin No, we are not, sir.

Mr. Eilberg Now what about the situation of the Angolan refugees who have fled?

Mr. Carlin Well, first of all, approximately 600,000 Portuguese were obliged to leave Angola during the recent strife in that country, and they've been returned to Portugal. And we – that is, USAID – has made a contribution.

Mr. Warren $35 million.

Mr. Carlin $35 million to the Government of Portugal to assist those returnees from Angola in Portugal. Apart from that, we have made a special contribution to ICEM of $1 million to – as part of an appeal. The ICEM Director appealed to ICEM member governments for funds for the resettlement of those returnees from Angola, and our response was $1 million. ICEM is currently developing programs to move some of those people to countries in Latin America and elsewhere.

Mr. Eilberg Have any of these people entered the United States? Angolan refugees?

Mr. Carlin Not to my knowledge.

Mr. Eilberg And what can you tell us about the stateless Christian refugees from Lebanon?

Mr. Carlin During the heat of the battle in the Lebanon, sir, some 2700 Christian refugees – Armenians, Assyrians, and others – were lifted from Beirut to Athens. And in Athens they were processed for resettlement. Approximately 2400 of them have been accepted by the U.S. and are physically here today.

A number of the balance have been accepted by other countries: Australia, Canada, etc. There are approximately 100 still in Athens awaiting resettlement.

Mr. Eilberg What types of assistance is the United States providing to them, whether here or in Athens?

Mr. Carlin We contributed to their care and maintenance in Athens through the UNHCR the amount of $910,000; and as I indicated earlier, we took the majority of them, accepted them for immigration to this country. Incidentally, many of them had been in processing in Beirut for the U.S. previously, so it was a matter of continuing the processing in Athens.

Mr. Eilberg Are we doing anything for them here?

Mr. Carlin   No, we are not, sir. The voluntary agencies of course sponsor their resettlement and they have followed that up, sir.

Mr. Eilberg   How did the stateless Christian refugees come to the United States?

Mr. Carlin   Well, they were processed in Athens and when they were movement-ready, visaed and movement-ready, they were moved by ICEM.

Mr. Eilberg   And what was their legal basis for their coming here? Was it parole?

Mr. Carlin   It was a combination, sir, of using conditional entry numbers and non-preference visa numbers.

Mr. Eilberg   No parole?

Mr. Carlin   No parole. No, sir.

Mr. Eilberg   What about Kurdish refugees from Iraq?

Mr. Carlin   Early in 1976, there were some 2000 Kurds in Iran, Kurds from Iraq in Iran, seeking resettlement. They had been identified by the UNHCR. Again, the UNHCR appealed to the international community to open their doors to them. Of the 2000, we agreed to take up to 400, and we ended up taking just over 300. They are physically here today. The balance of that original 2000 were accepted by other countries: Western European countries, Canada, and Australia.

Mr. Eilberg   And the voluntary agencies are taking care of those people?

Mr. Carlin   Voluntary agencies provided the sponsorships for those who came to this country; yes, sir.

Mr. Eilberg   Without any U.S. government assistance?

Mr. Carlin   We did provide care and maintenance support. They stopped down in Frankfurt for immigration processing, and we provided care and maintenance in Frankfurt, I think, to the tune of $150,000. Other than that, we expended no funds on them.

Mr. Eilberg   Do you have any information on the recent parole of the 4000 Russian Jews in Rome? Have they departed Italy, and have they been brought here?

Mr. Carlin   We understand, sir, that that action is very well underway. I think some have physically been moved since the program started last month. When we recommended that particular action, we estimated that there would be in excess of 4000 Soviet refugees in the pipeline in Italy as of the turn of the year, and that estimate proved to be quite true. However, during the month of January, the INS and our consular officers issued either conditional entry numbers or non-preference visa numbers to, I think, some 1200–1400 of these refugees.

Mr. Eilberg   In addition to the 4000?

Mr. Carlin   No. This was included within the 4000, and with respect to the special parole action we had stipulated that it would apply to those who had arrived in Italy prior to December 31, 1976. So the effect of the issuance of conditional entry and non-preference numbers to about 1400 diminished our ability to use up, fully utilize, the 4000.

So we have recommended now to the Commissioner of the Immigration and Naturalization Service that we extend the date, the deadline, from December 31 to April 1, in order to fully utilize the 4000 numbers. I think this is fully justified, sir, because Soviet refugees continue to arrive in Rome at the rate of about 700 per month; so unless we do that, there will just be a new backlog in some months' time.

Mr. Eilberg   I missed the numbers that they used.

Mr. Carlin   I think it was approximately 1400.

Mr. Eilberg   This, of course, was not consistent with the agreement or consultation with the members of the Judiciary Committee of both Houses. We had authorized 4000, and intended for those 4000 that were there at that time.

Mr. Carlin   That was our intention as well, sir; and it seems that while we were awaiting a final approval for extending the deadline, processing is proceeding satisfactorily in Rome. If the Commissioner agrees to extend the deadline, we will be able to take full advantage of the 4000 parole numbers.

Mr. Eilberg Does he have the authority to do that without having to go through consultation?

Mr. Carlin I can't give you an answer to that, sir, but I think it's his intention to consult with your committee, sir, and with the appropriate committee on the Senate side.

Mr. Eilberg Well, we wish that you would go ahead and do it without waiting to consult with us.

Mr. Carlin In the meantime, the action continues in Italy. We've made this proposal to the INS very recently.

Mr. Eilberg And finally, what about refugees from Rhodesia, Namibia, South Africa and Angola?

Mr. Carlin This is a serious problem at the present time and it's rapidly worsening, with more and more refugees coming out of those countries. There are over 400,000 Angolans outside Angola at the present time, plus many new refugees from Rhodesia, Namibia and South Africa. Once again, in response to an appeal from UNHCR, we have recently made a special contribution of $1 million for assistance to these refugees.

Mr. Lowman The UNHCR has appealed for $3.25 million. We made a contribution of $1 million in response to that appeal.

Mr. Carlin And I would add, sir, that the refugee situation in Africa seems to be worsening; it's a matter that we have under very close review.

Mr. Eilberg Now, when the request was made to you from the UNHCR for a monetary contribution, what are the mechanics involved in making that decision and giving them the money?

Mr. Carlin Well, first of all, I would mention that the UNHCR appeal went not only to us, but to the international community. When we got his appeal, we considered it in the State Department. We sought information and advice from our embassies in the countries where the refugees were situated. When we made our judgment in the matter, we then recommended a draw-down from our refugee emergency fund, and this goes all the way through OMB to the White House. Finally, the President makes the final decision. And that's what happened in this case.

Mr. Eilberg And can you tell us, with regard to the last category, you mentioned a dollar figure that we've given, and you said the situation is worsening. Could you just expand on that a little bit?

Mr. Carlin Well, there's still a very unsettled situation in Angola which seems to be producing more and more refugees from that country. The strife in Rhodesia and in South Africa is also accounting for more and more refugees, particularly young student types; and when they get out to countries like Botswana, Swaziland, etc., they need special attention. And part of our support, part of the UNHCR's efforts, is to provide education for some of those young Africans coming out. In many cases, their education was interrupted in their home countries, so part of the emphasis is on education of those refugees who get out. But it's all a result of the turmoil, the unsettled conditions in Southern Africa at the present time.

Mr. Eilberg Mr. Carlin, gentlemen, you've been very helpful, and your supply of information is inexhaustible. And we continue to admire the kind of work that you do, and thank you very much for your cooperation with the subcommittee. The subcommittee is adjourned.

(Whereupon, at 12.10 p.m., the hearing was recessed subject to the call of the chair.)

ANNEX 1

Migration and Refugee Assistance

A.1 Approximate numbers of refugees accepted by the United States, 1945–1976, under various immigration programs

Legislative or Other Base of Program	Duration of Program	Beneficiaries of Program	Number Admitted
President Truman's Directive of December 22, 1945	1945–48	Displaced persons from European countries who refused repatriation after World War II	40,324
Displaced Persons Act of 1948	1948–52	Displaced persons and escapees from East European countries and ethnic Germans expelled from East European countries	409,696
Refugee Relief Act of 1953	1953–56	Expellees, escapees and refugees from Europe, the Middle East and the Far East	189,021
Act of July 29, 1953	1953–56	Orphans	466
Act of September 11, 1957 (Public Law 85–316)	1958–59	German expellees, Dutch nationals displaced from their homes in Indonesia following that country's independence, families of U.S. resident aliens and refugee-escapees from Communist countries or from countries within the general area of the Middle East	29,462
Act of July 25, 1958 (Public Law 85–559)	1958–59	Hungarians who fled their country following the 1956 revolt (conversion of their parole status to that of resident alien)	30,751
Act of September 2, 1958 (Public Law 85–892)	1958–60	Portuguese nationals displaced from their homes in the Azores Islands because of natural calamity and Dutch nationalists displaced from their homes in Indonesia following that country's independence	22,213

Act of September 22, 1959 (Public Law 86–363)	1959–60	Families of resident aliens admitted to the U.S. under the Refugee Relief Act	1,820
Act of July 14, 1960 (Public Law 86–648 "Fair Share Act")	1960–65	Refugee-escapees from Communist countries in Europe or from countries in the general area of the Middle East	19,754
President Kennedy's Parole Directive of May 23, 1962	1962–65	Chinese refugees in Hong Kong	15,000
Cuban Refugee Program (January 1, 1959–June 30, 1976)	Since Jan. 1959	Cubans who have fled to the U.S. since the advent of the Castro regime in Cuba in 1959	660,054
Act of October 3, 1965 (Public Law 89–236) Immigration and Nationality Act, as amended (7th Preference Provision)	Since 1/1/66	Refugee-escapees from Communist countries or from countries in the general area of the Middle East	95,874
Admitted with immigration visas under provisions of the Immigration and Nationality Act, without regard to refugee status	1945–1976	No restrictions as to beneficiaries	205,000 (est.)
Indochinese Refugee Parole Program	1975–1976	Vietnamese refugees (129,000), Cambodian refugees (6,000) and Laotian refugees (10,000)	145,000
Parole programs for various groups of refugees	Since Oct. 1964	Miscellaneous categories of refugees	15,709
			1,880,144

A.2   U.S. contributions to refugee assistance 1945–75

Summary

A.	Through Intergovernmental Organizations:	$1,291,300,000
B.	Through Direct U.S. Programs:	3,020,800,000
	GRAND TOTAL	$4,312,100,000

Through Intergovernmental Organizations

		$ (*millions*)
1. UNRRA (United Nations Relief and Rehabilitation Administration	1945–48	29.0

2.	IGCR (Intergovernmental Committee for Refugees)	1946–46	3.0
3.	IRO (International Refugee Organization)	1947–51	237.1
4.	UNKRA (United Nations Korean Reconstruction Agency)	1952–55	23.0
5.	Unified Command Emergency Relief for Korea	1950–54	61.0
6.	UNHCR (United Nations High Commissioner for Refugees)	1951–75	31.1
7.	U.N. Relief for Palestine Refugees	1949–50	16.0
8.	UNRWA (United Nations Relief and Works Agency for Palestinian Refugees in the Near East)	1950–75	617.0
9.	ICEM (Intergovernmental Committee for European Migration)	1952–75	133.0
10.	WRY (World Refugee Year)	1960	6.0
11.	Special Programs by UNHCR		
	a. Assistance for East Pakistani Refugees in India	1971–72	90.9
	b. Assistance to refugees returning to Southern Sudan	1974	10.0
	c. Assistance to Ugandan Asians	1974	1.6
	d. Exchange of Persons Pakistan/Bangladesh	1973–74	4.5
	e. Refugees returning to Mozambique	1975	.9
	f. Refugees returning to Guinea-Bissau	1975	1.0
	g. Refugees and displaced persons on Cyprus	1975	20.7
	h. Indochina refugees in Thailand	1975	5.0
	i. Indochina refugees outside their country of origin	1975	.5
		SUB-TOTAL	1,291.3

Through direct U.S. programs

12.	U.S. Occupation (Europe)	1945–51	300.0 (est.)
13.	U.S. Occupation (Korea)	1945–48	70.0 (est.)
14.	Hungarian Refugees	1956–57	18.0
15.	USRP (United States Refugee Program, formerly the United States Escapee Program)	1952–75	71.4
16.	FERP (Far Eastern Refugee Program)	1954–75	18.3
17.	South Vietnamese Refugees in South Vietnam (AID programs and previous)	1954–75	572.5
18.	Laotian Refugees in Laos (AID program)	1961–75	104.3
19.	Cambodian Refugees in Cambodia (AID program)	1974–75	42.1

20.	PL-480 Food Programs (All Areas) (excluding portions allocated as part of regular contributions to certain programs, e.g. UNRWA and East Pakistani Refugees in India)	1954–75	347.9
21.	Tibetan Refugees	1959–69	4.0
22.	Cuban Refugees in USA (HEW)	1961–75	1,080.9
23.	Southern African Student Programs	1962–75	20.1
24.	Burundi Refugees		.4
25.	Soviet Refugees	1952–75	133.5
26.	Refugees from Cambodia and Vietnam	1975	228.7
27.	Refugees from Cambodia and Vietnam (HEW)	1975	6.1
28.	Refugees from Laos	1975	2.6
			3,020.8

A.3 U.S. assistance to refugees for fiscal year 1976

Categories of Refugees Assisted	Program Managed By	Source of Funds	Amount of Program Assistance $	Value of P.L. 480 Funded By Department of Agriculture[1] $	Total $
Refugees in Europe and elsewhere from European Communist countries	State	Foreign assistance	2,591,000	—	2,591,000[2]
Chinese refugees in Hong Kong and Macao	State	Foreign assistance	290,000	—	290,000[2]
Refugees moved from Europe, the Near East and other areas	Intergovernmental Committee for European Migration (ICEM) – State	Foreign assistance	3,000,000[3]	—	3,000,000[2]
Various categories of refugees worldwide	United Nations High Commissioner for Refugees (UNHCR) – State	Foreign assistance	1,168,000	—	1,168,000[2]
Refugees from the Soviet Union	State	Foreign assistance	20,300,000	—	20,300,000
Refugee students from southern African countries in the U.S.	State	State	238,492	—	238,492[4]
Refugee students from southern Africa in other African countries	State	Foreign assistance	200,000	—	200,000[2]
Refugee students from South Africa, Namibia and Rhodesia	AID	Foreign assistance	262,550	—	262,550
Palestine Arab refugees	U.N. Relief and Works Agency for Palestine Refugees in the Near East (UNRWA) – State/AID	Foreign assistance	38,700,000	—	38,700,000

Cuban refugees in the United States	HEW	Foreign assistance	85,000,000	—	85,000,000
The Indochina Refugee Program	State	State	127,647,000	—	127,647,000
Indochina refugees in the U.S.	HEW	HEW	105,418,000	—	105,418,000[4]
Special Lao Refugee Program	State	Foreign assistance	7,136,000	—	7,136,000[4]
Support by UNHCR of Indochinese refugees in Thailand	State	Foreign assistance	—	—	—[5]
Displaced Cypriots	UNHCR/AID	Foreign assistance	29,800,000	—	29,800,000[4]
Refugees returning to Mozambique	UNCHR/AID	Foreign assistance	615,000	—	615,000
Stateless Christian refugees from Lebanon	UNHCR/State	Foreign assistance	910,000	—	910,000
Kurdish refugees	UNHCR/State	Foreign assistance	150,000	—	150,000
Returnees from Angola in Portugal	AID	Foreign assistance	35,000,000	—	35,000,000
Refugees and returnees from Angola	AID	Foreign assistance	8,131,429	—	8,131,429
Refugees in Lebanon	AID/ICRC	Foreign assistance	4,000,000	—	4,000,000
P.L. 480 Food for Peace – Worldwide	AID	Agriculture	—	5,151,000	5,151,000
TOTAL			470,557,471	5,151,00	475,708,471

[1] At Commodity Credit Corporation costs.
[2] Includes obligations incurred in calendar year 1976.
[3] Includes national migrants to Latin America.
[4] Includes obligations incurred in the Transition Quarter.
[5] Excludes $6.24 million included under the Indochina Refugee Program and $3.16 million included under the Special Lao Refugee Program.

ANNEX 2

A.4   Number of refugees from Eastern Europe assisted by the U.S. government, 1972–1977

	ACTUAL					EST.
	1972	*1973*	*1974*	*1975*	*1976*	*1977*
Refugees from the Soviet Union						
To Israel	31,274	33,249	16,842	8,395	7,216	7,000
To countries other than Israel	800	1,951	5,238	7,195	8,545	11,000
TOTAL	32,074	35,200	22,080	15,590	15,761	18,000
Refugees from other Eastern European countries	6,453	5,474	4,973	4,197	4,587	6,000
TOTAL	38,527	40,674	27,053	19,787	20,348	24,000

ANNEX 3

Countries receiving boat cases from Vietnam

The overall program for those refugees has been and continues to be an activity of the UNHCR. We admitted 517 in the past few months as part of a parole program for 11,800 Indochinese, which has now ended. UNHCR reports that other countries have responded to appeals as follows:

France	580
Australia	475
Canada	130
FRG	105
Norway	80
Netherlands	60
Belgium	25
UK	25
Austria	20
Switzerland	12
Taiwan	6
TOTAL	1,518

Moreover, Hong Kong, a port where first asylum is given to those ultimately going on to other countries, has accepted 25 for permanent resettlement. Altogether over 2,000 of these refugees have been resettled between July 1976 and the end of February 1977.

ANNEX 4

A.5 Refugees moved under the auspices of the Intergovernmental Committee for European Migration in 1975–76

	1975	*1976*
Australia	966	730
Canada	2,589	2,949
Israel	10,817	9,392
New Zealand	165	150
South Africa	514	68
Other countries	291	93
Latin America		
Argentina	231	83
Bolivia	11	3
Brazil	127	108
Chile	17	23
Colombia	86	41
Ecuador	24	16
Paraguay	1	—
Peru	21	4
Venezuela	222	131
Central America, Panama and the Caribbean	568	454
Europe		
Austria	219	247
Belgium	254	238
Bulgaria	20	—
Denmark	246	207
East Germany	26	68
Finland	31	3
France	6,696	11,918
FRG	269	566
Greece	2	—
Hungary	142	31
Ireland	25	1
Italy	346	73
Luxembourg	38	14
Netherlands	145	586
Norway	189	235
Poland	4	—
Portugal	—	15
Romania	380	49
Spain	21	25
Sweden	880	880
Switzerland	114	175
Turkey	2	2
U.K.	864	570
U.S.S.R.	—	46
Yugoslavia	22	11

ANNEX 5

Supplementary information concerning the effect given to the 1951 United Nations Convention and the 1967 Protocol relating to the Status of Refugees

The UNHCR is very active in promoting the objectives of the 1951 Convention and the 1967 Protocol relating to the Status of Refugees, and in exercising his statutory watchdog function of overseeing the proper implementation of these international treaties by nations which are parties thereto. A matter of particular importance and concern is the provision in both the Convention and the Protocol which prohibits the *refoulement* or forcible return of a refugee to any territory where his life or freedom would be threatened on account of his race, religion, nationality, membership of a particular social group or political opinion. Over the years there have been a number of instances in which Contracting States to the Convention or Protocol have violated their obligation in this regard and have carried out the *refoulement* of refugees. The UNHCR invariably reacts promptly and vigorously in such cases in taking the matter up with the Contracting State concerned. It is not UNHCR policy, however, to publicize such negotiations in any manner which would name the offending State and thus subject it to international embarrassment. Such negotiations are pursued quietly and, as the High Commissioner reported to the UN General Assembly at its last session, 'in an open and constructive dialogue, in accordance with the responsibilities entrusted to the High Commissioner by the General Assembly'. The High Commissioner – still without naming names – brings such matters forcefully to the attention of the UNHCR Executive Committee and, through his Annual Report, to the attention of the UN General Assembly. In both of these fora he regularly deplores the reported instances of *refoulement* and calls upon all States to observe the humane principles of the Convention and Protocol. The UNHCR has used similar means to protest instances in which refugees have been subjected to violence or abduction.

Several years ago the UNHCR distributed to all Contracting States to the Convention or Protocol a very extensive questionnaire which, article by article, called upon such States to report in detail the extent to which they had carried out all of their obligations under these instruments, including the listing of pertinent laws and regulations enacted or adopted. This exercise was pursued by the UNHCR with great determination. It constituted a strong pressure upon States parties to the Convention and Protocol to discharge faithfully their obligations thereunder.

ANNEX 6

Supplementary information concerning the United States Government and its relations with the United Nations and the UNHCR

As previously stated to the Committee, the United States requested both the UN Secretary General and the UN High Commissioner for Refugees to become involved with providing assistance to the displaced persons in Cyprus.

The United States also appealed directly to the Secretary General to arrange for the High Commissioner to assume responsibility for coordinating effective international assistance for the relief and resettlement of the refugees escaping from Vietnam in boats. Since the time when the High Commissioner assumed such role the United States has repeatedly brought to his attention the importance which we attach to this matter and has urged him to redouble his efforts toward assuring a fully effective response to the problem by the international community.

The United States Government, through Secretary of State Kissinger's Lusaka speech of April 27, 1976, has made it clear to all concerned including the United Nations that we place a high priority on the provision of assistance to refugees from Southern Africa. Since then we have on several occasions, both in the UNHCR Executive Committee and otherwise, reiterated our interest to the High Commissioner for Refugees and asked him to take urgent steps to assure that Southern African refugees receive effective UNHCR assistance.

For some time after the emergency in Iran of the problem of Kurdish refugees from Iraq, the UNHCR took no active steps to assist these refugees. The United States, through the Department of State, intervened on several occasions with the UNHCR with the view to securing UNHCR assistance for the Kurds. Subsequently, the UNHCR placed several thousand of the Kurdish refugees under the UNHCR mandate and successfully undertook a relief and resettlement program in their behalf.

In 1968, after the invasion of Czechoslovakia, some 60,000 Czech refugees fled to nearby countries, chiefly Austria. The United States, acting both through direct unilateral approach and in concert with other countries through the UNHCR Executive Committee, pressed the UNHCR to extend assistance to the Czech refugees. This was subsequently done, through contribution by the UNHCR to the Austrian Government of funds earmarked for assistance to the Czech refugees.

Publicly, the allocation of UNHCR funds as between countries is carried out on a non-priority basis. The annual global budget is prepared by the UNHCR and submitted for approval, with justification for each project, to the 31-nation UNHCR Executive Committee at its annual meeting in the fall of each year. Funds are allocated according to the scope and nature of each refugee problem to be assisted. Urgent, priority needs which may develop in certain areas – particularly those arising between sessions of the Executive Committee – are met by the UNHCR by drawing on the $2 million UNHCR Emergency Fund, with appropriate notification by the High Commissioner to members of the Executive Committee.

The Annual Report of the UNHCR is sent to and reviewed by the UN General Assembly, as an agenda item at its regular annual session. On this occasion – as in the meetings of the UNHCR Executive Committee – the United States delegation has every opportunity to express its views and to urge and vote for action by the UNHCR in areas of particular concern to the United States. Apart from the sessions of these multilateral bodies, the United States through the Department of State maintains close and continuous contact with the UNHCR on a direct basis, chiefly with UNHCR headquarters in Geneva. This is done by the United States Mission in Geneva, acting upon both general and particular instructions from the Department of State, and by the Department itself through direct contact with the High Commissioner himself or with the United States Office of the UNHCR at the seat of the United Nations in New York. Through these means the United States is able to communicate its views and recommendations to the UNHCR on a regular basis, to stay closely in touch with developments concerning UNHCR activities, and to exert every effort toward influencing the UNHCR in matters related to UNHCR protection measures, the financial level of UNHCR programs, the areas in which the UNHCR participates and actual priorities carried out in practice by the UNHCR.

ANNEX 7

Supplementary information on instances of limited response by the United States Government to UNHCR appeals for funds or resettlement opportunities

There have been instances in which the United States has not responded, or has responded in a limited manner, to appeals of the UN High Commissioner for

Refugees for funds or for resettlement opportunities in this country. With the fall of Vietnam in 1975 the United States has not provided funds to the UNHCR program of assistance for displaced persons within that country or in the neighboring country of Laos.

The United States has responded in a limited way to UNHCR appeals for assistance to refugees from Chile and refugees in Argentina. In the case of Chile the United States agreed to accept a total of 400 families from Chile and Peru, involving approximately 1,100 persons. Other governments accepted approximately 19,000 refugees. A US contribution of $500,000 was made available to the UNHCR for this special program.

The High Commissioner has estimated that there are over 10,000 refugees in Argentina, one thousand in dire circumstances. The United States also responded in a limited way in 1972 when the Ugandan government expelled some 35,000 Asians from that country. The United States accepted only 1,900 persons among that group.

ANNEX 8

A.6 Transfers from Foreign Assistance Appropriations to Migration and Refugee Assistance Appropriations by Presidential Determination, FY 1963 – FY 1976

		$	$
FY 1963			none
FY 1964			none
FY 1965			none
FY 1966			271,000
Unnumbered	Refugees from Cuba	271,000	
FY 1967			none
FY 1968			125,000
P.D. 68–3	Refugee needs in connection with the Middle East crisis	125,000	
FY 1969			5.706,000
P.D. 69–4	Czechoslovak and other refugees from communist countries in Europe	5,706,000	
FY 1970			5,752,000
P.D. 70–2	Czechoslovak and other refugees from communist countries in Europe	5,752,000	
FY 1971			10,000,000
P.D. 71–15	Refugees from East Pakistan (Bangladesh) in India	5,000,000	
P.D. 71–19	Refugees from East Pakistan (Bangladesh) in India	5,000,000	
FY 1972			8,850,000
P.D. 72–01	Refugees from East Pakistan (Bangladesh) in India	5,000,000	
P.D. 72–06	Assistance to selected emigres (purchase of annuities)	1,850,000	
P.D. 72–14	Refugees from the Soviet Union going to Israel	2,000,000	
FY 1973			4,000,000
P.D. 73–01	Refugees returning to the Sudan	2,500,000	
P.D. 73–06	Asians expelled from Uganda	1,500,000	
FY 1974			10,000,000

P.D. 74–06	Exchange of Persons – Pakistan and Bangladesh	4,400,000	
P.D. 74–24	Assistance to Palestinian refugees	4,200,000	
P.D. 74–25	Assistance to refugees in and from Chile	1,400,000	
FY 1975			10,000,000
P.D. 75–06	Assistance to Soviet refugees going to other than Israel	5,000,000	
P.D. 75–13	Assistance to refugees from South Vietnam and Cambodia	5,000,000	
P.D. 76–02	Assistance to refugees from Laos and authority to use funds made available under P.D. 75–13 for this purpose Use of P.D. 75–13 and P.D. 76–02 funds		
	Cambodia/South Vietnam 2,277,454		
	Laos 2,722,546		
FY 1976			6,800,000
P.D. 76–03	Assistance to refugees from Laos	6,800,000	

A.7 Draw-downs by Presidential Determinations from the Emergency Refugee and Migration Assistance Fund, 1 July 1976 – 31 January 1977

Transition Quarter			6,360,000
P.D. TQ–2	Assistance to Soviet refugees not resettling in Israel – CY 1976	5,300,000	
P.D. TQ–4	Assistance to Kurdish refugees	150,000	
P.D. TQ–5	Assistance in Greece to stateless Christian refugees from Lebanon	910,000	
FY 1977, through January 31, 1977			7,300,000
P.D. 77–3	Resettlement of Angolan refugees who have fled to Portugal	1,000,000	
P.D. 77–4	Relief and resettlement of Latin American refugees	1,200,000	
P.D. 77–7	Assistance to Soviet refugees not resettling in Israel – 1977	2,000,000	
P.D. 77–9	Assistance to African refugees	1,000,000	
P.D. 77–11	Contribution to the UNHCR's Indochinese refugee program in Thailand	2,100,000	

Index

Page numbers *in italics* denote illustrations.